PART TWO:
REFLECTIONS ON THE SEQUEL

Edited by Paul Budra and Betty A. Schellenberg

What do *Paradise Regained* and *Terminator 2* have in common? They are both sequels, both chronological extensions of narratives that were originally envisioned as closed and complete works. *Part Two* explores the phenomenon of secondary narrative by studying the conditions that determine its production and reception. The volume encompasses works of poetry, drama, prose, and film, moving from Homer to Hollywood. Each piece is grounded in a specific genre or period while engaging a broader historical or theoretical perspective.

PAUL BUDRA and BETTY A. SCHELLENBERG are with the department of English at Simon Fraser University.

THEORY/CULTURE

General Editors:
Linda Hutcheon, Gary Leonard,
Janet Paterson, Paul Perron, and Jill Matus

Edited by PAUL BUDRA
and BETTY A. SCHELLENBERG

Part Two:
Reflections on the Sequel

UNIVERSITY OF TORONTO PRESS
Toronto Buffalo London

© University of Toronto Press Incorporated 1998
Toronto Buffalo London
Printed in Canada

ISBN 0-8020-0915-8 (cloth)
ISBN 0-8020-7895-8 (paper)

Printed on acid-free paper

Canadian Cataloguing in Publication Data

Main entry under title:

Part two : reflections on the sequel

(Theory/culture)
ISBN 0-8020-0915-8 (bound)   ISBN 0-8020-7895-8 (pbk.)

1. Sequels (Literature).   2. Motion picture sequels.   I. Budra, Paul Vincent,
1957– .   II. Schellenberg, Betty A., 1956– .   III. Series.

PN56.S477P37 1998   809   C98-931324-7

University of Toronto Press acknowledges the financial assistance to its
publishing program of the Canada Council for the Arts and the Ontario Arts
Council.

For Our Very Own Sequels:
Christian & Max
Samuel & Luc

Contents

viii   Contents

Acknowledgments

We wish to thank Simon Fraser University and the Social Sciences and Humanities Research Council of Canada for their generous financial support of this project. We would also like to thank Suzanne Rancourt, Kristen Pederson, and Barbara Porter at the University of Toronto Press for their efforts, and Linda Hutcheon for her support. The judicious criticism of the Press's readers – Martin Kreiswirth, Alison Lee, Heather Murray, and Joseph Natoli – made a valuable contribution to this volume's final shape. Matthew Wispinski, Bill Souder, and, especially, Wendy Smith made valuable contributions in the assembling and correcting of the manuscript, for which we are grateful. Scholars who were part of the formative stages of this book include Nancy Copeland, Leith Davis, James Nohrnberg, and John Pierce; our thanks to them for their thought-provoking contributions to our discussions. Two of our institutional colleagues must be singled out for special mention: Kathy Mezei offered constructive enthusiasm for this project from the beginning, while Carole Gerson offered sage advice on ushering the book through the publishing maze. Finally, we are sincerely grateful to the contributors who made this volume possible; all editors should have the like privilege of working with scholars who are at once professional, congenial, and punctual.

PAUL BUDRA
BETTY A. SCHELLENBERG

PART TWO: REFLECTIONS ON THE SEQUEL

Introduction

PAUL BUDRA and
BETTY A. SCHELLENBERG

This project was born in the discovery of common territory shared by the two apparently disparate research fields of eighteenth-century English print culture and late twentieth-century film. That common territory was the sequel. What, we found ourselves asking, do Samuel Richardson's 'cult-novel' *Pamela* and the movie *The Terminator* have in common that might have led both to generate a sequel? This initial question broadened into a general curiosity about the sequel as a recurrent phenomenon, whether in the form of the *Little Iliad, Paradise Regained, Anne of Avonlea,* or *Friday the 13th, Part 4;* the sequel has become an almost-predictable footnote to the narratives of Western history. What configuration of 'author,' original narrative, and audience, in what cultural conditions, explains a sequel?

While the ubiquity of the sequel might make such a question appear unavoidable, virtually nothing has been written about the phenomenon. A few studies have focused on the popularity of novel continuations in the nineteenth and early twentieth centuries, or on film sequels.[1] The most extensive study to date of a form of sequelization in the English language is Helge Nowak's *'Completeness is all': Fortsetzungen und andere Weiterführungen britischer Romane als Beispiel zeitübergreifender und inter-kultureller Rezeption.* Nowak concentrates on late twentieth-century rewritings of earlier works such as Daniel Defoe's *Robinson Crusoe* and Charlotte Brontë's *Jane Eyre* in order to isolate the transhistorical and cross-cultural dynamics of reception and intertextuality, using the theories of Hans Robert Jauss and Gerard Genette. This study is valuable in its exploration of a very particular form of the sequel, the retrospective rewriting of a culturally formative narrative; at the same time, its concerns are too specific to provide an overview of the conditions influencing the sequel in its wide range of temporal, generic, and media manifestations.[2]

If little attention has been paid to the sequel as genre, those generalizations that have been made in the course of discussion of particular cases have tended to coalesce around the nature of the sequel's relation to audience expectation. Roger Sharrock, in his 1966 study of John Bunyan's continuation of *The Pilgrim's Progress*, muses that, in the case of a sequel, 'the unknown explorer of a single personal theme finds himself a writer with a public; the second novel is a writer's book, self-conscious, the work of an artist with a style ... looking for a theme.'[3] Sharrock's originary account of the author as heroic individualist, mirroring Bunyan's narrative of the solitary Christian struggling through the hostile wilderness of this world, is oddly disjunctive with its own sequel of a public making a writer and demanding that a text be moulded into a desired image. The latter formulation is, indeed, suggestive of Michel Foucault's work on the author function and of recent theoretical interest in the history of print culture and its creation of a reading public.[4] Poststructuralism and cultural materialism have taught us that the public sphere in which the original text takes its place must be considered both as a marketplace and as a discursive space, which can, in both of these forms, be constructed not only by writers, publishers, texts, and readers, but also by other actors such as agents, pirates, advertisers, imitators, and reviewers.[5]

If Sharrock's statement invites deconstruction and historicization, so do those common-sense generalizations about the sequel which more explicitly place the phenomenon in the marketplace. Phil Wilhelm, one of the film-makers of the 1997 video short *Hillbilly Hercules 2: Lost in New York City*, facetiously encapsulated the stereotype when he explained to *The New York Times* that there is no *Hillbilly Hercules 1* 'because sequels always make more money.'[6] At least three centuries earlier, in early English print culture, the sequel seems already to have been notorious as an exploitative device, a cynical ploy to sell an inevitably inferior new text on the basis of an earlier work's success. Thus, Daniel Defoe, in his preface to the 1719 *Farther Adventures of Robinson Crusoe*, argues that the work is 'every Way as entertaining' as its precursor, 'contrary to the Usage of Second Parts'; Samuel Richardson hopes that his 1741 continuation of *Pamela* after the heroine's marriage will enjoy 'the good fortune, which *few continuations* have met with, to be judged not unworthy the *First* Part'; and the 1753 preface to Sarah Fielding's *The Adventures of David Simple, Volume the Last* begins with the admission that 'sequels to Histories of this kind are ... generally decried, and often with ... good Reason' because of their authors' 'building so much on public Approbation as to endeavour to put off a second-rate insipid Piece, void of the Spirit of the first.'[7]

Writing about Samuel Richardson's continuation of his enormously popular first novel, *Pamela*, Terry Castle, in her 1986 *Masquerade and Civilization: The Carnivalesque in Eighteenth-Century English Culture and Fiction*, takes into account the modern 'economy of literary production' in explaining the sequel, summarizing what she herself calls the 'commonplace' that 'sequels are always disappointing' because they are 'an attempt to profit further from a previous work that has had exceptional commercial success.' At the same time, Castle's interest in the carnivalesque of subversive desire leads her to invoke a mysterious, irrational undercurrent which arouses this apparently calculated commercial impulse. She begins with a precursor text that possesses extraordinary qualities; thus 'only charismatic texts, those with an unusually powerful effect on a large reading public, typically generate sequels.' The sequel's own destiny is a 'tragedy,' Castle goes on, in that 'it cannot literally reconstitute its charismatic original' – this despite its readers' 'secret mad hope' for repetition, a desire that they already know must be disappointed. As an extreme case, Richardson's sequel 'seems almost to insult us, to affront our expectations, including our very desire for repetition.'[8] Castle's Gothic explanation of the sequel as the fantastic, inevitably deformed outgrowth of an uncontrollable desire coupled with, while pitted against, an aesthetically and morally debased profit motive ultimately obscures the very analysis of the economy of literary production and reader response which it initially appears to offer.

In short, an audience's desire to re-experience in some way a memorable story, an author's response to that desire, and the inevitably changed conditions which make it impossible to achieve a precise repetition of the experience are clearly germane to the sequel phenomenon. At the same time, the precise object of that audience desire; the aesthetic, psychological, or economic barriers to its fulfilment; the role of the original (or secondary) writer in creating and responding to audience desire; the mediating or interfering forces operating in the spheres which author, original text, and audience inhabit – all are variables which have been oversimplified or assumed or simply overlooked in the commonplace model of the sequel which we have been reviewing. Our purpose in this volume, then, is to problematize, examine, elaborate on, and nuance, in turn, the following assumptions:

1 / *that the origins of the sequel can be located solely in unique qualities of a precursor text which combine to form its 'charisma.'* The precursor's

'charisma' must be understood as a complex interaction of cultural factors and mediations. What ideological and material forces might bear upon an author's initial production of such a text and upon its dissemination to an audience? What makes an audience receptive to this text more than to another? Or, to put it another way, what is the role of the charismatic text in creating a particular audience, whether defined by age, education, gender, or taste?

2 / *that the precursor's charisma generates audience desire for repetition, be it of style or story, which, in turn, leads an author to attempt to exploit that audience desire.* In what circumstances does receptivity take the form of a desire for repetition? Is repetition, in fact, what the audience is seeking? Is the 'pretext's' charisma inextricably bound up with its claim to originality,[9] and, if so, how will the requirement of originality be satisfied together with the demand for the familiar? How is audience desire communicated to the text's original producer? Again, it appears likely that the desire for a sequel might be mediated by various apparatuses for bringing cultural products and consumers together. Furthermore, the original text's producer might be drawn towards a sequel for motives other than purely commercial ones, including a wish to revisit some aspect of the original text; or to correct a known response to that text; or to further increase her or his cultural status with a prepared, relatively defined audience, using the first text as a pretext. And when the sequel author is not the 'original' author, so that an initial recipient and new producer are collapsed into one, what is the new configuration of first author, second author, and audience surrounding the narrative and its continuation?

3 / *that the sequel inevitably fails.* Is the sequel indicative of a *distinctively* inorganic, or morally tainted, relation among artist, narrative object, and audience? Does the sequel indeed fail? By what criteria is such failure measured? If the sequel's production is governed by complex local forces, is not such complexity characteristic of the forces influencing all cultural productions, and therefore as variously liable to result in success or failure?

As these questions indicate, it has seemed to us that the sequel bears examination, not simply for its own sake, but as a phenomenon for which the tensions that always intersect at the site of narrative are thrown into high relief: tensions between the individual text and its precursors, tensions between the producer of the text and her or his audience, tensions between the aesthetic and the material aspects of artistic production, tensions between the ideal of unmediated transmission of meaning and the vagaries of reception. In other words, we believe that the sequel is not unique, but uniquely representative in its extreme typicality.[10] And, as a corollary to this premise, while the general questions to be asked about every sequel might be the same, and the same as those to be asked about virtually all narrative objects, the individual sequel also presents a heightened image of the *particular* cultural moment which it inhabits.

Given this point of departure, the first step in this examination – indeed, the only way in which it could be conducted – was to locate individual sequels in the authorial, aesthetic, market, and social conditions governing their production. Thus we invited a group of scholars to reflect with us on the sequel as it might be located in the historical moment, the genre, the medium, most familiar to each of them, using the theoretical framework which seemed most illuminating of the sequel manifestation they were examining. Then we asked them to exchange these observations, testing those about other sequelizations with their own. In so doing, we hoped to deconstruct the common-sense model of the sequel which we had encountered, moving from specific cases to any broader generalizations which might offer themselves.

But, first, we established a working definition of the sequel as an inevitably inadequate, but necessary, artifice which would allow us to maintain common points of reference in our separate pursuits. Our understanding of the phenomenon as 'extremely typical' meant that its features blurred with those of a wide variety of intertextualities; thus, we set boundaries to the term that would allow us to define a meaningful and manageable inquiry within this vast field. The word 'sequel,' sharing with the word 'sequence' the Latin root *sequi*, 'to follow,' betrays, of course, the phenomenon's fundamental temporality. Chronological extension of a narrative was therefore our starting point,[11] to which we added the criterion of a precursor narrative that was originally presented as closed and complete in itself (whether or not it was, in fact, conceived as such by its author). In this we excluded the latter parts of a serial publication or of an announced series, for example, while including continuations by writers other than the first, whether such continuations were authorized or not, and even if the sequel was created years, perhaps centuries, after the original narrative. We included 'prequels,' works in which the internal chronological relation to the pretext narrative is prior, as well as before-and-after extensions.

Our criterion of chronological extension also led us to exclude the related and fascinating category of non-sequential rewritings or adaptations, such as the numerous versions of Arthurian legends, post-colonial

retellings of *Robinson Crusoe,* or film adaptations of novels, simply be-
cause such rewritings did not fit the requirement of internal sequentiality.[12]
In what proved a more permeable boundary, we initially excluded spatial
or tangential expansions of an original story, works which might be
called 'spin-offs,' such as Tom Stoppard's *Rosencrantz and Guildenstern
Are Dead,* or clusters of texts, such as Sir Walter Scott's Waverley novels.
As the discussions, in this collection, of Trollope's Palliser novels, Bennett's
Five Towns stories, and Montgomery's Avonlea series suggest, the distinction between chronological extension and spatial expansion appeared
ultimately to be one of degree rather than of kind, and it at times became
impossible to distinguish the sequel neatly from related narrative
outgrowths.

In the course of their particular pursuits, then, our contributors pushed
at the boundaries of our definition, while confirming some, and nuancing
all, of the commonplaces with which we began.

In their essays, Alexander Leggatt, Carole Gerson, and Paul Budra explore the nature and implications of the 'unkillable' protagonist. They
look at specific fictional characters who, at their first public appearance,
resonated within and beyond their ordinal narratives to create a cult of
personality that invited narrative extension to keep them 'alive.' Whether
they are Scythian conquerors, incorrigible carousers, red-haired orphans,
or homicidal monsters, such characters suggest narrative possibilities
which are not exhausted by their original fictions. Thus they pressure
their authors and texts for continuance, often resulting in a Frankenstein-
like scenario of competition between the character's creator and her or
his creation.

Lynette Felber and Mary Ann Gillies, on the other hand, look at narrative worlds that are greater than the sum of their individual parts. In such
cases, it is this world – not any specific character – and its elaborated
atmosphere, geography, and society, in short its culture, that are charismatic. Readers want to continue inhabiting the intricate social and political networks of the Pallisers or the Five Towns district, re-entering this
alternative reality through a seemingly inexhaustible succession of narrative representations. Hence the resultant 'sequels' may combine to form a
cluster work of narratives rather than a temporally linear sequence.
Unlike the author who creates a charismatic protagonist, furthermore,
these authors, as the possessors of the vision upon which a desirous
audience depends, seem able to retain a satisfying ascendancy over their
fictional worlds and audiences.

Perhaps the purest form of narrative charisma is that explored by Lianne McLarty in her essay on the regenerative capacity of social identity in popular narrative. Readers or viewers may find the arrangement of events within a narrative so attractive that they want to re-experience that story without disturbance of its enabling cultural ideologies. In order to offer such untroubled continuity, characters and plots must be rehabilitated to absorb or deflect critique. The action-film sequel domesticates its male hero, for example, while deflecting motiveless violence to irrational women and explaining away racism as the mere perception of oppression on the part of its victims; thus, gendered and racialized structures of power may be remodelled while remaining fundamentally untouched. The story continues, and the story remains the same.

Their examinations of the nature of an original narrative's charisma led a number of our contributors to elaborate on the meaning of repetition with respect to the sequel. Thus several of the essays in this collection challenge Castle's paradigm of an audience consumed by the 'secret mad hope' of 'a repetition that does not look like one, the old story in a new and unexpected guise,' only to be inevitably disappointed by its impossibility, or by the refusal of the author to realize those hopes.[13] In effect, the dynamic is always more complex: the audience knows it is seeking repetition-with-variation, and ideally 'the management of a skilfull Hand' will produce that 'beautiful Novelty' which Sarah Fielding in 1753 compares to 'a melodious Variation on the same Notes,'[14] a sequence of narrative satisfactions that is at once a variation upon, and ultimately comparable to, the audience's first experience. The solutions to this undeniable challenge range from the increase in scale characteristic of the action film, relying on familiarity offset by heightened thrills (see Lianne McLarty); to the foregrounding of previously subordinate narrative lines in the case of a charismatic fictional world which the audience wants to see as fully realized as possible (see Felber, Gillies); to Milton's implication that two narratives may be historically sequential, but spiritually coincident (see Samuel Glen Wong); to the strategy employed by the nineteenth-century popular novelist Charlotte Yonge of inserting familiar characters and moral principles into an entirely new generic atmosphere (see June Sturrock). Whatever the solution, the balance between repetition and variation can be successfully struck, and, when it is, the result is anything but the 'tragedy' of which Castle warns.

Testing any definition of the sequel also inevitably raises the question of the author function. As Andrew Taylor demonstrates, posthumous continuations of *The Canterbury Tales* by a number of authors can be seen as complements to, and commentaries on, Chaucer's text rather than as sequels legitimate or spurious, and were possible in an era in which the author function was still fluid. Similarly, Ingrid Holmberg shows us that in antiquity the traditions of oral literature had to solidify into a fixed canon that became 'Homer' before other texts could be seen as linear narrative extensions of the *Iliad* and the *Odyssey*. Once that function was being actively defined in modern culture, however, producers of texts began to assert ownership of the originals as their unique creations, thereby also claiming the right to control over any subsequent productions. Thus, Betty Schellenberg notes the tendency on the part of male novelists, at least, at an early point in this process of definition, to invoke the image of paternity in denouncing spurious continuations. In the transition towards the model of the author as authority, Leggatt traces a strange rivalry between the playwrights Shakespeare and Marlowe and the too-popular Falstaff and Tamburlaine for their audience's allegiance, ending in the authors' exercising of their right to murder their creatures. Not long after this, Wong suggests, even the work of a Milton generally portrayed as the individual genius toiling on in defiance of a shifting and unappreciative readership can be understood in an entirely new way when viewed from the perspective of the spiritually insecure reader.

The individualism of the modern writer paradoxically makes of the sequel an opportunity for its author to revisit the original text and to respond, in turn, to the response of its audience. For the early modern playwright, this may mean telling metatheatrical jokes about a larger-than-life hero (see Leggatt); for the didactic novelist, qualifying an earlier tendency to social subversion (see Schellenberg) or affirming the fixity of religious and social tenets despite changing popular tastes (see Sturrock); for the realist, delineating change over time (see Felber); for the aging and world-weary writer, offering an escape from political uncertainty (see Gerson).

Indeed, as our contributors discovered, the most acclaimed modern sequels attest to the limitations of an adversarial author–audience paradigm as a means of explaining textual creation: the author 'dragged at the chariot wheels' (Montgomery, qtd. in Gerson) of her originating text in response to the demands of a merciless public is, in fact, participating in an increasingly sophisticated and specialized complex of production and consumption which, at its best, serves the purposes of all its participants. The insertion of the literary agent into this complex arguably locates in the early twentieth-century publishing world the potential for the most mutually expedient furthering of these interests (see Gillies).

More recently, the primacy of the author is no longer assumed and the scales have tipped in favour of the pressure to maintain an established market through steady production. Thus contemporary screenwriters and film directors sign the rights to their creations over to film production houses, which then hire teams of artists to manufacture sequels, often in direct response to the perceived audience desires and anxieties which fuelled the success of the original movie (see McLarty). At one remove from a transparent response to the dictates of the popular market, the postmodern horror movie self-consciously seeks out collective anxieties of the moment and offers them back to its audience as a fantasy of stability and power in the form of the monster-hero (see Budra).

The postmodern novelist, despite situating her- or himself at a critical distance from the popular marketplace, nevertheless acknowledges with the film-maker the Death of the Author. In an intertextual universe within which the name of the author no longer demarcates an inviolable territory, every text is a sequel to every other text, and, as Michael Zeitlin demonstrates, postmodern sequels select and establish their own prequels, 'subjecting them in the process to more or less radical programs of fragmentation, distortion, and rearrangement' (161). Zeitlin suggests that the quintessential postmodern sequel is the post-Freudian narrative, which disrupts and thereby makes visible traditional Western narratives and their obsessions. Alternatively, as Thomas Carmichael argues, the sequel allows the self-consciously postmodern author to foreground representational practices by creating a text that is inherently dependent upon at least one previous text. The sequel, by definition, is extravagantly intertextual, and so conveniently formalizes the artifice of narrative, opening up the construction of history and meaning for critical query. And thus we come full circle to this introduction's initial premise of the sequel's extreme typicality as a figure for the operative conditions of a field of narrative at any given cultural moment. More apropos of the fate of the sequel as form, its predictable recurrence in Western narrative history is being recognized for what Holmberg's discussion of the epic cycle reveals it to be – a sign of the circumscription and hierarchalization of the intertextual which have accompanied the writing of narrative. In the words of Fredric Jameson, cited by both Carmichael and Budra, 'neither space nor time is "natural" in the sense in which it might be metaphysically presupposed,'[15] and the sequel's dependence on spatio-temporal narrative assumptions makes it, in turn, dependent on, and revealing of, a particular culture's investment in those assumptions.

When the essays in this collection are themselves organized as a chronological sequence according to their subjects, it becomes clear that shifts in the cultural complex precipitate not only interrogations of the author function, but also re-evaluations of reading and representation that result in shifting ascendencies of narrative forms. Generally, it is the ascendant form that is likely to be responded to as charismatic and produce a demand for extension. And, as a rule, this form will be, in this time of dominance, popular, even populist. If the essays collected here are roughly charted by the historical–cultural periods and by the narrative forms they address, the results serve as a broad overview of a chronological shift in sequel forms:

Period	Sequelized narrative mode
Antiquity	myth
Middle Ages	catalogue/compendium
Renaissance	theatre
Eighteenth to twentieth century	novel
Late twentieth century	film

This alignment of the sequel with the dominant populist mode implies a powerful conservatism in narrative extension, a conservatism which depends upon, and realizes, the sequel's inherent potential for stabilization through repetition across textual boundaries. A brief account of each of the essays in this collection in turn will illustrate in more detail this tendency of the sequel to serve the interests of consolidation and conservation, manifested variously in the canonization of a body of texts, in an author's assertion of control over her or his characters, in the perpetuation of a social status quo through reinterpretation of an original text, in the reaffirmation of values and stereotypes across storylines, or in the reifying of intertextual extension itself as a transhistorical and cross-cultural constant.

In the first essay in this collection, 'Homer and the Beginning of the Sequel,' Ingrid Holmberg examines the body of narratives known as the epic cycle which have been preserved in fragmentary form as prequels and sequels to the monumental texts of the *Iliad* and *Odyssey*. She contrasts the narrative inclusiveness and flexibility of the oral tradition, of which both the epic cycle and the Homeric epics were a part, with the exclusiveness and rigidity of the fixed texts of the *Iliad* and *Odyssey*. Her conclusion posits that the fixity and canonization, whenever they occurred, of the *Iliad* and *Odyssey* in turn forced the other narratives of the epic cycle to assume fixity and narrative linearity in relationship with these texts, thus creating prequels and sequels.

In 'The Curious Eye and the Alternative Endings of *The Canterbury Tales*,' Andrew Taylor looks at the continuations of *The Canterbury Tales* written by various successors of Chaucer, each apparently committed to conserving the master's text yet dissatisfied both with Chaucer's failure to recount the pilgrims' return trip and with the ending that he provided, the daunting Parson's Tale. Taylor sees in these sequels a rejection of Chaucer's model of textual apprehension through solitary study in preference for an emerging model of reading as visualization, exemplified in the pilgrimage-guidebook genre. From another point of view, the satisfactions of the manual which can be consulted repeatedly are giving way to the demands of linear narrative. *The Canterbury Tales* sequels, then, offer an example of the tension between the requirements of continuity and those of revision that can emerge through the cultural shifts dividing an originating text from its extensions.

In 'Killing the Hero: Tamburlaine and Falstaff,' Alexander Leggatt examines the phenomenon of the dramatic sequel in the English Renaissance. He demonstrates how William Shakespeare and Christopher Marlowe, responding to public and commercial demand, made sequels around their most popular dramatic characters only to find themselves overshadowed and confined by their creations. Leggatt traces these playwrights' assertion of authorial power over their work, an assertion that results in what might be called 'homicidal sequels,' sacrificing character to author. Even in such extreme cases, however, authorial self-assertion is in part a function of the protagonist's popularity, a popularity that allows the protagonist to survive his author.

Samuel Glen Wong considers the critical problem of Milton's composing a sequel to the 'sublimely sufficient *Paradise Lost*' (70) by tracing a series of verbal iterations that variously simplify, circumscribe, multiply the effects of, and even transcend the reader's experience of that epic. While Wong acknowledges such iteration's practical goal of opening a space, at once psychic and physical, in which a sequel can reside, he notes as well a more radical effect: narrative sequence is subverted by the cosmic frame of the Alpha and Omega, precursor and sequel are 'draw[n] ... together, not as sequence, but as sublimely coincident utterances' (82). *Paradise Regained* and *Paradise Lost* therefore come to inhabit the same time, subtly transformed by iteration into coeval works where sequence, in the end, dissolves.

In '"To Renew Their Former Acquaintance": Print, Gender, and Some Eighteenth-Century Sequels,' Betty Schellenberg uses her discussion of the eighteenth-century English novel sequel to speculate on the connection between the shift towards a market system of literary production and the professionalization of the author, most specifically the female author. She argues that, while publishing success provided novel writers with an identifiable audience, it also left them vulnerable to criticism and unauthorized imitation. Whereas for male writers this new sense of social authority and public scrutiny is figured in tropes of paternity and proprietorship, such a stance was not available to the female writer. Thus women such as Sarah Fielding, Frances Sheridan, and Sarah Scott present their sequels to their audiences as sites for the gathering of an intimate community of friends, within which they nevertheless can assert their own status as professionals and moral authorities.

Shifting from print culture's influence on the sequel's author to its influence on the sequel's content, June Sturrock, in 'Sequels, Series, and Sensation Novels,' her study of Charlotte Yonge's 1856 *Daisy Chain* and its 1864 sequel, *The Trial*, shows how Yonge succeeded in carrying both her loyal audience and her affirmation of 'feminized and domesticated Christianity' from the family chronicle to the plot-driven sensation novel. Yonge condemns the wildly popular new subgenre for its dependence on sexual crime and its denial of individual moral responsibility, yet exploits its possibilities for dramatic expansion of the moral logic of influence, reward, and punishment that governs the familiar domestic narrative. By reinserting her characters into the sensation novel, Yonge presents an argument for the authority over the public and over the contemporary of those values which she had previously vindicated in the private and the seemingly timeless.

In *Phineas Finn* and *Phineas Redux* by Anthony Trollope, the sequel is used to place change in high relief, rather than smooth it over: it is precisely the variation upon a repeated pattern which is of greatest interest to author and reader. Thus, Lynette Felber uses the position of the Phineas novels as a pair within the larger Palliser sequence to explore the historical and generic point of articulation between sequel and sequence, arguing that, for Trollope, and for the Victorian and the modernist reader, the potential for continuation without closure and for multidimensional elaboration pushes the novel in the direction of the anticlimactic and the encyclopedic, ultimately the 'meganovel.' This pressure towards expansion meets its counter-force in the increasing limitations placed upon sequentiality by readers who can no longer be trusted to share knowledge of a charismatic original or to read in chronological order.

Approaching the late nineteenth- and early twentieth-century pressures on our working definition of the sequel from the perspective of Pierre Bourdieu's theories of cultural production, Mary Ann Gillies argues in

'The Literary Agent and the Sequel' that the conditions which result in strictly chronological continuations cannot, in fact, be distinguished from those producing subsequent texts of any sort. Specifically, she examines the role of the literary agent in not only channelling, but creating, the readerly desires that enable sequels. Using the case of J.B. Pinker as the agent of Arnold Bennett, Gillies argues that it was Pinker's financial support, analysis of target audiences, pacing of Bennett's production, and packaging advice which enabled the popularity, critical acclaim, and financial success of Bennett's Five Towns works. Thus, the sequel becomes only one of a range of production strategies generated by the cultural and material conditions of authorship.

Whereas Gillies's essay profiles an apparently successful balance struck among author, original text, and audience through the mediation of the literary agent, Carole Gerson's account of Lucy Maud Montgomery's unhappy servitude to publishers, a charismatic character, and a demanding audience – '"Dragged at Anne's Chariot Wheels"' – reveals the underside of the literary marketplace in the first half of the twentieth century. This story, however, is in itself a complex one: Montgomery's production of the Anne of Green Gables stories was shaped not only by the exigencies of the American market which any commercially ambitious Canadian writer had to court, but also by her own ambivalence about her publishing success and the process of sequelization upon which it depended. Ultimately, the literary historian is faced with the probability that Montgomery's autobiographical records are themselves narratives retrospectively shaped to reflect the *Anne* phenomenon. Gerson suggests that Montgomery's experience of sequelization became the governing plot of her own life. The way is prepared, one is tempted to argue, for the postmodern consciousness of life as text and of the death of the author as sole creator of the text.

In his contribution to this volume, Michael Zeitlin uses the narrative fiction of Donald Barthelme to elaborate the idea of a distinctively postmodern sequel, a sequel in which the conventional narrative extension is subverted and complicated because the sequential assumptions of narrative itself have not survived modernity. Postmodern sequels, Zeitlin finds, will select, incorporate, and transform their originating narratives at the same time that they complete them. Looking at Barthelme's radical extensions of Freud's *Totem and Taboo* in *The Dead Father*, Zeitlin uses psychoanalytic discourses to trace in Barthelme's dark narrative at once the ego's attempt at revenge against the father and a culture's ambivalent relation to the master narratives buried in 'the ironically self-conscious but still dark and troubled discourses of American postmodernism' (170).

Thomas Carmichael, in turn, draws attention to the simultaneity of the sequel's narrative and metanarrative levels and its relation to the frenetic circulation of images that marks the postmodern condition. Reminding us that the sequel's claim to authority is entirely dependent upon its intertextual traces, Carmichael focuses on John Barth's *LETTERS* and Marx's *Eighteenth Brumaire of Louis Bonaparte* to demonstrate how the postmodern sequel must reject repetition for the more contingent consecutiveness that is the process of history and difference. Barth's *LETTERS*, in Carmichael's formulation, is a test case for such rejection, critiquing, as it does, the sequel as a mode of narrative representation while elaborating upon the origins of representational authority.

In 'Recurrent Monsters: Why Freddy, Michael, and Jason Keep Coming Back,' Paul Budra looks at the phenomenon of horror-movie sequels, tying the open-endedness of contemporary horror narratives to the epistemological and ontological instability that is the postmodern reality. The postmodern horror movie uses ideological incoherence as the origin of its monster and reifies this incoherence formally: a happy ending is impossible because closure is impossible. Sequels are inevitable and serve, paradoxically, to stabilize the putative monsters of the films, for it is the monster, and the monster only, who will live on into Parts two, three, four, and so on. The horror-movie sequel terrifies, then, because it bestows the charisma of stamina upon monstrosity, making the audience complicit in the brutal certainties of homicidal madness as the only (but false) alternative to the monstrosity of its own postmodern condition.

Lianne McLarty looks at the most popular contemporary form of the sequel, the blockbuster movie, in her essay '"I'll be back": Hollywood, Sequelization, and History.' Finding an intertextuality in the contemporary popular film sequel that is consistent with a postmodern culture in which texts beget texts, McLarty examines the adjustments that film sequels make to incorporate or displace challenges to the white, patriarchal power structures which their precursors have represented. Concentrating on science-fiction and action sequels, McLarty illustrates how they reconfigure representations of sexual and racial oppression, not in order to acknowledge critique and shifts in ideology, but rather to absorb opposition and promote a 'domesticated,' perhaps even more powerful, patriarchal authority.

With this series of reflections on the sequel, we do not claim to be exhaustive or encyclopedic or definitive. Theoretically, we might wish to pursue further the possibility that the phenomenon of readerly desire for repetition-with-variation is particularly acute at certain historical junctures, or, to put it another way, that the sequel is possible only under certain (repeating) cultural conditions. Historically, geographically, and generically, we are aware of the absence here of continuations of sacred texts such as the Bible, of precursors and sequels not originating in Europe or North America, and of sequelization in media such as television or the popular song. And our definition might have extended to continuations that cross linguistic, media, and cultural boundaries. We have, however, discovered that the sequel phenomenon is far from boring, far from a monument to flawed and unfulfilled intentions, far from tragic. On the contrary, we have found it to be a revealing instance of the unique and intricate relations among author, narrative, and audience within any cultural moment, relations that govern the generation and circulation of all stories.

Notes

1 See, for example, Janet Husband, *Sequels: An Annotated Guide to Novels in Series* (Chicago: American Library Association, 1982); Heidi Ganner-Rauth, '"To be Continued?" Sequels and Continuations of Nineteenth-Century Novels and Novel Fragments,' *English Studies* 64 (1983): 129–43; Robert K. Morris, *Continuance and Change: The Contemporary British Novel Sequence* (Carbondale: South Illinois UP, 1972); Robert A. and Gwendolyn Wright Nowlan, *Cinema Sequels and Remakes, 1903–1987* (Jefferson, NC: McFarland, 1989).

2 Helge Nowak, *'Completeness is all': Fortsetzungen und andere Weiterführungen britischer Romane als Beispiel zeitübergreifender und interkultureller Rezeption* (Frankfurt am Main: Lang, 1994).

3 Roger Sharrock, *John Bunyan: 'The Pilgrim's Progress'* (London: Arnold, 1966) 43–4.

4 Michel Foucault, 'What Is an Author?' *Language, Counter-Memory, Practice*, ed. Donald F. Bouchard; trans. Donald F. Bouchard and Sherry Simon (Ithaca: Cornell UP, 1977) 113–38; for print culture and the public sphere, see Jürgen Habermas, *The Structural Transformation of the Public Sphere: An Inquiry into a Category of Bourgeois Society*, trans. Thomas Burger with Frederick Lawrence (Cambridge: Polity, 1989), and Benedict Anderson, *Imagined Communities: Reflections on the Origin and Spread of Nationalism*, rev. ed. (London: Verso, 1983). See also Martha Woodmansee and Peter Jaszi, eds., *The Construction of Authorship* (Durham, NC: Duke UP, 1994).

5 In order to avoid awkward multiplication of terms, throughout this introduction we frequently use 'author' and 'text,' although they are only, in fact, referential to the medium of print, to apply more broadly to all producers of narratives and their recited poems, dramatic works, published books, and films.

6 'Hokum Hero,' *The New York Times*, 15 June 1997, 12.

7 Daniel Defoe, 'The Preface' [to *The Farther Adventures of Robinson Crusoe*], *Robinson*

Crusoe, 3 vols. (Oxford: Blackwell, 1927) 1.ix; Samuel Richardson, *Pamela*, ed. Mark Kinkead-Weekes, 2 vols. (London: Dent, 1962) 2.v; Sarah Fielding, *The adventures of David Simple*, ed. Malcolm Kelsall (Oxford: Oxford UP, 1969) 309–10.

8 Terry Castle, *Masquerade and Civilization: The Carnivalesque in Eighteenth-Century English Culture and Fiction* (Stanford: Stanford UP, 1986) 133–4.

9 We are drawing here on one of Nowak's terms for the original text, 'Prätext,' translated as 'pretext,' because of its appealing double sense of originating narrative and excuse for a sequel. Nowak also speaks of 'Prätext' and 'Folgetext' as a means of avoiding the evaluative connotations of 'original' and 'sequel' (as creative and imitative, respectively), which become particularly marked when the sequel is produced by a second author (17, 20n.6).

10 This formulation is used by Catherine Gallagher in *Nobody's Story: The Vanishing Acts of Women Writers in the Marketplace, 1670–1820* (Berkeley and Los Angeles: U of California P, 1994) xv, to describe women authors in early English print culture.

11 It should be noted that even this apparently self-evident starting point does not cover all uses of the term 'sequel.' A search of the *English Short-Title Catalogue*, for example, reveals that, in Restoration and eighteenth-century English usage, at least, title reference to a sequel was no guarantee of narrative form; of 250 located titles containing the word 'sequel,' a considerable proportion indicate moral or scientific treatises, political pamphlets, songs, or non-narrative poems published in response to, or continuation of, another text in the same genre. In these cases sequentiality exists only at the level of publishing history rather than as an internal feature of the secondary text.

12 Our definition parts company with that of Nowak, who studies continuations using the original as a 'hypertext' (Genette's term); that is, she is interested in any set of at least two texts in which the following text bears an extensive and direct relation to the pretext's contents as a kind of prototype (Nowak 17–18, 58). Thus, she includes not only continuations of unfinished narratives such as Jane Austen's *Sanditon*, but also the many rewritings of *Robinson Crusoe*, including Michel Tournier's *Vendredi* and J.M. Coetzee's *Foe*, which are not primarily chronological extensions.

13 Castle, *Masquerade* 134–5.

14 Fielding, *David Simple* 310.

15 Fredric Jameson, *Postmodernism or, The Cultural Logic of Late Capitalism* (Durham, NC: Duke UP, 1991) 367.

Homer and the Beginning of the Sequel

INGRID E. HOLMBERG

Most of us are familiar with the fact that the *Iliad* and the *Odyssey* are the earliest extant works of literature in Western culture. These two enormous, carefully crafted epics appear to rise out of the darkness of the essentially preliterate Greek Bronze Age as two solitary pillars. On the one hand, the *Iliad* depicts mortality as an inescapable reality through its representation of its hero, the doomed Achilles; on the other hand, the *Odyssey*, through its polytropic, ever-moving hero, presents us with the fantasy of escaping mortality. Accordingly, the two epics are frequently cited as the respective beginnings of tragedy and comedy; along similar lines, John Peradotto, in *Man in the Middle Voice*, has recently analysed them as examples of the closed mythic and open-ended folkloric narrative. The survival of these two narratives over so many centuries testifies to the continuing cultural significance of their themes. The cultural prominence and popularity of these two texts, then, in addition to the many references to other potential narratives embedded within these same texts, would seem to provide (almost insist upon) opportunities for the creation of additional narratives or texts which depend upon and complement the Homeric narratives, that is, prequels or sequels. And, indeed, a body of literature extant only in fragments and summaries, obscure to most modern readers, does survive in the form of prequels and sequels to the *Iliad* and *Odyssey*. An examination of early Greek epic poetry and the oral tradition, however, reveals that the so-called prequels and sequels of the Homeric epics were created independently of those epics, and perhaps even prior to them.[1] The narratives of the epic cycle came to be understood as prequels and sequels to the Homeric epics only under the force of the dominance, canonization, and most particularly the fixation (through either the rhapsodic tradition or writing) of the texts of the monumental Homeric epics.

The whole epic cycle ranges from the marriage of heaven and earth to the death of Odysseus. It includes various subnarratives or smaller cycles which form the central core of much ancient Greek literature: the war of the Titans, the story of Oedipus, a *Thebaid* (the story of the struggle over the rulership of Thebes by Oedipus's sons), and the *Epigoni* (the renewal of that conflict by the next generation of warriors). The Trojan cycle is part of this large narrative and begins immediately following the *Epigoni*, with the *Kypria*. The Trojan cycle includes what survive as six titled narratives (attributed in the ancient sources to a variety of authors, including Homer) which surround the *Iliad* and the *Odyssey*: the *Kypria*, which relates the events prior to the Trojan War and the *Iliad*; the *Aethiopis*, which relates the events immediately following the *Iliad* such as the death of Achilles; the *Little Iliad*, which relates events following the death of Achilles and the end of the war; the *Iliou Persis* (destruction of Troy), which also relates the end of the war; the *Nostoi*, which relates the returns of the Greek heroes to Greece; and, finally, the *Telegony*, which concerns the death of Odysseus. These narratives are preserved for us through three main sources: the first are the fragmentary references and quotations in the works of ancient authors such as Athenaeus, Plutarch, and Pausanias, among others; the second is an incomplete set of epitomes by Proclus attached to two manuscripts of the *Iliad*; and the third is the summary of the Trojan cycle by Proclus called the *Chrestomathy* ('Things Useful to Learn') and preserved in Photius's *Biblioteca* ('Library'; 319A17), itself, in turn, a summary of literature and genres from the ninth century A.D.[2]

Since antiquity, the fixed narratives of the epic cycle have been subordinated to the fixed Homeric epics in several ways, with the result that, in the late second century A.D., Clement of Alexandria can confidently assert that the narratives of the *Chrestomathy* are the prequels and 'sequel' of the *Iliad*.[3] The consensus that the narratives of the epic cycle are prequels and sequels created to complement the Homeric epics seems to have arisen through a combination of factors. First, the epic cycle was fixed and written down after the establishment of the Homeric texts and under their influence; thus the chronological posteriority of the establishment of the fixed narratives of the cycle yields to the assumption that these narratives were, in fact, *created* as dependents upon the Homeric epics.[4] Second, although the cyclic narratives are sometimes attributed to Homer, sources dating back at least to Pindar establish a tradition of assigning to the minor epics distinct authors who are often affiliated with Homer as his disciples or as continuers of his tradition.[5] The authors of the cyclic poems were also assumed to have been younger than Homer, and therefore the texts are generally dated post-700 B.C.[6] Third, these narratives were considered aesthetically inferior to the *Iliad* and the *Odyssey*: according to Photius, Proclus said that the poems of the cycle were preserved and studied not for their artistic nature so much as for the sequence of events.[7] A telling example of this judgment is a *scholion* on *Odyssey* 7.115 which complains that epithets in the epic cycle do not match the excellence of those in Homer, and merely function to fill out a verse conveniently.[8] Aristotle (*Poetics* 1459b) judges the *Kypria* and the *Little Iliad* to be much more episodic than the unified *Iliad* and *Odyssey*, and therefore inferior to them.[9]

Perhaps the most important factor in the reception and reputation of the epic cycle has been the work of the Hellenistic Alexandrian scholars who collected, compiled, and edited much ancient Greek literature. These scholars, who remain some of the most influential editors and commentators on Greek literature, were unaware of the oral tradition of archaic Greek poetry. As a result, they firmly established the practice of interpreting the cyclic narratives as later compositions which provided further storylines for unexplained or allusive references in the *Iliad* and *Odyssey*, and which could not have functioned as influences on the Homeric poet. The Alexandrians explained Homer by Homer, and were largely responsible for discrediting the epic cycle.[10]

This approach to the epic cycle continued until the early twentieth century, when one major Homeric scholar could write that 'the effect of the *Iliad* and the *Odyssey* was still so strong that sequels or introductions met with a public.'[11] The epic cycle still suffers, too, from aesthetic judgments by modern scholars: Malcolm Davies, in his book on the epic cycle, writes, 'Why, for instance, publish literal translations of those tiny portions of confessedly second-rate epics that happen to have survived?'[12] As Lynette Felber notes in this volume, however, the perceived inferiority of sequels is 'an aesthetic judgment, not a narrative law.'[13] In the present essay, I will challenge the long-held assumptions that the poems in the cycle were created as prequels and sequels to Homeric epics, and that they are aesthetically inferior to them. I will do this through a consideration of the mode of production of narrative in the oral tradition from which both the epic cycle and the Homeric epics sprang. This may provide scholars with a new perspective from which to interpret and appreciate the creation of the Homeric epics, the relationship of the epic cycle to those epics, and the beginning of the sequel.

The *Iliad* and the *Odyssey* did not spring full-blown from the head of Homer, whoever or whatever he was; nor did they exist in quite the solitary splendour I described in my introductory comments. These very long poems were the result, as we now know through the pioneering work of Milman Parry and his student Albert Lord, among others, of an extensive oral epic tradition.[14] Oral-traditional narrative is characterized by its fluidity, its lack of boundaries and closure, and its inherent capacity for spontaneous shortening and lengthening in every compositional production. Its nature defies the notion of prequel and sequel, involving the chronological priority of the charismatic text, and the reopening of a closed text with which modern readers are familiar.[15] This oral tradition may have reached back beyond even the Greek Bronze Age depicted in the poems, to early Indo-European speakers.[16] The oral tradition formed a huge, interconnected, variegated web of legendary and mythical narratives which comprised the *corpus* of the epic cycle, part of which were the stories of Achilles and Odysseus which eventually became the *Iliad* and *Odyssey*. The events which are the focus of the *Iliad* and the *Odyssey*, therefore, were always already part of a universalizing mythical/legendary narrative which surrounded them with events occurring both before and after them.[17] Ross Scaife argues on the basis of art-historical evidence that the *Kypria*, and by implication other narratives of the epic cycle, were initially received as favourably as, or even more so than, the narratives of the *Iliad* and *Odyssey*.[18] Nevertheless, out of this massive body of mythological literature, the *Iliad*, in particular, and the *Odyssey*, secondarily, have been constructed since antiquity as the primary, original texts to which various prequels and sequels accrete. At some stage, the narratives of the *Iliad* and the *Odyssey* were distinguished from the traditional material, were canonized, and became highly charismatic texts.

The fixation of the narratives of the *Iliad* and the *Odyssey* as charismatic texts forced the narratives of the epic cycle into a relationship of priority and posteriority to them, which in the context of the oral tradition had existed only very loosely, if at all. The epic cycle, through time, began to assume a more formal, sequential structure. Recent scholars acknowledge the common narratives which existed before the fixation of the *Iliad* and the *Odyssey*, and the effect of that fixation on the epic cycle.[19] Latacz, in particular, refers to the epic cycle as we have it as a 'post-Homeric version of the Troy saga.'[20] Yet because of that very fixation and canonization of the Homeric epics, a process which distinguished the Homeric epics from the epic cycle and oral tradition of their origin, it is also likely that the epic cycle has been allowed to retain some pre-Homeric elements of the oral tradition.[21] The fragmentary evidence of the cycle reveals its origins in the oral tradition in a way which has been foreclosed to the *Iliad* and the *Odyssey* simply because of their canonization and exclusivity. The epic cycle, in particular, reveals its ties with the oral tradition through the elements of flexibility, repetition, and inclusiveness. Conversely, the fragments of the epic cycle can also shed some light on how the Homeric epics sought to distinguish themselves from established traditional narrative patterns.[22]

The first narrative of the Trojan cycle is the *Kypria* in eleven books (all the epics or parts of epics surrounding the *Iliad* and *Odyssey* are much shorter than the two monumental poems in the forms in which we have them). Although the text of the *Kypria* which Proclus preserves in many instances seems to presuppose the *Iliad*, I suggest that the text represents a tradition shared by both narratives rather than an imitation of, and reference to, the fixed narrative of the *Iliad* by a text composed to complement that *Iliad*.

The beginnings of the *Kypria* and the *Iliad* demonstrate the difficulty of determining the interrelationship of these narratives, and complicate the notion that the *Kypria* is the 'prequel' to the *Iliad*. In Proclus's *Kypria*, the plot is explained by Zeus's planning (*bouleuetai*) with Themis to bring about the Trojan War.[23] The opening lines of the *Iliad* refer to the plan (*boule*) of Zeus being fulfilled.[24] These lines are provided with a *scholion* which quotes lines in verse (Proclus' epitome is in prose) from the *Kypria* which contain the same phrase for the plan of Zeus as the *Iliad* does, and which outline Zeus's plan to relieve Earth from the burden of mankind's population by causing both the Theban and Trojan wars.[25] The *scholion*'s commentary explains the severity of Zeus's punishment as resulting from the lack of reverence among mankind. The connection which the *scholion* to the *Iliad* makes between the plan of Zeus in the *Iliad* and the plan articulated in the *Kypria* indicates that the former plan at least in part refers to the plan of Zeus for the diminishing of mankind. Nevertheless, the plan of Zeus in the *Iliad* has, since the Hellenistic Age, been interpreted as referring primarily to Zeus's plan for Achilles – in other words, as separate from the rest of the Trojan cycle; accordingly, the plan of Zeus in the *Kypria* has been read as dependent upon, and an imitation of, the beginning of the *Iliad*. Thus begins the construction of the *Kypria* as a prequel to the *Iliad*.

My own emphasis on the independence of the *Kypria* does not preclude other interpretive options. The reference to the *boule* of Zeus in the *Iliad* may be an acknowledgment of the common store of myth which the *Kypria* and *Iliad* share, or it may simply stand on its own within the *Iliad*. Given the self-consciousness of the poet of the *Iliad*, there is also the distinct likelihood that the *boule* of Zeus at *Iliad* 1.5 refers both to the plan in the *Kypria* and to Zeus's plan for Achilles in the *Iliad*.[26] My point is that once the *Iliad* and the *Odyssey* achieved a fixed status and became exemplars of the epic genre, other narratives of the epic cycle were forced into a less prominent position, eventually being read as simply extensions of the *Iliad* and *Odyssey*, when all the narratives, including the *Iliad* and the *Odyssey*, had previously existed on a relatively equal footing. The *Kypria*, along with the other Trojan epics, finds itself literally and figuratively relegated to the rank of explanation, footnote, and prequel to the text of the Homeric poems.

The *Kypria* also contains an example of another characteristic which is considered a sign of the inferiority of the epic cycle: repetition of stories between apparently segregated minor epics. Both Achilles and Odysseus are depicted as hiding in order to escape conscription, events scrupulously avoided by the Homeric poet. Odysseus pretends to be mad, but he is detected by Palamedes, a revelation which is later punished by Palamedes' death by drowning at the hands of Odysseus, according to one variant.[27] Achilles' feminine disguise is not referred to by Proclus, but is related in a *scholion* to the *Iliad*, dubiously assigned to the *Kypria*.[28] According to this *scholion*, Peleus hides Achilles in disguise as a girl on Scyros, where he meets Deidamia and sires Neoptolemus. Proclus does relate in the *Kypria* Achilles' marriage to Deidamia on Scyros after Achilles has wounded Telephus and the Greeks have been scattered by a storm on their first attempt to sail to Troy. The *Little Iliad* also says that Achilles is driven by a storm to Scyros after his expedition to Telephus's land.[29] Without attempting to unravel the complexities of Achilles' visits to Scyros and the necessary chronologies for Neoptolemus's conception if he is to be old enough to fight at Troy, suffice it to say that both the *Kypria* and the *Little Iliad* seem to have included at least one trip by Achilles to Scyros.[30] The reference by the two cyclic epics illustrates the potential for overlapping narratives and repetition of the same episodes associated with an oral tradition in which each poet had great flexibility in constructing an inclusive narrative. Although the prequels and sequels are presented as named narratives with beginnings and endings, this repetition and overlap indicates the influence of the oral tradition rather than its disorganization and inadequacy.[31]

Proclus says that the *Iliad* follows the *Kypria* and that the *Iliad* is, in turn, followed by the *Aethiopis* of Arctinus of Miletus.[32] The *Aethiopis* is preserved by Proclus and is in two fragments, one of which may be spurious. As with the *Kypria*, the *Aethiopis* was probably written down expressly to complement and expand upon the *Iliad*.[33] The narrative of the *Aethiopis*, however, appears from the type of stories it relates to be one of the most ancient of the cyclic epics: its main incidents are the conflicts between Achilles and two Trojan allies, Penthesilea and Memnon. Christian Kopff has recently argued, relying upon some of the same notions of flexibility and repetition that I have addressed, that the *Aethiopis* may also have included Priam's supplication of Achilles which we have in *Iliad* 24, and that *Iliad* 24 may have conversely included the death of Penthesilea (an *Amazonia*) featured in the *Aethiopis*.[34]

In the second conflict, Memnon, son of Eos, kills Antilochus, the great friend of Achilles (see *Iliad* 23 for Antilochus as a clever young chariot-eer); Achilles, in turn, kills Memnon, who is granted immortality; and Achilles, himself killed by the combination of Paris and Apollo, is granted immortality. Achilles' contest with Memnon seems to parallel signifi-cantly Achilles' encounter with Hector in the *Iliad*. The two events differ, however, in ways which illuminate the agenda of the Iliadic author. The most prominent of these is the immortality which is available to both Memnon and Achilles from their divine mothers in the *Aethiopis*: Memnon receives immortality from Eos (dawn) and Achilles is transported by his mother, Thetis, to the White Island. Although I would hesitate to suggest that the Memnon/Achilles scenario is the early paradigm of the Hector/Achilles antagonism, it does seem likely that the Homeric poet may have had the Memnon/Achilles story in mind, and sought to distinguish and deepen his own narrative by denying his heroes the salvation of immor-tality. The Homeric poet therefore distinguishes his poem from the cyclic tradition of Achilles' immortality, as well as from the possibility of im-mortality for mortals in general which runs through the cycle, by an explicit denial of these variants.

Proclus's *Aethiopis* ends with the quarrel between Ajax and Odysseus over the arms of Achilles; a *scholion* to Pindar's *Isthmian* 3.53, the only fragment definitely connected with the *Aethiopis*, says that the *Aethiopis* relates Ajax's suicide. Severyns gives credence to this fragment, asserting that the author of the *Aethiopis* would not have ended his narrative without including the suicide. The *Little Iliad* in four books, by Lesches of Mitylene, begins with this same dispute over the arms and Ajax's suicide; therefore, it apparently renews part of the *Aethiopis*. It is not unlikely that in the oral tradition there were versions of Ajax's suicide in both the *Aethiopis* and the *Little Iliad*, but that Proclus eliminated one in the inter-ests of a smoother overall narrative.[35] The *Little Iliad* also relates the story of Odysseus's seizure of the Palladium: Odysseus, disguised as a beggar, meets with Helen (a scene narrated by her in *Odyssey* 4), and, either on this same mission or on a separate one, Diomedes and Odysseus steal the Palladium out of Troy, the most important condition for the fall of Troy.[36] The *Iliou Persis*, however, informs us that the Palladium stolen by Odysseus was a copy, and that Aeneas, a remaining member of the Trojan royal family, had hidden it and subsequently escaped with it.[37] These repetitions again betray the flexibility of the narratives of the epic cycle before they achieved their fixed status as prequels and sequels.

The narrative of the *Little Iliad* intervenes between two poems attributed to Arctinus of Miletus: the *Aethiopis*, discussed above, and the *Iliou Persis* (Sack of Troy). Interestingly, its status within the epic cycle seems to mirror the cycle's status in relation to the Homeric epics. The *Little Iliad*'s sharing of many incidents and episodes with both the *Aethiopis* and the *Iliou Persis* has led a number of scholars to conclude that the *Aethiopis*, the *Little Iliad*, and the *Iliou Persis* were originally one undifferentiated poem called the *Little Iliad*. The argument against this theory, as Davies puts it, is that Proclus does divide these three epics up carefully by the number of books assigned to each, and that he would not do so unless they were distinct works.[38] The intervention of the *Little Iliad* by Lesches between two poems ascribed to Arctinus in combination with these overlappings has led other scholars to speculate that Lesches composed the *Little Iliad* to fill in the narrative gap left by Arctinus between his poems.[39] Like the poets of the epic cycle who have been said merely to have filled in gaps left by the magisterial Homer, the author of the *Little Iliad* is often disparaged in contrast both with other cyclic poets and with Homer. Severyns repeatedly explains passages in the *Little Iliad* which differ from the *Aethiopis* and the *Iliou Persis* as rather hapless innovations (rather than alternative traditions), and finds the style of Lesches 'romanesque.'[40]

The two remaining narratives of the epic cycle, the *Nostoi* and the *Telegony*, also might invite the label 'romanesque.' Both have extremely episodic and disunified plots. Many of the episodes in the *Nostoi* closely parallel descriptions of events in the *Odyssey*, although this does not prove that one was dependent on the other; it seems, rather, representative of the oral tradition. The *Telegony*, the final book of the epic cycle preserved by Proclus, is a very strange and even less well-known part of the epic cycle; it suffers the humiliation of being described by Severyns as a 'misérable poème,' a harsh judgment but one which, to a certain extent, encapsulates the attitude to sequels in general.[41] A study of the *Telegony*'s far-fetched plot would certainly have contributed strongly to Aristotle's and Aristarchus's opinions that the epic cycle was far inferior to Homer's finely crafted epics.[42] The events depicted in the *Telegony*, like events of several of these other minor epics, are also assigned to other narratives: the scholar Eustathius attributes the story to a version of the *Nostoi* rather than to the *Telegony*.[43]

I began this essay by discussing the oral tradition of poetic composition of which the *Iliad*, the *Odyssey*, and the poems of the epic cycle are all products. The *Iliad* and the *Odyssey* survive intact as magnificent examples of the highest level of achievement of that tradition; the epic cycle survives for us only in a very few quotations and in the second-hand summary of Proclus in Photius. The survival of both the two large epics and the epic cycle in the fixed forms that we have is directly dependent upon preservation in writing at some point; the relative degree of survival in writing reflects literary–historical judgments about the value and excellence of the narratives (as does the survival of all ancient classical literature: *Oedipus Tyrannus* has been judged more valuable for preservation in the canon than, for example, Aeschylus's trilogy about Achilles, which supposedly incorporates a homosexual relationship between Achilles and Patroclus). Before the *Iliad* and the *Odyssey* achieved fixed form, both they and the rest of the epic cycle were part of the oral tradition in which narratives were composed by an individual bard according to the contingencies of the occasion and of his audience.

In the oral tradition, then, prequels and sequels did not and could not exist. In the oral tradition, the *Iliad* and the *Odyssey* by Homer did not exist as defined texts with beginnings, endings, and an author, even if the stories or versions of the stories circulated. From literary references and artistic sources, it is clear that the *Iliad* and the *Odyssey* of Homer were recognized as pre-eminent epics from the eighth century onward in Greece (which is why the introduction of writing in the eighth century is often used to explain the fixed nature of their texts).[44] It is tempting to attribute this pre-eminence to an arguably superior aesthetic quality of these narratives in comparison with the rest of the cycle, as is often done, but this excludes other possibilities which are not available for modern scholars to explore, such as political and historical exigencies in the archaic Greek world.[45] The narratives of the epic cycle were constructed as prequels and sequels, not by the forces of capitalism, but by the power of charismatic texts and by the aesthetic priorities of literary historians in establishing a canon. All the other episodes and narratives in the epic cycle, loosely affiliated as they were, now became secondary to these works. The effect of the *Iliad* and the *Odyssey* on these narratives is significant. It is my contention that the fixedness of the *Iliad* and the

Odyssey, the attribution of an author, and the definition of boundaries by inclusion and exclusion forced the poems of the epic cycle, perhaps for their own survival, into a similar pattern of definition. And because the *Iliad* and the *Odyssey* were the first to achieve prominence, the other narratives of the epic cycle arranged themselves in relation to those narratives as sequels and prequels, with fixed limits and authors.[46] Yet, given their origins in the oral tradition, for both the epic cycle and the *Iliad* and the *Odyssey*, the construction of distinction and exclusion was and is as much a fiction as the purported authors assigned to each.[47]

Unlike more modern primary texts and sequels, which begin with a unique text which then itself generates sequels and perhaps prequels, in the archaic epic tradition the charismatic text arises from a context which already contains that text's prequels and sequels. It seems, therefore, that the emergence of the *Iliad* and the *Odyssey* from the overarching narrative of the oral tradition, their canonization and preservation, was also the birth of the prequel and sequel.

The proximity to, and the dependence of, the Trojan cycle on the oral tradition is revealed precisely through the uncertainty of its narratives. Commentators since the Alexandrian times have complained that the boundaries of the *Kypria*, the *Aethiopis*, the *Little Iliad*, the *Iliou Persis*, the *Nostoi*, and the *Telegony* encroach upon each other, and that there seem to be different versions of the same episode available for individual epics. As I have suggested, a more fruitful approach to these inconsistencies might be to understand them as remnants of the living oral tradition, and to accept the inherent multiplicity, rather than insisting upon determining the one true version. The unity, perfection, and exclusion of the *Iliad* and the *Odyssey* created, along with the prequel and sequel, a lack of appreciation for the multiplicity of the oral tradition. The *Iliad* and *Odyssey* themselves brook almost no variants: their beginnings and endings are clearly fixed, with only minor variables possible, and they do not repeat other episodes in the epic cycle. Jasper Griffin, in an important article entitled 'The Epic Cycle and the Uniqueness of Homer,' argues that Homer excludes so much from the epic cycle because it is fantastical, bizarre, inappropriate for the modest and discreet Homeric poet.[48] I speculate that the Homeric poet does not omit events from the epic cycle out of a dislike for bizarreness or some false modesty (one need only look at the episodes in Odysseus's wanderings for bizarreness, or the song by Demodocus about Ares and Aphrodite for sexual frankness), but rather specifically in order to establish his own narratives as unique and individual, as not part of an amorphous tradition, and as supremely exclusive.

The oral tradition of the epic cycle as I have presented it comprises what may essentially be read as one large, universalizing text. This state of composition seems to resemble Todorov's description of the nature of narrative: 'In a certain sense, all texts can be considered as parts of a single text which has been in the writing since the beginning of time. Without being unaware of the difference between relations established *in presentia* (intratextual relations), and those established *in absentia* (intertextual relations), we must also not underestimate the presence of other texts within the text.'[49] The notion of 'other texts within the text' resembles the overt interpenetration of episodes from one text to the other which the Trojan cycle preserves for us; again, this aspect of intertextuality in the *Iliad* and the *Odyssey* is discernible only in the form of allusion and is repressed as much as possible in these narratives' striving towards unity and closure. Jonathon Culler, too, proposes for all texts a unity which the oral tradition of the epic cycle exhibits clearly: 'literary works are to be considered not as autonomous entities, "organic wholes," but as inter-textual constructs: sequences which have meaning in relation to other texts which they take up, cite, parody, refute, or generally transform. A text can be read only in relation to other texts, and it is made possible by the codes which animate the discursive space of a culture.'[50] Unlike literature following the *Iliad* and the *Odyssey*, the stories of the epic cycle existed, not as 'autonomous entities,' but as intertextual constructs. The establishment of the primary texts of the *Iliad* and the *Odyssey* began the process of asserting narrative closure (and opening) against a tradition which seems to have been based upon unselfconscious and overt intertextuality. The creation of the *Iliad* and the *Odyssey* inaugurated the autonomous text, to which other texts then must relate as either prequels or sequels.[51]

The effects of the literary uniqueness of the *Iliad* and *Odyssey* were widespread. Their narrative fixation engendered a lack of appreciation for the multiplicity of narrative and enforced a linear way of looking at its creation, opening the way for the possibility of both prequels and sequels. Not surprisingly, the dominance of the *Iliad* and the *Odyssey* in the epic genre and their comparatively lacklustre prequels and sequels seem to have precluded much further work in epic in early Greece. Other narrative genres emerged or became prominent, such as lyric, various types of prose writing (travelogues, histories, philosophy later), and tragedy. It is notable that all of these genres assert clearly their debt to the monumental Homeric epics at the same time that they identify their own uniqueness. Lyric often relies on Homeric language and allusions; historians often situate their narratives by citing the Trojan War (both Herodotus and Thucydides refer to the Trojan War in the first paragraphs); the tragedies explicitly employ narratives and themes from the epic cycle (but only once from the *Iliad* or the *Odyssey*!).[52] Plato's anxious relationship to Homeric poetry and tragedy is well known, manifesting itself in a compulsion to distinguish philosophy from epic and tragic poetry at the same time that he stoops to using characters and techniques from those very genres when it suits his purpose. In myriad ways, Greek literature builds upon the foundation of the *Iliad* and the *Odyssey*, which, in turn, is an important component in Roman literature, which provides the basis for ecclesiastical and early European literature. Although the connections to the *Iliad* and the *Odyssey* inevitably become tenuous, they do exist. In a playful yet polemical move, I might assert that Western European literature since the ascension of the *Iliad* is little more than a sequel to that very text.[53]

Notes

1 See Malcolm Davies, 'Prolegomena and Paralegomena to a New Edition (with Commentary) of the Fragments of Early Greek Epic,' *Nachrichten der Akademie der Wissenschaft in Göttingen 1 phil.-hist. Kl.* 2 (1986): 98.

2 Albin Lesky, *History of Greek Literature*, trans. James Willis and Cornelis de Heer (London: Methuen, 1957) 79, and Thomas W. Allen, *Homer: The Origins and the Transmission* (Oxford: Oxford UP, 1924) 51–3.

3 Scholion (marginal comment) *Protrep.* 2.30; Lesky, *History of Greek Literature* 79.

4 See G.L. Huxley, *Greek Epic Poetry: From Eumelos to Panyassis* (Cambridge, MA: Harvard UP, 1969) 123–4, 141; Allen, *Homer* 64–5. Gregory Nagy, *Pindar's Homer: The Lyric Possession of the Epic Past* (Baltimore: Johns Hopkins UP, 1990) 73, comments on the paradox of the written epic cycle being later than Homer although the narratives of the epic cycle may represent an earlier version in the oral tradition; see also Malcolm Davies, *The Epic Cycle* (Bristol: Bristol Classical, 1989) 3–5, and Malcolm Davies, 'The Date of the Epic Cycle,' *Glotta* 67 (1989): 100.

5 See Davies, 'Prolegomena' 100, for a discussion of the attribution of authors to the minor epics. Pindar fr. 265 (Sn.) states that Homer gave Stasinos the *Kypria* as a dowry (see Loeb fr. 2 = Allen *testimonia*).

6 The Alexandrian scholars repeatedly refer to the cyclic sources as *neoteroi* or 'younger,' although this is not an unproblematic connection (Davies, 'Prolegomena' 109). Nagy, *Pindar's Homer* 19 n.9, points out that attribution to a specific author becomes more 'exclusive' as time progresses.

7 Davies, *Epic Cycle* 8; Huxley, *Greek Epic Poetry* 123–4; Albert Severyns, *Le cycle épique*

dans l'école d'Aristarque (Paris: Les Belles Lettres, 1928) 245.

8 'The epithets are not thrown in casually in the manner of the epic cycle, but the individuality of each tree is observed through each epithet': Severyns, *Le cycle* 156.

9 Huxley, *Greek Epic Poetry* 124; Lesky, *History of Greek Literature* 83. Ross Scaife, 'The *Kypria* and Its Early Reception,' *Classical Antiquity* 14 (1995): 170–4, however, challenges the aesthetic terms of Aristotle's judgment, and see below.

10 Severyns, *Le cycle* 247 and 159; although it should be noted that the most influential Homeric scholar, Aristarchus, despite his derogatory attitude to the cycle, always included in his *scholia* and commentary the tradition he denied, thereby preserving it for posterity. His predecessor Zenodotus was not so fastidious, and whatever he rejected was in general excised completely from his commentary. Both Severyns and Davies (*Epic Cycle* 2) note that beginning with the Alexandrians the term 'cyclic' became identified with the inferior status of cyclic poetry.

11 Allen, *Homer* 69.

12 Davies, *Epic Cycle* iv.

13 Felber 118; see also Carole Gerson 145–6, this volume.

14 Albert Lord, *The Singer of Tales* (Cambridge, MA: Harvard UP, 1960), and Milman Parry, *The Making of Homeric Verse: The Collected Papers of Milman Parry*, ed. Adam Parry (Oxford: Oxford UP, 1971).

15 Terry Castle, in an aside in a work on the eighteenth-century novel, comments that sequels arise from a 'charismatic text' which encodes 'talismanic mythic material,' thereby articulating 'underlying cultural fantasies,' gratifying 'pervasive cultural wishes,' and having 'an unusually powerful effect on a large reading public': see *Masquerade and Civilization: The Carnivalesque in Eighteenth-Century English Culture and Fiction* (Stanford: Stanford UP, 1986) 133–4.

16 Gregory Nagy, *The Best of the Achaeans* (Baltimore: Johns Hopkins UP, 1979) 2.

17 Severyns, *Le cycle* 261.

18 Scaife, 'Kypria' 164–5.

19 Joachim Latacz, *Homer: His Art and His World*, trans. James P. Holoka (Ann Arbor: U of Michigan P, 1996) 61, 75–8; Jonathon Burgess, 'The Non-Homeric *Cypria*,' *Transactions of the American Philological Association* 126 (1996): 78–9, acknowledges the eventual function of the epic cycle as prequel and sequel, but asserts that the epic cycle was not necessarily dependent upon Homer at the moment of its fixation.

20 Latacz, *Homer* 75.

21 See Latacz, *Homer* 76; Burgess, 'Non-Homeric *Cypria*' 78–9.

22 See Richard Janko, ed., *The Iliad: A Commentary*, vol. 4, G.S. Kirk, general ed. (Cambridge: Cambridge UP, 1992) xi and 347, for Homer's variation from the oral tradition.

23 Allen fr. 1 = Loeb fr. 1. The Alexandrian scholars Aristophanes and Aristarchus substitute Thetis for Themis here, obviously assimilating this planning session with the plans of Zeus and Thetis for Achilles in *Iliad* 1 (Severyns, *Le cycle* 247). If, as the various commentaries and *Kypria* claim, the purpose of the wars is to punish mankind for lack of reverence, Themis, the goddess of holy law, would be the likely candidate as Zeus's assistant.

24 *Iliad* 1.5.

25 Loeb fr. 3 = Allen fr. 1.

26 Proclus's *Kypria* ends with Zeus's plan (*Dios boule*) to relieve the Trojans through Achilles' withdrawal. This *boule* does seem to resonate with the Iliadic *boule* as a means of connecting the narratives.

27 Proclus only mentions Palamedes' death, while Pausanias cites the *Kypria* as relating his drowning death at the hands of Diomedes and Odysseus (Loeb fr. 19 = Allen fr. 21).

28 *Scholion* to *Iliad* 19.326 = Davies *incertum fragmentum* 4. See Severyns, *Le cycle* 289–91.

29 Loeb fr. 5 = Allen fr. 4.

30 Severyns, *Le cycle* 338, suggests that Achilles was hidden on Scyros as a boy, as in the uncertain Cyprian fragment; that he returned to Scyros as a man, according to the *Little Iliad*; and that Proclus incorporates both by having Achilles actually marry Deidamia on this second visit, even though Neoptolemus was previously conceived.

31 See Burgess, 'Non-Homeric *Cypria*' 87 ff., on the process of demarcation. Burgess argues that the non-Proclus fragments indicate that the *Cypria* did not end where Proclus said it did (81) and may have in fact narrated the whole Trojan War, that is, including the *Iliad* narrative even at the date of fixation (85, 91). The shared treatment of the same themes may resemble, on a less complex scale, Samuel Glen Wong's notion of 'coincident utterances,' in this volume (82).

32 Allen 105.20–2 = Loeb fr. 1.

33 Severyns, *Le cycle* 313–14, 318.

34 E. Christian Kopff, 'The Structure of the Amazonia (Aethiopis),' in *The Greek Renaissance of the Eighth Century B.C.: Tradition and Innovation*, ed. Robin Hagg (Stockholm: Astroms, 1983) 59 and 61.

35 Severyns, *Le cycle* 324–5; Davies, *Epic Cycle* 60.

36 Loeb fr. 1 = Allen pp. 106–7 divides Odysseus's entry into Troy into two distinct visits; Apollodorus V.13 describes it as one visit. Severyns argues that the *Little Iliad* innovates by dividing Odysseus's entry into Troy into two episodes, one derived from Helen's Odyssean rendering, the other from the story of the Palladium from the *Iliou Persis*.

37 Loeb *Iliou Persis* fr. 2 = Davies *fragmentum dubium*; Davies, *Epic Cycle* 79, is highly sceptical of this latter story from Dionysius Halicarnassus, and suspects it of lateness because of its convenient connection with the Roman and Vergilian myth of Aeneas.

38 Davies, *Epic Cycle* 7 and 63; Huxley, *Greek Epic Poetry* 147.

39 Severyns, *Le cycle* 356–7; Allen, *Homer* 74.

40 Severyns, *Le cycle* 331, 333, 352. See Nagy, *Pindar's Homer* 76, for an alternative interpretation which valorizes Lesches.

41 Severyns, *Le cycle* 409: 'Eugammon de Cyrène a fait tomber l'épopée plus bas encore que Lesches, dont il éxagère les défauts jusqu'à l'invraisemblance. Une oeuvre comme la *Télégonie* marque la fin du genre épique, annonce un genre nouveau, celui du roman en prose.' The more moderate Lesky, *History of Greek Literature* 83, calls this the 'most surprising' part of the epic cycle, combining old tradition with new invention.

42 In the *Telegony*, Odysseus is killed by Telegonus, his own son by Circe. Following the mistaken patricide, Telegonus, accompanied by Penelope and Telemachus, takes his father's body back to Circe, where Circe makes them all immortal and they intermarry (Circe to Telemachus; Penelope to Telegonus). 'This is a second-rate Greek epic's equivalent of "they all lived happily ever after"': Davies, *Epic Cycle* 94.

43 *Nostoi* Loeb fr. 4 = Allen fr. 9

44 I hesitate to assign a date for this occurrence: it could be the date at which writing was introduced to Greece in the late eighth century and the monumental texts of the *Iliad* and *Odyssey* were perhaps written down, or it could be a later date when the *Iliad* and *Odyssey* became fixed texts through rhapsodic stabilization. Latacz, *Homer* 61,

attributes the organization of the epic cycle to the establishment of a written text of the *Iliad* and *Odyssey*.

45 It is virtually impossible to ascertain why the narratives of Achilles and Odysseus, out of the whole corpus, became focal narratives, but from the later prominence of the *Iliad* and the *Odyssey* it may be surmised that Achilles and Odysseus may very well have been charismatic focuses from very early on. This is especially compelling when one considers Nagy's claim that the essential Achilles narrative can be traced back to Indo-European myth. Along with others, Latacz is still wedded to the idea that the success of the *Iliad* and *Odyssey* is due to their 'originality of perspective' (*Homer* 75). Nagy, *Pindar's Homer* 70, reasserts his argument that the Homeric epics achieved their prominence through an impetus towards 'pan-Hellenism.' Gillies, in this volume, cites material and cultural forces as causes of both original narratives and their prequels and sequels.

46 'The *Iliad* and *Odyssey* would appear to have been preserved in written texts earlier than the other poems of the Epic Cycle, which seem to have gradually assumed the status of sequels to or anticipations of the Homeric epics. By the time they took on the stable and permanent form of which we possess fragmentary knowledge, they would have been accurately termed "post-Homeric"': Davies, *Epic Cycle* 5.

47 J. Hillis Miller, 'The Problematic of Ending,' *Nineteenth-Century Fiction* 33 (1978–9): 3–7, discusses the fictionality imposed by the beginnings and endings of novels: 'The aporia of ending arises from the fact that it is impossible ever to tell whether a given narrative is complete. If the ending is thought of as tying up in a careful knot, this knot could always be untied again, by the narrator or by further events, disentangled or explicated again' (5). He continues, 'No novel can be unequivocally finished, or for that matter unequivocally unfinished' (7).

48 Jasper Griffin, 'The Epic Cycle and the Uniqueness of Homer,' *Journal of Hellenic Studies* 97 (1977): 40, 43: 'In the Cycle both heroism and realism are rejected in favour of an over-heated taste for sadistically coloured scenes; more striking, even more perverse effects are once again what is desired' (45).

49 Tzvetan Todorov, *The Poetics of Prose*, trans. Richard Howard (Ithaca, NY: Cornell UP, 1977) 244.

50 Jonathon Culler, *The Pursuit of Signs: Semiotics, Literature, Deconstruction* (Ithaca, NY: Cornell UP, 1981) 38. 'Intertextuality thus becomes less a name for a work's relations to particular prior texts than a designation of its participation in the discursive space of a culture: the relationship between a text and the various languages or signifying practices of a culture and its relation to those texts which articulate for it the possibilities of culture. The study of intertextuality is thus not the investigation of sources and influences as traditionally conceived; it casts its net wider to include anonymous discursive practices, codes whose origins are lost, that make possible the signifying practices of later texts' (103).

51 My argument does not intend to deny conscious use of intertextuality by later authors, or unconscious intertextuality in all types of texts. The creation of the *Iliad* and the *Odyssey* changed the face of narrative in that texts either did not reveal or were not aware of intertextuality, or recognition of intertextuality became a conscious literary device rather than the mode of composition.

52 This is the much disputed *Rhesus* of Euripides.

53 See also Michael Zeitlin, who is open to a more extended notion of sequel and intertextuality, referring to 'this bottomless hierarchy of texts' (this volume 162).

The Curious Eye and the Alternative Endings of *The Canterbury Tales*

ANDREW TAYLOR

Just as those who in physical books only have regard for thick letters and capitals for play and curiosity will never be good clerics, so those who only acquire knowledge in the book of God for the sake of pleasure and curiosity and only have regard for that which is beautiful and delectable to the eyes, nor use these things for the love and knowledge of God, will never be led through them to the perfect vision of God.
John Bromyard[1]

Visualisers ... are exposed to a special danger. The vivid and precise images which arise before us, owe much of their character and detail to sources which are quite outside the poet's control.
I.A. Richards[2]

It is widely known that Chaucer left *The Canterbury Tales* unfinished, or at least that he deviated from his original plan to have the pilgrims tell tales both on the way to Canterbury and on the return, abandoning his story-tellers at their arrival on the outskirts of town. Instead of the final series of tales, instead of a tale at all, Chaucer concluded by offering, through the Parson, a monumental prose treatise, which has daunted or irked many a modern reader. What is rather less well known is that one of Chaucer's immediate successors, apparently dissatisfied with his ending, provided an alternative which actually took the pilgrims into Canterbury. In this sequel we can see a near contemporary pitting his understanding of the pleasures of a book against Chaucer's and resisting the more austere reading practice that Chaucer's own conclusion seems to demand.

This particular struggle took place before notions of the author's proprietorial rights and the integrity of the literary work had been fused together in mutual reinforcement. Vernacular writers in the Middle Ages only gradually achieved the status of the modern author or the patristic *auctor* and, without a strong restraining principle of ownership, their writings flowed into each other in a stream of translations, free adaptations, reworkings, abridgements, and expansions.[3] Chrétien de Troyes's twelfth-century romance *Perceval*, for example, gave rise to a number of sequels whose total length was several times that of the original, and most medieval readers probably were not conscious of where the work of Chrétien stopped and that of his continuators began. On the other hand, Chaucer's cultural authority, and the relative stability of vernacular poetry by his day, gave rise to a rather different pattern, one of deliberate imitation rather than continuation. A host of fifteenth-century poets proclaimed Chaucer as their master, borrowing his themes, images, rhetorical figures, and turns of phrase, in elaborate tribute. On a few occasions, however, these poets went a step further and wrote sequels; Robert Henryson wrote *The Testament of Cresseid* as a sequel to *Troilus and Criseyde*; John Lydgate and an anonymous author both added a last Canterbury tale. Indeed, Chaucer is perhaps the first medieval English writer whose authorial status was sufficiently developed that his works might engender a proper sequel, that is, the first English writer whose works were both sufficiently popular to invite continuation and sufficiently well defined that a continuation would not necessarily blend into them.[4]

The struggle between Chaucer and his early continuators, especially the anonymous author of the *Tale of Beryn*, follows a pattern that becomes increasingly familiar in the age of print, prefiguring some of those discussed elsewhere in this volume. Like Falstaff and Tamburlaine; Sherlock Holmes, Phineas Finn, and Anne of Green Gables; Batman, Mad Max, and the Terminator, Chaucer's pilgrims acquire a life of their own. The sequels in which these various characters reappear testify not only to their popularity, but to the extent to which they have begun to wander in an alternative reality, as if they were people (if not quite real people). This illusionism fosters strong loyalties in readers, as Arthur Conan Doyle found when he tried to kill off Holmes and as L.M. Montgomery found when she tried to escape from Anne of Green Gables. When an author reaches the point where she can write that her heroine 'is as real to me as if I had given her birth,' as L.M. Montgomery did of Anne, the heroine is no longer fully hers.[5] If characters are popular enough, they can defy authorial privilege; authors may try to abandon them, but others ensure they return.

But if 'success breeds sequels,' to echo Alexander Leggatt in this volume,[6] so, too, does a difficult ending, one which refuses the reader the appropriate form of closure. As Dickens separated Pip and Estella in the first ending of *Great Expectations* only to be coerced into reuniting them in a revised version, as Shaw separated Henry Higgins and Eliza Doolittle only to have them reunited in *My Fair Lady*, so Chaucer defied his readers' curiosity and left his pilgrims on the edge of Canterbury only to have others complete the journey for him. The sequel thus becomes not just an act of homage, but also an act of resistance to the author's more severe artistic or didactic purpose.[7] Before considering the early sequels to *The Canterbury Tales*, then, it is worth considering the kind of ending they rejected. As we shall see, Chaucer's ending is particularly difficult not just because it abandons the tale-telling characters in favour of explicit moralizing, but also because it shifts to an entirely different genre, that of a particular kind of instructional manual, and in doing so demands an entirely different kind of reading.

I

The Parson's so-called tale is something of a critical embarrassment. Although it seems well to the pilgrims to end 'in som vertuous sentence' (X 63), the Parson's long prose piece is hardly what is required. As the Host pointedly reminds him, the 'sonne wole adoun' and he would do well to be 'fructuous and that in litel space' (70–1).[8] Instead, the Parson provides a comprehensive treatise that would take at least two hours to deliver. A 'long, prosy, and unleavened sermon, totally devoid of comedy, character, or narrative interest,' according to one reader, 'ill-tempered, bad-mannered, pedantic, and joyless,' according to another, the piece seems bound to fail with both pilgrims and readers.[9] Various solutions, some rather desperate, have been proposed by modern critics to cope with this frustrating ending. Many, reluctant to suggest that Chaucer simply blundered, either dismiss the Parson's Tale as a piece of unfinished business or parcel it together with the Retractions as a deathbed renunciation which, however sincere, remains a regrettable lapse from Chaucer's humane good humour and no true part of his literary work.

There is, however, a strong argument that Chaucer did not simply abandon the *Tales* and that the Parson's Tale must be seen, not as an unfinished or stop-gap measure, nor as a mere extraliterary gesture of piety, but as a calculated denial of the more worldly taste for narrative.[10] Chaucer, according to this argument, closes by deliberately breaking the fellowship of storytelling and directing a reader – rather than a listener-

towards pious, solitary meditation. The trajectory is discernible long before we reach the Parson's Tale; as we move from the Canon Yeoman's revelations of alchemical chicanery to the sordid fable of the Manciple, we follow a 'degenerative sequence' that calls into question the poetic enterprise of the Tales.[11] When, in the Manciple's Tale, the god of poetry, Phoebus, is exposed as a vindictive cuckold and the tale-bearing crow as a malicious voyeur, poetry, tale-telling, and perhaps even language itself are revealed as brutally deceptive.[12] All this prepares us for the final section, where storytelling is finally abandoned and we move 'from the public delights of a "fable" to the private spiritual refreshment of a "meditacioun."'[13]

If we accept the Parson's Tale as a proper ending, however, the question of its genre becomes crucial. It has long been recognized that the Parson's Tale is, strictly speaking, neither a tale nor a sermon, but a compilation of two penitential manuals.[14] Many, however, persist in referring to it as a sermon. The common assumption appears to be that a penitential manual could be delivered as if it were a sermon, and that the difference between the two was minor. Even Siegfried Wenzel, while careful to stress that the tale is 'not formally a sermon or homily,' allows that it might be classified as a sermon 'as long as one understands by "sermon" no more than an extended *discourse* on a religious or moral subject, especially if directed by a cleric to a group of *listeners*.'[15] Most critics, from F.N. Robinson on, have been less cautious and have referred to the Parson's Tale as a sermon without further qualification. All this assumes that the Parson's Tale, rather like the Pardoner's, is intended to be appreciated in its entirety as if it were an actual oral discourse, 'spoken by a parish priest to a group of listeners.'[16] A penitential manual, however, bears roughly the same relation to a sermon that a textbook does to a popular lecture. Such manuals, whose primary purpose was to instruct a priest so that he might hear confession, were on occasion used by preachers as collections of material, but their contents were never delivered verbatim. The preacher might use the themes and material, and even in places the structure, of the manual, but he had to rework the material extensively before he could deliver it with any hope of success.[17] Schematic, encyclopedic, and unadorned, a manual such as the Parson's Tale would indeed be dull and ineffective if delivered as a sermon and would testify to a pitiful incompetence on the part of the man who attempted to preach it. As long as we conceive of the tale as a discourse delivered to the pilgrims, it remains a failure. What Chaucer provides, however, is not a sermon, nor an imitation of spoken discourse of any kind, but rather a doctrinal manual, one which could possibly also be used for devotional reading and self-scrutiny, but was intended neither to be heard or read through at a sitting nor to be visualized as a dramatic performance. As we enter the elaborate scholastic divisions of the Parson's Tale, the world of the pilgrims recedes and we no longer feel their wearied presence.

More is at stake in classifying the Parson's Tale as a penitential manual than just nicety of terminology. By abutting a penitential manual to his collection of tales, Chaucer creates an ending which is radically disruptive and challenging, far more so than it would have been had he concluded with some shorter moral discourse along the lines of the Pardoner's Tale.[18] *The Canterbury Tales* is, for the most part, written to be read aloud. However much they may benefit from the repeated consultation and cross-referencing that book ownership allows, the tales make use of conventions associated with oral delivery and are thus well suited to dramatic reading.[19] When read privately, on the other hand, they require 'the silent reader to resist the tyranny of the eye and to *hear*' and 'treat the reader not just as a hearer, but as a member of an audience or group of hearers,' thus inscribing the reader into an imaginary community.[20] The Parson's Tale, however, is better suited for studying, that is, for piecemeal and largely solitary but repeated consultation; taken all at once, it is indigestible. The Ellesmere glossator, for one, appears to have understood the Parson's Tale in this way, for he provides abundant Latin glosses in this section, giving visual definition to the page, which would assist readers to find their way back to passages and to memorize them.[21]

Chaucer's transition, in other words, demands not just that the reader abandon earlier frivolity, but that the reader start using the book in a fundamentally different way. Rebuking the expectations he established in his earlier tales, and breaking the imaginary fellowship of both pilgrims and listeners, Chaucer calls his reader to self-examination and studious consultation using the penitential manual as a guide. The Parson's Tale thus has much in common with the tradition of devotional contemplation often known as *meditatio*, as Thomas Bestul has argued. Although, for the most part, the Parson's Tale is free of images, many of those it does use, such as the blood that spurts from under Christ's nails when he is bound, are common in northern devotional literature.[22] Such images were intended to provoke intense affective piety, in which the penitent reader would become a direct witness to Christ's suffering, but they represent only a transitional stage in religious meditation and must eventually be abandoned for more purely intellectual contemplation. The Parson's Tale leads in the same direction, weaning the reader from 'the image-bound world of fables and fiction, on a progress toward the prayer of the Retraction.'[23]

II

The Parson's Tale is truly a difficult ending, and it is hardly surprising that some of Chaucer's actual readers resisted. His ending requires us to read with almost monastic discipline; indeed, the tradition of *meditatio* developed in the monasteries as a form of the daily religious reading that was part of the *opus dei* and was gradually adopted by pious laypeople. Yet it is precisely this pious labour that is rejected by Chaucer's Monk, as if the very pattern of future resistance were prefigured in *The Canterbury Tales* itself:

> This ilke Monk leet olde thynges pace,
> And heeld after the newe world the space,
> He yaf° nat of that text a pulled hen,   °gave
> That seith that hunters ben nat hooly men,
> Ne that a monk, whan that heis recchelees,°   °heedless of rules
> Is likned til a fissh that is waterlees –
> That is to seyn, a monk out of his cloystre.
> But thilke text heeld he nat worth an oystre;
> And I seyde his opinion was good.
> What sholde he studie and make hymselven wood,°   °mad
> Upon a book in cloystre alwey to poure,
> Or swynken° with his handes, and laboure,   °work
> As Austyn bit?° How shal the world be served?   °St Augustine commanded
>
> (A 175–87)

Here, at the very beginning of his work, Chaucer lays out the opposition between two possible approaches to reading, as if to anticipate the struggle his own book will engender. On the one hand, we have what a medieval allegorist might call the Pride of Life: fine horses; fur-lined robes; well-greased boots; a jingling bridle; and the joys of hunting, courting, and feasting – all of which elicit the quick sympathy of the genial narrator and the rough good fellowship of the Host. On the other hand, we have the sterner demands of the Benedictine rule, in which reading is like digging in the field, humbling labour for a sinner. One reader will pore over a book in an act of mental encloistration, while the other will seek the joys of the vicarious hunt. One reader will hear in the question 'How shall the world be served?' only the genial narrator's acquiescence to the Monk's pragmatism, while the other will hear a grim allusion to religious duty betrayed. Rightly or wrongly, many readers have followed the Monk, rejecting the penance of solitary study and trying to win back the world of fables and images Chaucer abandoned when he rewrote his ending.

One short example of such a sequel is the Benedictine monk John Lydgate's introduction to his *Siege of Thebes*, an epic of nearly five thousand lines that echoes Chaucer's Knight's Tale. In the *Siege*, as in many of his works, Lydgate acknowledges Chaucer as his poetic master while endeavouring to assume something of Chaucer's poetic authority. This Oedipal relationship is emphasized in the prologue when Lydgate has himself join the pilgrims on their return, temporarily supplanting Chaucer the pilgrim, the one prominent absence from the group.[24] Here the pleasures of storytelling revenge themselves on the demands of meditation, as Lydgate the monk is dragged from his breviary by the Host:

> Come forth, Daun John, be your Cristene name,
> And lat us make some manere myrth or play!
> Shet youre portoos,° a twenty devel way!   °breviary
> It is no disport so to patere and seie.°   °say pater nosters
> It wol make your lippes wonder dreye.
> Tel some tale, and make thereof jape,
> For be my rouncy,° thou shalt not eskape.   °horse
> But prech not of non holynesse;
> Ginne° some tale of myrth or of gladnesse,   °Begin
> And nodde not with thyn hevy bekke.°   °nose (beak)   (160–9)[25]

This brief prologue seems intended primarily to establish the *Siege* as a continuation of Chaucer's canon; Lydgate abandons his pilgrims after fewer than two hundred lines and never returns to them. It is Chaucer's themes and Chaucer's style that he will emulate. His brief re-creation of the pilgrimage, however, remains a testimony to the appeal of the fellowship of characters emblematized by their bluff governor Harry Bailey.

Only a proper sequel, one which reintroduces favourite characters, can offer the full satisfaction of rejoining this fellowship, however, and in this regard Lydgate's brief introduction is disappointing. A more extensive revival of Chaucer's pilgrims was offered sometime in the early fifteenth century by an anonymous writer, possibly a Canterbury monk, who added a long and complex story, the *Tale of Beryn*, recounting the legal misfortunes of a young nobleman who becomes a merchant.[26] The Beryn-author gives this story, appropriately enough, to the Merchant, but it is the less dignified pilgrims who capture his fancy. He prefaces the new tale with a second prologue, running to more than seven hundred lines, which begins by mustering the pilgrims at the Checker of the Hope, a well-known Canterbury inn.

> They toke hir in° and logged hem at mydmorowe, I trowe,   °their inn
> Atte Cheker of the Hope, that many a man doth knowe.
> Hir° Host of Southwork that with hem went, as ye have herd tofore,   °Their
> That was rewler of hem al, of las and eke of more,
> Ordeyned hir dyner wisely or they to chirch went
> Such vitailles as he fond in town and for noon other sent.[27]

Roughly half of the new prologue is devoted to the misadventures of the Pardoner, now demonstrating an aggressive heterosexuality, as he pursues the tapster, a young widow named Kit. The other half of the prologue takes us on a tour of Canterbury with the pilgrims, visiting first the cathedral and then the town and ramparts:

> The Knyght and al the feleshipp, and nothing for to ly,
> When they were all i-logged,° as skill wold and reson,   °lodged
> Everich after his degre, to chirch then was seson°   °time
> To pas and to wend, to make hir offringes,
> Righte as hir devocioune was, of sylver broch and rynges.
> Than atte chirche dorr the curtesy° gan to ryse,   °social custom
> Tyl the Knyght of gentilnes that knewe righte wele the guyse°   °manner
> Put forth the prelates, the Person and his fere.°   °companions   (130–7)

What follows is, in effect, a guide to the medieval shrine, describing the correct procedures to be followed – or not to be followed – by the visitor. On entering the cathedral, the pilgrims are asperged by one of the local monks, and the Friar, presuming upon his religious rank, tries to assist to get an opportunity to see the Nun's (or Nuns') face. The Pardoner, the Miller, 'and other lewde sotes' (147) wander around, 'counterfeting gentilmen' and trying to identify the heraldic blazons on the windows and interpret the stories, until the Host rebukes them and sends them up to the altar. Here they all pray to Saint Thomas and kiss the relics. Before they leave, the pilgrims buy – or, in the Miller's case, steal – souvenirs, which leads to a revealing exchange between the Miller, the Pardoner, and the Summoner:

Then, as manere and custom is, signes there they boughte,
For men of contre° shuld know whom they soughte.   °their neighbours
Ech man set his sylver in such thing as they liked.
And in the meenwhile, the Miller had i-piked°   °stuffed
His bosom ful of signes of Caunterbury broches,
Huch° the Pardoner and he pryvely° in hir pouches   °Which   °secretly
They put hem° afterward, that noon of hem it wist.°   °them   °knew
Save the Sompnour seid° somwhat and seyd to hem, 'List   °saw
Halff part!' quod he pryvely, rownyng° on hir ere.   °whispering
'Hussht! Pees!' quod the Miller, 'Seist thowe nat the Freere,
Howe he lowreth under his hood with a doggish ey?
Hit shuld be a pryvy thing that he could not aspy.
Of every craft he can somewhat, Our Lady gyve hym sorowe.'
'Amen,' tho quod the Sumpnour, 'on eve and eke on morowe!
So cursed a tale he told of me, the devil of hell hym spede –
And me! – but yf I pay° him wele and quyte wele his mede,   °repay, fee
Yf it hap homward that ech man tell his tale,
As we had hiderward, thoughe I shuld set at sale°   °put on display
Al the shrewdnes that I can, I wol hym nothing spare
That I nol touch his taberd somwhat of his care.'°   °would not touch his garment
                                     (revenge myself) somewhat to his sorrow
                                                                      (171–90)

The Beryn-author obviously found the pilgrims too lifelike to abandon, and with the Summoner's threat to avenge himself on the Friar on
the return journey, the Beryn-author even hints that an entire second
cycle of tales is in the offing. His efforts, while clumsy, show his appreciation of the social comedy of his model, the General Prologue and the
narrative links between the early tales, in which the characters reveal
themselves through their animosities. Not all the Beryn-author's suggestions are fully convincing, particularly those which normalize Chaucer's
range of sexual errancy. Quite apart from the Pardoner's transformation
into a more conventional heterosexual lecher, the Wife of Bath is now so
tamed that she, the great wanderer-by-the-way, proposes to the Prioress
that they retire to the garden to rest while the men tour the town (281–6).
With the more traditional rogues, however, the Beryn-author does better,
drawing them into a tight visual cluster in which their rivalries can once
more have free play.

Like those who quest after Lady Macbeth's children or the Wife of Bath's
former husbands, the Beryn-author might be accused of an unsophisti-
cated surrender to the facile pleasures of literary illusionism. His pro-

logue shows no appreciation of Chaucer's elaborate reworking of rhetorical conventions and is quick to abandon the detail of Chaucer's text for its own imaginings, a recurring failure of the undisciplined reader, as I.A. Richards laments. Yet the Beryn-author's response is one that seems to be encoded into the text of *The Canterbury Tales* itself, which provides just enough clues to incite the reader to speculation as to what the characters who are not actually speaking are doing (a recurring pleasure for the reader of a sequel).[28] At any rate, many other readers have engaged in such speculation. Kittredge, for one, does so repeatedly in his famous discussion of *The Canterbury Tales* as a roadside drama in which each separate tale exists as an expression of the character who tells it. For Kittredge it is the psychology of the pilgrims that is of primary concern and he explores this psychology with ingenuity. When he treats of the Clerk's Tale, for example, Kittredge describes what the Clerk has been thinking since the Wife finished her tale, biding his time through the tales of the Friar and the Summoner for his chance to respond. 'This is the opportunity for which the Clerk has been waiting,' Kittredge tells us, adding in passing that 'the Host, indeed, has no idea that the Clerk proposes to revive the discussion [and the Wife] has no inkling of what is in store, nor is the Clerk in any hurry to enlighten her. He opens with tantalizing deliberation and it is not until he has spoken more than sixty lines that he mentions marriage.'[29] For Kittredge, as each tale is delivered, the entire group is there, and the motives and thoughts of all members can be surmised, even if there are no direct allusions to them in the text.

Nor is Kittredge at all unusual in holding this view.[30] Bernard Bronson speculates even more freely on the professional rivalry of the Friar, the Summoner, and the Pardoner over the Wife of Bath:

All these men have a special interest – a very particular concern – with the Wife. When she talks, they are certain to be close at hand, and each of them gives careful study to her reminiscences, even to the point of interrupting with question and comment. This is no accident: she is their natural prey and they are stalking her. They are conscious rivals – not for the dubious privilege of becoming her sixth, but for her purse. Potentially, she is very vulnerable to some of the weapons they know how to use; and whether by working on her superstitions, or by blandishment, barratry, or blackmail, they mean to take their illegitimate toll ... This common aim exacerbates the mutual hatred of the Friar and Summoner, jealous of advantage with the Wife.[31]

By the time he has finished, Bronson has set the stage for a sequel of his own, in which the Wife and her predators finally confront each other directly, venting the hostilities within them as the three men attempt 'to take their illegitimate toll.'

Much of what makes this scenario credible is the apparent coincidence, which Bronson suggests is no coincidence at all, that all four repeatedly refer to and interrupt one another. If we visualize the action in a realistic space, as Bronson does, this implies that the four are actually riding close together. From the picture in the mind's eye of the pilgrims on the road, there springs a drama which continues to unroll beyond the textual hints that first suggested it. This spinning out of a secondary fantasy is what is entailed in the reading of a roadside drama, and it draws heavily on the visualization. It involves *seeing* the characters as if they were real people, riding, more or less, in real space, and then speculating on their dramatic interaction. This visualization is easier if the characters can be placed in locations that are already familiar; when the Beryn-author describes the Checker of the Hope as a spot 'that many a man doth knowe,' he is not just providing an easy rhyme for 'trowe' but emphasizing one of the attractions of his tale.[32] Social histories such as that of Sidney Heath, which seeks to capture the experience of *Pilgrim Life in the Middle Ages*, have a similar appeal (figure 1).[33] The pleasure of literary tourism and the pleasure of the picaresque roadside drama both lie in the reader's inner eye.

III

The conflict between the two kinds of conclusions, the kind Chaucer provided and the kind many would have preferred him to provide, might be described as a conflict between the two modes of textual apprehension first suggested through Chaucer's worldly Monk. One is cloistered study or meditation, the mode that the Monk rejects and that the Parson's Tale would seem to demand. The other, a more idle pleasure, was often associated with the term *curiositas*.[34] In many ways, the two seem polar opposites. *Curiositas*, according to Jean Gerson, the chancellor of the University of Paris in the late fourteenth-century, 'is a vice by which, once more useful things have been put aside, a man turns his attention to things which are less useful or things that are none of his business or things that may hurt him.'[35] *Curiositas* is an idle and vain curiosity of the kind which leads scholars to wilful perversity. It is born of scholarly pride, like its sisters, singularity and envy, and together they beget contention, argument, impudence, defence of error, love of one's own understanding, and persistence in one's perverse thoughts.[36] *Curiositas* can also, particularly among laymen or among women, manifest itself in an unwholesome fascination with visions or the religious

Figure 1 The Chequer of the Hope, Canterbury. From Sidney Heath, *Pilgrim Life in the Middle Ages* (London: T. Fisher Unwin, 1911), 207.

images which might induce them, since visions, too, can become a means of asserting personal authority against orthodox doctrine and its official guardians.[37] Or, as the Dominican preacher Bromyard notes, *curiositas* can take the form of a casual and self-indulgent delight in visual pleasure, in the trivialities of illuminated letters rather than the text or in the visual delights of the material world. *Meditatio*, on the other hand, is both an act of piety which fends off worldly distractions and a form of reading which, at least in its earlier development, involves the mouth and the heart, rather than the eye alone.[38] As the monk pores over the Bible, he chews the word of God, an image which occurs repeatedly in the works of Bonaventure and Saint Bernard and implies both the slow, ruminative internalization of the text through memorization and the actual mouthing of the words as they are subvocalized.[39] In short, while *curiositas*, which Zacher defines well as 'vagrant scrutinizing by the senses and intellectual wandering,' was evoked by metaphors of travelling, *meditatio* was evoked by metaphors of stasis and stability.[40]

In the late Middle Ages, however, meditation also came to be associated with the highly visual devotions of affective piety, and it is at this point that the distinction between *meditatio* and *curiositas* begins to break down. In late medieval devotional treatises, the reader is encouraged to 'make himself present in his mind' as a witness at central moments such as the Birth of Christ or the Passion, often drawing on techniques of mental visualization similar to those advocated by contemporary mnemonic treatises.[41] For example, in *The Blessed Lyf of Jesu Christ*, an early fifteenth-century translation by the Carthusian monk Nicholas Love of the pseudo-Bonaventurean *Meditationes vitae Christi*, the reader is instructed to 'make the in thi soule present to thoo thinges that bene here writen seyd or done of oure lord Jesu, & that bisily likyngly and abidyngly as thei [though] thou herdest hem [them] with thi bodily eres, or sey thaim with thin eyen done.'[42] This intense and cultivated visualization is in many ways similar to the practice of Kittredge, Bronson, and the Beryn-author, as they call up before their inner eye the travelling pilgrims. In particular, when the Beryn-author places his characters in a specific location which is well known to him, he is doing precisely what numerous devotional treatises recommend as the best way to imagine oneself as a participant at the Passion. Such intense devotional visualization could lead to dangerous extremes of affective piety and it was viewed with considerable apprehension by contemporary moralists such as Gerson.

The experience that the Beryn-author offers us is so much part of modern reading practice that we even have a term for it, 'armchair travelling,' but, in the late Middle Ages, such pleasures had not yet become commonplace and they provoked varied and contradictory responses. For those in the book trade, the new tastes offered commercial possibilities, and the period saw the extensive development of books designed to encourage imaginative journeying. Book illuminators, for instance, began to depict deep illusionistic space. In the lavish illustrations of the copy of Lydgate's *Siege of Thebes* commissioned by Sir William Herbert, now British Library MS Royal 18 D ii a, the reader's pleasure is enhanced by the addition of several illuminated landscapes, where one can journey as if for miles.[43] In the illustration of Calcas outside Troy, the eye travels back past the great brass horse, which glows on the page; past the walls of Troy and the tents outside it, with their taut ropes; past another castle in the distance and three ships on the river, their rigging just discernible; to the distant horizon, where the hills fade to a blue that is scarcely darker than the sky (folio 74). The famous illustration of the Canterbury pilgrimage on folio 148, which accompanies the *Siege of Thebes*, offers in the foreground a wealth of sharply delineated physical

Figure 2 British Library MS Royal 19 D iia, fol. 148r, Lydgate's *Siege of Thebes*.
By permission of The British Library.

details: the separate pebbles on the road, each one casting a small shadow, the eyes and ears of the horses, the spurs on the huntsmen, the decoration on the riders' harness, even the rings on the monk's left hand. In the background a woman stands at an open door, the beginning of a cityscape of houses, walls, and the church spires peeking above. Far in the distance a forest gives way to water meadows beside a small river, and beyond the river are hills and another forest (figure 2). This setting may not look much like Southwark, but it does offer a convincing illusion of space. As the pilgrims head out on their travels, the illuminated page becomes a gateway into a world in which we can accompany them.

These elaborate illuminations, with their deep space, are but one indication of how powerful the habit of fantasizing from a book had become by the late Middle Ages. The most elaborate and explicitly systematized example of this practice can be seen in a particular kind of guidebook that began to emerge in the late fourteenth century. These guides offered comprehensive listings of related shrines and the appropriate prayers for each, so that the reader could follow a precise devotional itinerary and thus acquire the same indulgences that a physical pilgrimage would bring.[44] Ironically, it is Gerson, the inveterate critic of excessive concentration on images, who provides the first model of this new genre, a guidebook for those who could not attend the jubilee celebrations in Rome.[45] If, as Peter Brown has suggested, the *Tale of Beryn* was written to celebrate the 1420 jubilee in Canterbury, then it would become a less systematic example of the same kind of work.[46]

As Walter Cahn argues, such guidebooks testify to both the continued religious commitment to pilgrimage and the growing unease at the licence and extravagance associated with it.[47] The virtual pilgrimage was a sanitized alternative to actual travel. Like all surrogates, however, mental travelling acquired something of the ill repute of the vice it supplanted. It was during this period that reading, long thought of as a kind of spiritual journey, became associated 'with sight-seeing or exploration, with the festiveness, awe, danger, loose talk and false tale-telling attributed to pilgrims and travellers.'[48] Chaucer, composing poetry during this period when the technologies of reading were in such a state of flux, presented the habit of solitary reading as both a source of spiritual refreshment and an antisocial and physically debilitating eccentricity. When *The Canterbury Tales* works first to elicit and then to suppress the pleasures of an imaginary journey, it is in keeping with these prevailing contradictions.

The responses *The Canterbury Tales* demands initially seem antithetical, but both depend on the power of the book to open an inner world, whether through the mental quietude of devotion which creates 'a chamber within the mind' or through curious fantasizing. If the commentary of Bromyard and Gerson, like Chaucer's Parson's Tale, shows the extent to which the new pleasures of textual journeying were regarded with dubiety in the late Middle Ages, the Beryn-author's sequel shows how widely these pleasures were enjoyed; like so many other sequels, it is both a tribute and a betrayal.

Notes

1 'Secundo, quia sicut in libro materiali, qui solum respiciunt literas crassas, & capi-

tales ad ludum, & curiositatem, nunquam erunt boni clerici, nec sic Dei, vel sui cognitionem acquirent ita qui creaturis utuntur ad voluptatem, & curiositatem potius, quam ad utilitatem, qui solum respiciunt illud, quod pulchrum & delictabile est occulis, nec eas ordinant, vel eis utuntur ad Dei cognitionem & amorem, nunquam per eas ad Dei perfectam ducentur visionem': John Bromyard, *Summa praedicantium* (Venice 1586), vol. 1: s.v. 'liber,' cap. iv, fols. 444v–5.

2 I.A. Richards, *Practical Criticism: A Study of Literary Judgement* (London: Routledge & Kegan Pal, 1929) 236.

3 Two of the more influential studies of the fluidity of the medieval text are provided by Paul Zumthor, *Essai de poétique médiévale* (Paris: Éditions du Seuil, 1972), and Bernard Cerquiglini, *Éloge de la variante: Histoire critique de la philologie* (Paris: Éditions du Seuil, 1989). The break between the medieval poetic composer and the proprietorial author, so famously discussed by Roland Barthes and Michel Foucault, should not be exaggerated, however. On the medieval *auctor*, see A.J. Minnis, *Medieval Theory of Authorship: Scholastic Literary Attitudes in the Later Middle Ages*, 2d ed. (Aldershot: Scolar, 1988), and Rita Copeland, *Rhetoric, Hermeneutics, and Translation in the Middle Ages: Academic Traditions and Vernacular Texts* (Cambridge: Cambridge UP, 1991).

4 In fact, many of the works of Chaucer's followers, including Henryson's *Testament of Cresseid*, were for a long time attributed to Chaucer himself. Walter Skeat provides a useful compilation of some of the less well-known pieces in *Chaucerian and Other Pieces ... Being a Supplement to the Complete Works of Geoffrey Chaucer* (Oxford 1897).

5 Gerson 152, this volume.

6 Leggatt 53, this volume.

7 My approach here diverges from that offered by Seth Lerer, who sees many of the fifteenth-century continuations of Chaucer as enacting textual patterns inherent in Chaucer's works themselves. Lerer thus locates 'the energies of fifteenth-century Chaucer reception and authorial self-definition in those moments of departure, dedication, or release that close the major fictions of the poet and that ground the literary identities of his inheritors': *Chaucer and His Readers: Imagining the Author in Late Medieval England* (Princeton: Princeton UP, 1993) 209.

8 All quotations from *The Canterbury Tales* are from *The Riverside Chaucer*, ed. Larry D. Benson (Boston: Houghton Mifflin, 1987).

9 John Finlayson, 'The Satiric Mode and the *Parson's Tale*,' *Chaucer Review* 6 (1971): 94–116; E. Talbot Donaldson, *Speaking of Chaucer* (Durham, NC: Labyrinth, 1983) 173.

10 See, for example, Siegfried Wenzel, 'Chaucer's Parson's Tale: "Every Tales Strengthe,"' *Europäische Lehrdichtung: Festschrift für Walter Nauman*, ed. Hans Gert Rözer and Herbert Wlaz (Darmstadt: Wissenschaftliche Buchgesellschaft, 1981) 86–98. A useful summary of the argument is provided by Wenzel in his notes to the *Riverside Chaucer* and by Thomas H. Bestul, the first to explore at any length the possibility that the Parson's Tale should be understood as a meditation, in 'Chaucer's Parson's Tale and the Late-Medieval Tradition of Religious Meditation,' *Speculum* 64 (1989): 600–19. For a positive assessment of the Parson's Tale as an act of personal expiation on the part of Chaucer, see Albert E. Hartung, '"The Parson's Tale" and Chaucer's Penance,' *Literature and Religion in the Later Middle Ages: Philological Studies in Honor of Siegfried Wenzel*, ed. Richard G. Newhauser and John A. Alford (Binghamton, NY: Medieval & Renaissance Texts and Studies, 1995) 61–80.

11 Donald R. Howard, *The Idea of the Canterbury Tales* (Berkeley: U of P, California: 1976) 304.

12 James Dean, 'Dismantling the Canterbury Book,' *PMLA* 100 (1985): 746–62; Britton J. Harwood, 'Language and the Real Chaucer's Manciple,' *Chaucer Review* 6 (1971–2): 269–79.

13 Glending Olson, *Literature as Recreation in the Later Middle Ages* (Ithaca, NY: Cornell UP, 1982) 158.

14 Siegfried Wenzel, 'Notes on the Parson's Tale,' *Chaucer Review* 16 (1982): 237–56.

15 Wenzel, 'Notes on the Parson's Tale,' 248; italics mine.

16 Wenzel, 'Textual Notes' 956.

17 W.A. Pantin, *The English Church in the Fourteenth Century* (Cambridge: Cambridge UP, 1948) 189–219. Even model sermon texts were subject to extensive modification when they were actually delivered to a particular audience. Gerard R. Owst offers what is still the fullest account of the dramatic power of actual sermon *exempla* in *Literature and Pulpit in Medieval England*, 2d ed. (Oxford: Oxford UP, 1961).

18 It has sometimes been suggested that the Pardoner's Tale was originally written for the Parson. See G.C. Sedegwick, 'The Progress of Chaucer's Pardoner, 1880–1940,' *Modern Language Quarterly* 1 (1940): 437–8.

19 The oral conventions were early recognized by Ruth Crosby, 'Chaucer and the Custom of Oral Delivery,' *Speculum* 13 (1938): 413–32, and have been discussed extensively by critics since. On the actual conditions of delivery, see Paul Strohm, 'Chaucer's Audience,' *Literature and History* 5 (1977): 26–41, and *Social Chaucer* (Cambridge, MA: Harvard UP, 1989) esp. 47–83.

20 J.A. Burrow, *Medieval Writers and Their Work: Middle English Literature and Its Background, 1100–1500* (Oxford: Oxford UP, 1982) 50; italics in original.

21 On the mnemonic value of various marginal decorations, including short glosses and running titles, see Mary Carruthers, *The Book of Memory: A Study of Memory in Medieval Culture* (Cambridge: Cambridge UP, 1990) esp. 244–8. It is worth noting, in regard to locating passages, that the Ellesmere manuscript, like most manuscripts of the period, was originally not paginated. On the importance of the headings and glosses in establishing the book as a collection of moral authorities, see A.I. Doyle and M.B. Parkes, 'The Production of Copies of *The Canterbury Tales* and the *Confessio Amantis* in the Early Fifteenth Century,' *Medieval Scribes, Manuscripts & Libraries: Essays presented to N.R. Ker*, ed. M.B. Parkes and Andrew G. Watson (London: Scolar, 1979) 190, and Ralph Hanna III, introduction to *The Ellesmere Manuscript of Chaucer's Canterbury Tales: A Working Facsimile* (Cambridge: D.S. Brewer, 1989) 10–11.

22 Bestul, 'Religious Meditation,' 608–9.

23 Bestul, 617.

24 A.C. Spearing, 'Lydgate's Canterbury Tale: *The Siege of Themes* and Fifteenth-Century Chaucerianisms,' *Fifteenth-Century Studies: Recent Essays*, ed. Robert F. Yeager (Hamden, CT: Archon, 1984) 338; see also Rosamund S. Allen, '*The Siege of Thebes*: Lydgate's Canterbury Tale,' *Chaucer and Fifteenth-Century Poetry*, ed. Julia Boffey and Janet Cowen (London: King's College London Medieval Studies, 1991) 122–42, and Nicholas Watson, 'Outdoing Chaucer: Lydgate's *Troy Book* and Henryson's *Testament of Cresseid* as Competitive Imitations of *Troilus and Criseyde*,' *Shifts and Transpositions in Medieval Narrative: A Festschrift for Dr. Elspeth Kennedy*, ed. Karen Pratt (Cambridge: D.S. Brewer, 1994) 89–108.

25 All quotations from the *Tale of Beryn* and most of the accompanying glosses are from the edition of John M. Bowers, *The Canterbury Tales: Fifteenth-Century Continuations and Additions* (Kalamazoo, MI: Medieval Institute Publications, 1992).

26 Bowers is of the opinion that 'the Canterbury Interlude and Merchant's tale of Beryn was in all probability written by a Christ Church monk attached to the shrine of St. Thomas à Becket' (*Fifteenth-Century Continuations*, 3). Richard F. Green suggests another possible identity, that of Thomas Astell, who had studied civil law at Oxford and was related to Henry Chichele, archbishop of Canterbury, in 'Legal Satire in *The Tale of Beryn*,' *Studies in the Age of Chaucer* 11 (1989): 61, n. 49. On the dating, see Bowers, *Fifteenth-Century Continuations* 57.

27 Bowers, *Fifteenth-Century Continuations*, lines 13–18.

28 This particular pleasure is often enhanced if the text is shared by a small community. June Sturrock notes a similar interest on the part of Charlotte Yonge, whose letters 'record the flow of gossip about her characters before, during, and after, the narratives in which they feature, to which she treated (or subjected) her friends' (112, this volume).

29 George Lyman Kittredge, 'Chaucer's Discussion of Marriage,' *Chaucer Criticism: The Canterbury Tales*, ed. Richard Schoek and Jerome Taylor (Notre Dame, IN: U of Notre Dame P, 1960) 138–9.

30 While dissent from the extreme version of Kittredge's thesis has become almost *pro forma*, the tendency to explain the tales in terms of a coherent psychology of the teller remains pervasive to this day. Robert M. Jordan offers a sustained critique of this tendency in 'Chaucer's Sense of Illusion: Roadside Drama Reconsidered,' *English Literary History* 29 (1962): 19–33, and *Chaucer's Poetics and the Modern Reader* (Berkeley: U of California P, 1987) ch. 6; Harold Bloom offers a spirited defence in his introduction to the casebook *Geoffrey Chaucer* (New York: Chelsea House, 1985); and H. Marshall Leicester, Jr, offers a useful reformulation, which appeals, not to an external self, but to 'a speaker who is a subject created by the text itself as a structure of linguistic and semantic relationships,' in *The Disenchanted Self: Representing the Subject in the Canterbury Tales* (Berkeley: U of California P, 1990) 10.

31 B.H. Bronson, *In Search of Chaucer* (Toronto: U of Toronto P, 1970) 63.

32 Psychological studies indicate that vivid visualization is comparatively rare in ludic reading, in part because of the mental energy it requires: see Victor Nell, *Lost in a Book: The Psychology of Reading Pleasure* (New Haven: Yale UP, 1988) esp. 216–18, 245–6. One reason to visualize the action occurring in familiar locations is that these locations provide images ready-made, as do book illustrations, and now films of books.

33 Sidney Heath, *Pilgrim Life in the Middle Ages* (London: T. Fisher Unwin, 1911).

34 See Christian K. Zacher, *Curiosity and Pilgrimage: The Literature of Discovery in Fourteenth-Century England* (Baltimore: Johns Hopkins UP, 1976) 18–41.

35 'Curiositas est vitium quo dimissis utilioribus homo convertit studium suum ad minus utilia vel inattingibilia sibi vel noxia': Jean Gerson, *Oeuvres complètes*, ed. P. Glorieux, 10 vols. (Paris: Desclée, 1960–73) 3.230.

36 Gerson 3.230.

37 Gerson 9.518 *et passim*.

38 Paul Saenger, 'Books of Hours and the Reading Habits of the Later Middle Ages,' *Scrittura e Civiltà* 9 (1985): 250–1.

39 Jean Leclercq, *The Love of Learning and the Desire for God*, trans. Catherine Misrahi (New York: Fordham UP, 1961) 18–22.

40 Zacher, *Curiosity and Pilgrimage* 29.

41 See Thomas H. Bestul, *Texts of the Passion: Latin Devotional Literature and Medieval Society* (Philadelphia: U of Pennsylvania P, 1996) 48–68. Henry of Lancaster provides

an English example only a generation prior to Chaucer: see Andrew Taylor, 'Reading the Body in *Le Livre de Seyntz Medecines*,' *Essays in Medieval Studies* 11, Proceedings of the Illinois Medieval Association (1994): 103–18.

42 Michael G. Sargent, ed., *Nicholas Love's Mirror of the Blessed Life of Jesus Christ: A Critical Edition Based on Cambridge University Library Additional MSS 6578 and 6686* (New York: Garland, 1992) 13. I have substituted *th* for the medieval Þ.

43 For descriptions of the manuscript see Lesley Lawton, 'The Illustration of Late Medieval Secular Texts with Special Reference to Lydgate's *Troy Book*,' *Manuscripts and Readers in Fifteenth-Century England*, ed. Derek Pearsall (Cambridge: D.S. Brewer, 1983) 41–9, and the anonymous typescript catalogue *Anglo-Flemish Art Under the Tudor: An Exhibition Held in the Department of Prints and Drawings, British Museum, 1954* (London n.d.) 1–16.

44 Margaret of York, Duchess of Burgundy, owned just such a collection, a guidebook to the seven principal churches of Rome, listing the saints and the various indulgences available to those who prayed to them, which is now in the Beinecke Library in Yale; MS 639: see Walter Cahn, 'Margaret of York's Guide to the Pilgrimage Churches of Rome,' *Margaret of York, Simon Marmion, and The Visions of Tondal*, Papers Delivered at a Symposium Organized by the Department of Manuscripts of the J. Paul Getty Museum in Collaboration with the Huntington Library and Art Collections, 21–4 June 1990, ed. Thomas Kren (Malibu, CA: J. Getty Paul Museum, 1992) 89–98, and Dagmar Eichberger, 'Image Follows Text: *The Visions of Tondal* and Its Relationship to Depictions of Hell and Purgatory in Fifteenth-Century Illuminated Manuscripts' 129–40 in the same collection.

45 Cahn, 'Margaret of York's Guide' 96–7.

46 Peter Brown, 'Journey's End: The Prologue to *The Tale of Beryn*' Boffey and Cowen, eds., *Chaucer and Fifteenth-Century Poetry* 143–74.

47 Cahn, 'Margaret of York's Guide' 29.

48 Howard, *Idea of the Canterbury Tales* 66.

Killing the Hero: Tamburlaine and Falstaff

ALEXANDER LEGGATT

Betty Schellenberg has seen the definitive transformation of the author into a professional supplying a market as an early eighteenth-century phenomenon (85, this volume). In one area, however, this development was in place much earlier. Elizabethan theatre was a commercial enterprise that survived by giving the public what it wanted. This meant that, as in the movie business, success bred sequels, as the author, having created a demand, had to keep feeding it. There are cases of popular plays breeding not just one successor, but two: *The Blind Beggar of Bednal Green*, an anthology of crowd-pleasing ingredients (pathos, disguise, fight scenes) by the team of Henry Chettle, John Day, and William Haughton, was followed by *The Blind Beggar of Bednal Green*, Parts Two and Three. William Haughton's domestic comedy *The Two Angry Women of Abingdon* was followed by *The Two Angry Women of Abingdon*, Part Two, and *The Two Merry Women of Abingdon*. These were unpretentious popular works, but even writers with aspirations to literary dignity caught the bug. George Chapman followed *Bussy d'Ambois* with *The Revenge of Bussy d'Ambois*. Ben Jonson followed *Every Man in his Humour* with *Every Man out of his Humour*; the latter is not strictly a sequel, since there is no carry-over in action or characters, but it is designed to sound like a sequel, and to cash in on the first play by the similarity of its title. The same motive seems to have inspired Shakespeare to write a play (now either lost or known under another title) called *Love's Labour's Won*.

Two of the best-known sequels of the period are the second parts of Marlowe's *Tamburlaine the Great* and Shakespeare's *Henry IV*. In both cases we can attribute the popularity of the original in large measure to a striking character who entered the public consciousness at once and stayed there. Contemporary allusions tell the story. Richard Levin's 1984 article, 'The Contemporary Perception of Marlowe's Tamburlaine,' collects a host of contemporary references to *Tamburlaine*. Audiences were clearly fascinated by the conqueror's power: 'mighty Tamburlaine' is a recurring formula (Levin 56). There are several allusions to his use of colour-coded banners during a siege – white on the first day, showing mercy, red and black on the next two days as his cruelty deepens – and to his tormenting of the Turkish emperor Bajazeth, keeping him in a cage and using him as a footstool (Levin 58–9). Much fun is made of the line in which he taunts the kings drawing his chariot: 'Holla, ye pamper'd jades of Asia! / What, can ye draw but twenty miles a day' (Part Two 4.3.1–2; Levin 59–60). The allusions are to both parts, and most of them come after Marlowe's early death; but we can see in them the continuing fallout from the impact of the first play, an impact that led Marlowe to produce a sequel in short order, and that led a number of other writers to produce flagrant imitations (Berek passim).

As time went on *Tamburlaine* looked old-fashioned, and became a byword for strutting bombast. The allusions become increasingly comic. Shakespeare's Falstaff, on whom much of the popularity of the *Henry IV* plays rested from the beginning, was protected from such a fate by being comic already. Even as Shakespeare went through the period of devaluation that every writer endures after death, Falstaff carried on. Two generations later, Leonard Digges testifies to his ability to fill playhouses:

> let but *Falstaffe* come,
> *Hall, Poines*, the rest[,] you scarce shall have a roome
> All is so pester'd.   (*Shakspere Allusion* 457)

In his commendatory verses to the Beaumont and Fletcher Folio (1647), T. Palmer notes, 'I could prayse *Heywood* now: or tell how long, / *Falstaffe* from cracking Nuts hath kept the throng' (*Shakspere Allusion* 513). From the beginning he was a byword for girth, as Tamburlaine was for bombast (*Shakspere Allusion* 61, 77, 97, 136; the list is not exhaustive). He is mostly remembered with joking affection; but his ability to irritate the respectable persists well through the seventeenth century, as writers complain of the slander done to the historical Sir John Fastolfe by Shakespeare's naming of the fat knight (*Shakspere Allusion* 486, 507–8). (Falstaff's original name, Oldcastle, evidently caused similar trouble.)

The ranting conqueror who delights in bloodshed and the fat knight for whom the better part of valour is discretion may at first seem to have little in common but popularity. But when we look to see where that popularity comes from, common factors emerge. Both are exhilarating monsters, free (it seems at first) from ordinary moral considerations, free even from the laws of nature and common sense. Cosroe, one of Tamburlaine's first victims, feels that in Tamburlaine and his followers he has encountered something new and inexplicable: 'The strangest men that ever nature made! / I know not how to take their tyrannies' (Part One 2.7.40–1). Tamburlaine sees himself as rewriting the rules of the cosmos and of nature, immune to ordinary injury, immune even to death:

> I hold the Fates bound fast in iron chains,
> And with my hand turn Fortune's wheel about;
> And sooner shall the sun fall from his sphere
> Than Tamburlaine be slain or overcome.
> Draw forth thy sword, thou mighty man-at-arms,
> Intending but to raze my charmed skin,
> And Jove himself will stretch his hand from heaven
> To ward the blow, and shield me safe from harm.   (Part One 1.2.174–81)

His expansiveness includes a desire to extend the known world, and to show his power over it by acts of renaming:

> I will confute those blind geographers
> That make a triple region in the world,
> Excluding regions which I mean to trace,
> And with this pen reduce them to a map,
> Calling the provinces, cities, and towns,
> After my name and thine, Zenocrate.   (Part One 4.4.81–6)

He is driven by a mind 'Still climbing after knowledge infinite, / And always moving as the restless spheres' and while he calls the end of his quest 'The sweet fruition of an earthly crown' (Part One 2.7.24–5, 29), clearly he is not content with one. He is like the movie monsters described in Paul Budra's essay (this volume), who acknowledge no boundaries. There seems no reason why he should ever stop.

Operating on a smaller scale, and very much preoccupied with the things of earth, Falstaff seems equally unstoppable. As he tells the story of his fight with the rogues in buckram, his assailants grow from two to eleven as he speaks, doing to arithmetic what Tamburlaine plans to do to geography: 'These four came all afront, and mainly thrust at me. I made me no more ado but took all their seven points in my target, thus' – then, moments later, 'These nine in buckram that I told thee of' (Part One 2.4.198–200, 209–10). Like Tamburlaine, he resists closure. If something tells him that his days as Hal's companion are numbered, he fights off that knowledge. When he and Hal improvise a play acting out Hal's coming interview with his father, Falstaff, impersonating Hal, pleads against the inevitable: 'but for sweet Jack Falstaff, kind Jack Falstaff, true Jack Falstaff, valiant Jack Falstaff, and therefore more valiant being as he is old Jack Falstaff, banish not him thy Harry's company, banish not him thy Harry's company – banish plump Jack, and banish all the world' (Part One 2.4.470–5). It is as though he is trying to hold off the end through sheer proliferation of words. When the extempore play is broken off with news that the sherriff and the watch are at the door, he tries to keep it going: 'Out, ye rogue! Play out the play. I have much to say in the behalf of that Falstaff' (Part One 2.4.479–80). At the end of Part One, he frustrates the closure of Hal's story by taking on himself the credit for killing Hotspur. He mocks even the final closure of death. For all the audience knows, he is killed by Douglas in hand-to-hand combat as Hal fights Hotspur. After Hal leaves, the fat knight and the rebel hero lie together on stage, both, it would seem, equally dead. Then Falstaff pops up, with the explosive word 'Emboweled?' (Part One 5.4.111). The joke against death is also a joke against theatre: at the level of performance, all deaths are as fake as this one. Once Falstaff has carried him into the tiring house, the actor playing Hotspur will come to life too.

As specialists in resisting closure, Tamburlaine and Falstaff seem ideal subjects for a sequel. Even if their popularity had not provoked it, something in their natures would have. So far, so logical. But when Marlowe and Shakespeare bring the characters back for a second outing, something happens. The simplest rule of sequel-writing is, play it again: more bombast, more jokes, more car-chases, more explosions. But nothing is ever quite the same the second time around. Shakespeare shows this in *King Lear*, when Lear, on his way to prison with Cordelia, wants to repeat over and over the scene of his reunion with her: 'When thou dost ask me blessing, I'll kneel down / And ask of thee forgiveness' (5.3.10–11). The powerful and moving action we watched minutes earlier becomes attenuated into fantasy; life has no replay button, and neither does theatre. Tamburlaine and Falstaff are both highly performative characters, and when they come back they try to keep their old performances going. But the plays in which they are embedded have moved on. For Marlowe and Shakespeare, as for Trollope in *Phineas Redux* (Felber, 119–20, this volume), sequel means deterioration.

Early in Part Two, Tamburlaine's queen, Zenocrate, who all along has seen him as human and vulnerable, asks him when he is going to settle down with the family:

Sweet Tamburlaine, when wilt thou leave these arms,
And save thy sacred person free from scathe,
And dangerous chances of the wrathful war?

He replies,

When heaven shall cease to move on both the poles,
And when the ground, whereon my soldiers march,
Shall rise aloft and touch the horned moon,
And not before, my sweet Zenocrate.   (Part Two 1.4.9–15)

He is contemplating Parts Three, Four, Five, and on, for ever. He does not make it to the end of Part Two. Falstaff tries to pretend, even to himself, that he still has his old relations with Hal, by Hal's choice, not his: 'God send the companion a better prince! I cannot rid my hands of him!' (Part Two 1.2.198–9). In fact Hal has effectively rid himself of Falstaff; they meet only once before the end, and the comedy of that scene has a nastier edge than before, showing Hal's increasing distance from his old companion. The audience sees the new relation clearly, but Falstaff seems not to; later in the play, alone and fooling no one but himself, he predicts, 'I will devise matter enough out of this Shallow to keep Prince Harry in continual laughter the wearing out of six fashions, which is four terms, or two actions, and a'shall laugh without intervallums' (Part Two 5.1.76–80). His fantasy of inexhaustible laughter is like Tamburlaine's fantasy of inexhaustible conquest. This is the fantasy that drives him into the trap of the rejection scene.

Marlowe used up most of his source material in Part One, with the result that Tamburlaine, who marched from action to action in the first play, spends much of the second having nothing to do. He appears in the second scene of Part One, but is held back till the fourth scene of Part Two, continuing to disappear for long stretches as the focus shifts to other characters. This looks at first like a way of building anticipation, but it quickly becomes a way of emphasizing his inactivity. He congratulates his followers on *their* conquests, having no recent ones of his own; he mourns the death of Zenocrate; he lectures his sons on the art of war. It is not until late in Act Three that he is back on the road again; the first battle in which he is engaged takes place offstage at the beginning of Act Four. Falstaff, too, does a lot of standing around and talking; he has no equivalent of the Gad's Hill robbery or the tavern play. It is characteristic of *Henry IV Part Two* in general that no one has much to do but wait for the old king to die, and the characters spend the play (which is longer than its predecessor) filling in time, in a remarkable anticipation of some classic plays of the twentieth century. Even the defeat of the rebels at Gaultree Forest entails not having a battle. As part of the filling-in that both plays require, Marlowe creates, contrary to his practice in Part One, two full subplots in which Tamburlaine is not involved, the stories of Sigismund and Orcanes, and of Theridamas and Olympia. Shakespeare expands the part of the Hostess, and creates the new characters Doll Tearsheet, Pistol, and Shallow. Shallow, in particular, takes over the scenes in which he appears, reducing Falstaff to his 'feed.'

Tamburlaine loses some of his uniqueness as members of the supporting cast take over his voice. Callapine tempts his jailor Almeda to release him with promises of wealth and splendour that recall Tamburlaine's wooing of Theridamas and Zenocrate in Part One (Part Two 1.3.19–53). At this point in the play, Tamburlaine has not even appeared, and the impression is that Callapine has moved into his space. Theridamas mourns Olympia in terms that recall Tamburlaine's mourning for Zenocrate, a mourning he tried to present as unique (Part Two 4.3.87–98).

More important, Tamburlaine confronts as never before the otherness of other people, embodied (literally) in his own sons. With his tendency to impose his imagination on the world, he expects them to be copies of himself. Though the oldest, Calyphas, resists, the other two compete for the honour of reproducing their father exactly:

TAMBURLAINE
    These words assure me, boy [Celebinus], thou art my son.
    When I am old and cannot manage arms,
    Be thou the scourge and terror of the world.
AMYRAS
    Why may not I, my lord, as well as he,
    Be term'd the scourge and terror of the world?
TAMBURLAINE
    Be all a scourge and terror to the world,
    Or else you are not sons of Tamburlaine.   (Part Two 1.4.58–64)

The mechanical repetition of the key phrase reflects Tamburlaine's expectation that the boys, far from having their own lives, will simply repeat his life; they will be sequels that reproduce the original exactly. But just the fact of having children, though he sees it as an answer to his mortality, has also reminded him of that mortality, as he admits, uncharacteristically, that age will one day slow him down. More disturbingly, he notes that the boys do not look like him, and this not only makes him question his powers of reproduction, but casts a flicker of doubt on his hold over Zenocrate:

> Their fingers made to quaver on a lute,
> Their arms to hang about a lady's neck,
> Their legs to dance and caper in the air,
> Would make me think them bastards, not my sons,
> But that I know they issu'd from thy womb,
> That never look'd on man but Tamburlaine.   (Part Two 1.4.29–34)

That classic male anxiety – you can never be absolutely certain who the father was – touches even Tamburlaine. Zenocrate's reassurance about his sons is not, in fact, totally reassuring: 'My gracious lord, they have their mother's looks, / But, when they list, their conquering father's heart' (Part Two 1.4.35–6). This makes their feminine side endemic, and their masculine side a matter of temporary whim. Extended through his offspring, Tamburlaine's power has thinned out in the process.

In the case of Falstaff, the otherness of other people is dramatized through the recurring issue of debt. In Part One, we are briefly made aware that he owes the Hostess twenty-four pounds, but the point is not developed; in Part Two, a whole scene is devoted to her unsuccessful attempt to arrest Falstaff for debt, and we get a glimpse of the price she is paying for trusting him: 'By this heavenly ground I tread on, I must be fain to pawn both my plate and the tapestry of my dining chambers' (Part Two 2.1.138–40). In Part One, we enjoy Falstaff's irresponsibility, and if the thought crosses our minds that someone has to pay the bills, we are not invited to dwell on it. In Part Two, we are. It is like going from Algy's cheerful insouciance about debt in *The Importance of Being Earnest* to Thackeray's brutal analysis in chapter 37 of *Vanity Fair* of 'How to Live Well on Nothing a Year.' Here and in Part Two of *Tamburlaine*, we see the other side of relationships in which the hero would prefer to think of himself as the only character who matters.

Existing in a sequel can also make a character subject to the passage of time. Movie audiences have been able to watch the ageing of the crew of the Starship Enterprise, and of the actors playing James Bond. Marlowe and Shakespeare build the process into the script, in a way that implicitly warns the audience not to expect further sequels. The character is not just ageing; he is about to be used up. We are getting near the end of the story. When Tamburlaine's son Amyras asks his father if he can have a chariot too, Tamburlaine's reply, 'Thy youth forbids such ease, my kingly boy' (Part Two 4.3.29), reveals that the chariot is not just an image of Tamburlaine's power, but a sign that he's no longer up to a long day's march. (The historical conqueror on whom Marlowe based his hero was known as Timur the Lame.) In Part One, Falstaff defies reality with a snappy one-liner as he attacks the travellers at Gad's Hill: 'They hate us youth' (Part One 2.2.85). In Part Two, still defending his eternal youth, he is reduced to claiming that he has always looked the way he does now: 'My lord, I was born about three of the clock in the afternoon, with a white head and something a round belly' (Part Two 2.4.185–7). But when it is late at night in the tavern, and Falstaff's guard is down, we hear the stark confession, 'I am old, I am old' (Part Two 2.4.270).

In Part One, Tamburlaine saw his skin as charmed; in Part Two, he gives himself his first wound (Part Two 3.2.110–14) and he bleeds as anyone would. The first twinge of the illness that kills him draws the defiant assertion 'Whatsoe'er it be, / Sickness or death can never conquer me' (Part Two 5.1.219–20). Not only does sickness conquer him, but he is reduced to taking ordinary medical advice; his physician warns him, 'I view'd your urine, and the hypostasis, / Thick and obscure, doth make your danger great' (Part Two 5.3.82–3). Falstaff's first line in Part Two is addressed to his page: 'Sirrah, you giant, what says the doctor to my water?' (Part Two 1.2.1–2). In Part One, Tamburlaine deals death to other people; it is a power over which he has complete control. In Part Two, death comes for him, first by taking Zenocrate. Her death entails his; he entreats her as she lies dying, 'Live still, my love, and so conserve my life, / Or, dying, be the author of my death' (Part Two 2.4.55–6). Up to this point language has been his weapon, at which he is unbeatable. Zenocrate's death triggers the usual avalanche of rhetoric, and Theridamas has to tell him, 'Ah, good my lord, be patient! She is dead, / And all this raging cannot make her live' (Part Two 2.4.119–20). All he can do is preserve her body, and carry it around with him till his own death. As he plans their burial together, we see that the experience of her death has finally made him think of his own. When death finally comes for him, it leaves him with a terrible sense of unfinished business: 'Give me a map; then let me see how much / Is left for me to conquer all the world' (Part Two 5.3.124–

5). (Falstaff's equivalent of this moment comes when he is dragged out of the tavern and back to the war: 'Now comes in the sweetest morsel of the night, and we must hence and leave it unpicked' [Part Two 3.4.366–7].) Tamburlaine has more sequels planned in his imagination, and his fantasy is that his sons will carry out his unfinished conquests, that in effect they will be him: 'My flesh, divided in your precious shapes, / Shall still retain my spirit, though I die' (Part Two 5.2.173–4). They see the same relationship, but read it differently; because they are so bound up with him, when he dies they die: 'no hope survives, / For by your life we entertain our lives' (Part Two 5.3.167–8). There is no *Tamburlaine the Great Part Three*.

Falstaff does not literally die at the end of Part Two, but the new king's rejection leaves him as good as dead. His resilience is gone, as we see when for once he flatly confesses a debt: 'Master Shallow, I owe you a thousand pound' (Part Two 5.5.73–4). As Tamburlaine has tried to reach beyond the end into a new action through his sons, Falstaff has projected himself forward into a new play (which he probably imagines as *Falstaff Part Three*) in which he is the new king's chief adviser. For a moment he tries to revive the fantasy – 'Do not you grieve at this. I shall be sent for in private to him. Look you, he must seem thus to the world' (Part Two 5.5.77–9). But when the Lord Chief Justice returns with orders for his arrest, he is reduced to helpless protest, 'My lord, my lord – ' which the Justice – mercifully? – cuts off: 'I cannot now speak. I will hear you soon' (Part Two 5.5.94–5). Like Tamburlaine, Falstaff has extended his power through language; some of his speeches in Part Two are of Tamburlainian length. But now, in the most literal sense, words fail him.

When we first saw Falstaff touched with the fear of death, the moment was ominously juxtaposed with the silent, unobserved entrance of Hal:

DOLL

> Thou whoreson little tidy Bartholomew boar-pig, when wilt thou leave fighting o'days and foining o'nights, and begin to patch up thine old body for heaven?
> *Enter [behind] Prince and Poins [disguised as drawers].*

FALSTAFF

> Peace, good Doll, do not speak like a death's head; do not bid me
> remember mine end.   (Part Two 2.4.228–33)

In her account of his death in the next play – there is a sequel after all, but not the one Falstaff imagined – the Hostess makes the point simply: 'The

King has killed his heart' (*Henry V* 2.1.88). Though the epilogue to *Henry IV Part Two* (to which we shall return) promises more Falstaff in the next play, the promise is broken. It is the last of a trail of broken promises scattered through both parts of *Henry IV*. But Shakespeare has his reasons. The rejection effectively kills the character; he has given us as much Falstaff as there is ever going to be. (The Falstaff of *The Merry Wives of Windsor* is frequently regarded as a separate character; in any case he is a Falstaff to whom the rejection has not yet happened.)

The epilogue, by dealing self-consciously with the author's relation to his audience, alerts us to another feature of theatrical sequels: they tend to be metatheatrical. Playing on the audience's memories of the first play, they also play on its awareness of itself as an audience which has been in this theatre before and seen these characters before. (As Liane McLarty has shown in this volume, the same self-referential quality is pervasive in film sequels [200]; to her examples may be added the repetition of the Turkish-swordsman gag in the second Indiana Jones movie.) Taunting the upstart jailor-turned-king Almeda, Tamburlaine recalls an equally ineffectual figure (played by the same actor?) in Part One: 'Look to him, Theridamas, when we are fighting, lest he hide his crown as the foolish King of Persia did' (Part Two 3.5.157–9). When Hal and Poins, disguised as drawers, burst from hiding with the words, 'Anon, anon, sir' (Part Two 2.4.281), they recall the running gag involving Francis the Drawer in Part One. Pistol's quotations from old plays mostly mean nothing now, but for the first audience he would have been metatheatre personified, and one of his quotations at least is still recognizable:

> Shall packhorses
> And hollow pamper'd jades of Asia,
> Which cannot go but thirty mile a day
> Compare with Caesars, and with cannibals,
> And Troiant Greeks?   (Part Two 2.4.162–6)

It is here in Shakespeare, not in his sons, that Tamburlaine lives on. Falstaff himself is increasingly metatheatrical in Part Two, analysing the sources of his own comedy, aware of himself as a well-known character. When Coleville of the Dale recognizes him, he knows it is because of his appearance: 'I have a whole school of tongues in this belly of mine, and not a tongue of them all speaks any other word but my name' (Part Two 4.3.18–20). There may even be something metatheatrical about his complaint at being trapped in the role of war hero, a role he has no desire to play: 'There is not a dangerous action can peep out his head but I am thrust upon it. Well, I cannot last ever. But it was alway yet the trick of our English nation, if they have a good thing, to make it too common' (Part Two 1.2.211–15). The popular character himself is complaining at being brought back for a sequel.

Tamburlaine was performed at the Rose, a playhouse now known (since its excavation in 1989) to have been much smaller than its successors the Globe and the Fortune. To us, it looks like an intimate chamber theatre. This means that Tamburlaine's expansive ambitions were acted out in a tight physical space. And they were limited in time, the two or three hours of an Elizabethan performance. The metatheatrical references we have just touched on look back, reminding us we are in a sequel. But there is another, subtler type of metatheatrical reference that looks forward, connecting with the sense of mortality we have already examined, linking the end of the play with the end of a life and insisting that this sequel is the last. Zenocrate, dying, imagines that she was allowed only so much life, only so much breath even, just as a stage play is allowed only so much time:

> I fare, my lord, as other empresses,
> That, when this frail and transitory flesh
> Hath suck'd the measure of the vital air
> That feeds the body with his dated health,
> Wanes with enforc'd and necessary change.   (Part Two 2.4.42–6)

Timing also enters into the portrayal of Tamburlaine's death. His doctor warns him, 'this day is critical, / Dangerous to those whose crisis is as yours,' adding, 'Yet, if your majesty may escape this day, / No doubt but you shall soon recover all' (Part Two 5.3.91–2, 98–9). It is as though he is saying to Tamburlaine, if you can get past six o'clock, past the ending of the play, you can survive. He doesn't. Ionesco's *Exit the King* begins with a formal announcement from the stage that in ninety minutes the play will be over and the king will be dead. In ninety minutes the play is over and the king is dead; so it is with Tamburlaine. Falstaff, too, gets to the end of his time by getting to the end of his play. Rejecting him, Henry V sees the Falstaff scenes of the two plays just ending as a bad dream from which he has awakened:

> I long have dreamt of such a kind of man,
> So surfeit-swelled, so old, and so profane,
> But being awaked I do despise my dream.   (5.5.49–51)

We recall that in *A Midsummer Night's Dream* the ending of a dream was equated with the ending of a play.

Both sequels, having challenged the notion of closure by their very existence, end by insisting on it. They make further sequels impossible: no more Tamburlaine, no more Falstaff. One possible reading of this is that both Marlowe and Shakespeare, having created glamorous criminal heroes, responded to the moralizing streak in their culture, and possibly in themselves, by turning against those heroes, diminishing them, showing their limitations, and finally despatching them. Certainly Marlowe, who shows elsewhere in his work a keen undercutting wit, seems to have been aware from the beginning that there was something ludicrous about Tamburlaine. A self-destruct mechanism is built into the opening of Part One, in the first words of the ineffectual King of Persia:

> Brother Cosroe, I find myself agriev'd;
> Yet insufficient to express the same,
> For it requires a great and thundering speech.   (Part One 1.1.1–3)

The invitation is open to all those later writers (including Shakespeare) for whom Tamburlaine's bombast became a target of fun. In 1753, Sarah Fielding claimed that no one would mind more Falstaff 'if he always appeared with the same Humour' as in Part One (qtd. in Schellenberg, this volume 93). But the sheer expansion of his role in Part Two, which begins to induce fatigue and overfamiliarity, may embody Shakespeare's challenge to his audience: how much more of this could you really take?

There is another possibility, more elusive but worth considering. Popular characters take off on their own, enter the culture, cease to belong to the writers who created them. All those allusions to Tamburlaine are allusions to him, not to Marlowe. So with Falstaff. Once created, they belong to anyone. Other writers, as Andrew Taylor has shown (this volume), felt free to appropriate Chaucer's characters. But these two plays stand at a crucial turning point in the history of authorship (Helgerson 199–200). In the 1590s, plays published anonymously outnumber by roughly two to one plays published with the name of the author. In the following decade, the number of anonymous plays holds steady, but the number of plays that name the author trebles, and those plays outnumber the anonymous ones, albeit by a small margin. In the collaborative enterprise that was theatre, authors were at first expected to remain nameless; the early title pages are far more likely to name the acting company. Several of Shakespeare's early plays were published anonymously; so was *Tamburlaine*. Yet the stamp of Marlowe's style is so distinctive that *Tamburlaine* is an 'anonymous' play whose authorship has never been in doubt. Falstaff's name appears on the title page of the first surviving quarto of *Henry IV, Part One*; Shakespeare's does not. But Shakespeare joins his creation on the title page of *Part Two*, and it is in connection with this play that his name first appears in the Stationers' Register. We are witnessing the birth of the dramatic author as a public figure with an individual claim to attention (Leggatt 130–9).

The legal recognition of the concept of literary property lay far in the future. But in asserting control over Tamburlaine and Falstaff by limiting their appearances, are Marlowe and Shakespeare exerting their authority as authors? As Schellenberg has shown, one of the functions of the sequel in later periods was 'to strengthen an author's claim to his literary property' (90). These characters do not belong to just anyone; they belong to their original creators. Yet in bringing them back for the sort of sequel that makes further sequels impossible, Marlowe and Shakespeare are both recognizing the power of what they have created and (like Prospero giving up his magic) calling a halt to the operation of that power. In so doing they escape the frustration – of which there are many later examples – of the author trapped by a popular character of his own making. Conan Doyle's abortive attempt to kill Sherlock Holmes is well known. As the title of Carole Gerson's essay in this volume shows, there were times when L.M. Montgomerey felt 'dragged at [the] chariot wheels' of Anne of Green Gables. Arguably, the definitive statement of the problem is Stephen King's *Misery*. King's hero, like Conan Doyle, makes a desperate attempt to kill his creation; have we caught Marlowe and Shakespeare responding to a similar problem in a similar way?

It may be objected that this is pure speculation. Playwrights of this period have left hardly any comments on their own work, and we have no statements by Marlowe or Shakespeare that their creations had got out of hand and must be destroyed. Or have we? The prologue to *Tamburlaine Part Two* explains why the sequel was written:

> The general welcomes Tamburlaine receiv'd,
> When he arrived last upon our stage,
> Have made our poet pen his Second Part,
> Where death cuts off the progress of his pomp,
> And murderous Fates throw all his triumphs down.   (Part Two Prologue 1–5)

If we stopped at the end of the third line, we would have the simple statement that Marlowe wrote the play in response to box-office pressure, to cash in on the success of its predecessor. But the full thought is: Tamburlaine's popularity made the author bring him back *in order to kill him*. That is what the sequel is for.

The epilogue to *Henry IV Part Two* is in many ways problematic, but we can see the same idea at work:

> One word more, I beseech you. If you be not too much cloyed with fat meat, our humble author will continue the story, with Sir John in it, and make you merry with fair Katharine of France. Where, for anything I know, Falstaff shall die of a sweat, unless already a' be killed with your hard opinions; for Oldcastle died a martyr, and this is not the man. My tongue is weary; when my legs are too, I will bid you good night; and so I kneel down before you, but, indeed, to pray for the Queen.   (Part Two Epilogue 24–33)

This last part of the epilogue, like the play itself, is presented as an afterthought. It includes the admission that the performer is getting tired; is the playwright too? It includes also the suggestion – the hope? – that the audience is getting tired of Falstaff. It promises, like the prologue of *Tamburlaine Part Two*, to bring him back in order to kill him. We could say that Shakespeare breaks that promise; but we could equally well say that he has already kept it. This is what *Henry IV Part Two* has done, and pretending to defer it to the future may be a sardonic joke on members of the audience who haven't noticed.

But if Marlowe and Shakespeare are trying to assert their authorial power by ending the characters on their own terms, it has to be said that they failed, as Conan Doyle was to fail. If we leave aside the problematic case of *The Merry Wives of Windsor*, Falstaff has survived as an advertising icon, an adjective, and a brand of beer. He has entered popular culture as well as high culture, and his life shows no signs of stopping. Outside university English courses, Tamburlaine has not survived under his own name, though he had a good long run after Marlowe's death. But (though muscles and explosives now do the work of rhetoric) so long as the unstoppable hero haunts the video shops, the spirit of Tamburlaine lives on. Shakespeare and Marlowe created heroes who impose the power of their imaginations on the world around them, and tried to show that power ultimately failing. Ironically it was their own power, the power to insist on closure, that failed in the end.

Works Cited

Berek, Peter. '*Tamburlaine*'s Weak Sons: Imitation as Interpretation before 1593.' *Renaissance Drama* n.s. 13 (1982): 55–82.

Helgerson, Richard. *Forms of Nationhood: The Elizabethan Writing of England*. Chicago: U of Chicago P, 1992.

Leggatt, Alexander. 'The Presence of the Playwright, 1580–1640.' *Elizabethan Theater: Essays in Honor of S. Schoenbaum*. Ed. R.B. Parker and S.P. Zitner. Newark: U of Delaware P; London: Associated UP, 1996. 130–46.

Levin, Richard. 'The Contemporary Perception of Marlowe's Tamburlaine.' *Mediaeval and Renaissance Drama in England* 1 (1984): 51–70.

Marlowe, Christopher. *The Complete Plays*. Ed. J.B. Steane. Harmondsworth: Penguin, 1969.

Shakespeare, William. *The Complete Works of Shakespeare*. 4th ed. Ed. David Bevington. New York: Harper Collins, 1992.

The Shakspere [sic] *Allusion-Book: A Collection of Allusions to Shakspere from 1591 to 1700*. Ed. John Munro and others. Vol. 1. London: Humphrey Milford, Oxford UP, 1932.

Echoes of Paradise: Epic Iteration in Milton

SAMUEL GLEN WONG

According to Thomas Ellwood, Milton was provoked into writing a sequel to *Paradise Lost*. Ellwood had been a student of Milton's in 1662, reading aloud to him in exchange for tutoring in Latin. The arrangement lasted only a few months, but they remained friends, and Milton asked his former pupil to read his epic in manuscript. Ellwood recalled the fateful result in an autobiography published forty years after Milton's death:

He asked me how I liked it, and what I thought of it; which I modestly, but freely told him: and after some further Discourse about it, I pleasantly said to him, Thou hast said much here of *Paradise lost*; but what hast thou to say of *Paradise found*? He made me no Answer, but sate some time in a Muse: then brake of that Discourse, and fell upon another Subject ... And when afterwards I went to wait on him there (which I seldom failed of doing, whenever my Occasions drew me to *London*), he shewed me his Second POEM, called *PARADISE REGAINED*; and in a pleasant Tone said to me, *This is owing to you; for you put it into my Head by the Question you put to me at* Chalfont; *which before I had not thought of.*   (French 4.417–20)

Though Ellwood is a vital source for biographers of Milton – prime witness to the period when, forced from the political arena, he quietly prepared his greatest poems – his tale of intervention has been difficult to accept. As W.R. Parker observes:

What the humourless young Quaker failed to realize, in his eager excursion into literary criticism, is that *Paradise Lost* (at least in its printed version) has a number of very pointed and eloquent things to say of 'paradise found.' We may conjecture, therefore, that the poet's silence was compounded of disappointment and moody self-criticism. Had he failed to communicate his belief in a 'paradise within' or was Ellwood merely a careless reader? (597)

In a more recent biography, A.N. Wilson expresses similar doubts:

It is a touching story. 'He asked me how I liked it and what I thought of it' will ring true in the ear of anyone who has written anything designed for a public readership ... But one should not imagine that Milton immediately sat down and began to dictate *Paradise Regained* on Ellwood's helpful suggestion. Milton's silence, and changing of the subject, might very likely reflect a slightly wounded fear that Ellwood had not read the ending of *Paradise Lost* very carefully. (229)

For Parker and Wilson – and in this they echo modern critical consensus – *Paradise Lost* possesses precisely what Ellwood says that it lacks: paradise found in the vision of a 'paradise within.'

The encounter between Ellwood and Milton's biographers epitomizes the difficulty of reading the paradise poems as sequence. How does *Paradise Regained* succeed *Paradise Lost*? in what sense is it a sequel? Ellwood neatly resolves such questions in a story where he is the cause and *Paradise Regained* the effect, and the failing of a first epic is remedied by a second: 'Thou hast said much here of *Paradise lost*; but what hast thou to say of *Paradise found*?' Parker and Wilson reject his etiology, arguing that in its psychic restoration of paradise *Paradise Lost* prevents the essential terms of *Paradise Regained*. Where Ellwood sees incompletion that demands a sequel, they discern a sublime comprehension that precludes one. In these competing critical narratives, the problem of epic sequence is cast in radical terms of deficiency and plenitude that suggest the essential tension implicit in the very idea of a sequel to *Paradise Lost*. Is it a necessary or superfluous gesture? a vital supplement or brilliant work of supererogation?

In what follows, I consider Milton's epic sequence in terms inspired by these dissonant readings, specifically by tracing a series of verbal echoes: common words – like 'paradise' itself – that bind the epics in an elaborate play of redundance and transformation. My focus on iteration, which serves Milton virtually as a poetic principle, is inspired by the striking verbal economy Ellwood imposes on the poems, the antonymic shift from 'paradise lost' to 'paradise found' that, in his story, enables the imagination of a sequel. For Ellwood, epic meaning hinges on a word transformed in recurrence – a way of reading Milton in profound sympathy with his practice. If Ellwood suggests a method, the modern critique of his account informs my analysis as well. For iteration complicates the ideal of a sublimely sufficient *Paradise Lost* and shows how *Paradise Regained* extends its precursor in the very words they share. In the prophetic and recursive operation of iterated words, *Paradise Regained* and *Paradise Lost* become subtly coeval works where sequence, in the end, dissolves.[1]

Intimate Bonds

From title to closing words, *Paradise Regained* is a tissue of repetitions, verbal echoes of *Paradise Lost* that *en masse* reveal the depth of their negotiation of common epic territory. Seemingly cursory iterations, upon consideration, reveal the intimacy of their bond and the remarkable consistency of Milton's verbal imagination:

> Here passion first I felt,
> Commotion strange, in all enjoyments else
> Superior and unmoved, here only weak
> Against the charm of beauty's powerful glance.   (*PL* 8.530–3)

Adam confesses to his weakness for Eve in a conversation with Raphael, who will gently chastise him. The moment is prepared for from the first appearance of Adam and Eve in the epic and is a crucial part of the elaborate choreography of a fall that will entail, on the part of Adam in particular, a willing submission to passion.[2] Though the narrative prompts us to judge – couching the admission in a dialogue with an angel sent to admonish as well as encourage – we are aware that Adam's human weakness is not entirely without virtue. While this guileless confession is filled with foreboding, it also intimates the bonds of affection that will form the foundation of his postlapsarian life with Eve. In a narrative where their sin is a fact of history, Adam's fatal weakness will be translated into a very real strength. And, as Milton links beauty to weakness in *Paradise Lost*, so he does again in *Paradise Regained*:

> For beauty stands
> In the admiration only of weak minds
> Led captive; cease to admire, and all her plumes
> Fall flat and shrink into a trivial toy,
> At every sudden slighting quite abashed.   (*PR* 2.220–4)

In the course of discussing possible actions against Christ, Satan rejects the suggestion of Belial, 'after Asmodai / The fleshliest incubus,' who would seduce Christ with the 'daughters of men' (2.154). The strategy has succeeded before, but Satan knows that in Christ he faces a new kind of adversary and accuses his cohort of falsely measuring all others by his own lust.

Satan's abuse of Belial is itself a sign of corruption: a degeneration of the strained courtesy that marked the Parliament of Hell in *Paradise Lost* from which this debate is descended. Yet the most striking transformation here lies in the unsettling echoes of beauty and weakness. In these shared words, the passion of Adam is made consonant with the dissolution of Belial.[3] As Satan mocks Belial's weakness for the flesh in ironic counterpoint to Raphael's reproval of Adam, linking discordant scenes of angelic instruction and demonic dispute, Adam's own weakness is revisited, and both serve as prelude to the inevitable triumph of Christ in the desert. The iteration is subversive, enjoining the reader to make comparisons that revise the moral and spiritual terms of *Paradise Lost*. It is also hyperbolic: the extreme comparison of Belial to Adam may be no sooner entertained than rejected, but in that instant the vital issue – must superior wisdom resist superior beauty? – is defined. Such certainty comes at a cost; the intimate psychology of temptation that leads to Adam's fall vanishes from a sequel whose hero is proof against temptations of the flesh. One echo achieves a series of dissonant effects: Christ and Adam are sharply distinguished yet again; the emotional subtlety of the earlier epic is rejected in favour of a stringent moral clarity;[4] and the stern vision of *Paradise Regained* supersedes the humanity of *Paradise Lost*.

Through such repetitions as these, the moral and emotional language of *Paradise Lost* is rewritten word by word in *Paradise Regained*. In the course of a debate over the relative merits of 'Moses' law' (*PR* 4.225) and the 'sage philosophy' (4.272) of the Gentiles, Satan urges Christ to consider the precepts of the 'Peripatetics, and the sect / Epicurean, and the Stoic severe' (4.279–80). Christ rebuffs Satan, revealing his profound knowledge of Gentile philosophy:

> The Stoic last in philosophic pride,
> By him called virtue; and his virtuous man,
> Wise, perfect in himself, and all possessing,
> Equal to God, oft shames not to prefer,
> As fearing God nor man, contemning all
> Wealth, pleasure, pain or torment, death and life,

Which when he lists, he leaves, or boasts he can,
For all his tedious talk is but vain boast,
Or subtle shifts conviction to evade.
Alas what can they teach, and not mislead;
Ignorant of themselves, of God much more,
And how the world began, and how man fell
Degraded by himself, on grace depending?   (*PR* 4.300–12)

In his general rejection of ancient philosophy, Christ singles out the Stoic who, 'in philosophic pride,' may be said to re-enact a version of the fall: 'fearing God nor man' and worshipping instead a false self-sufficiency. In his discourse, and by his coming, Christ contextualizes the seeming wisdom of the Stoics, reminding Satan of the history that subverts their teaching. The passage is knit together by a series of internal echoes that describe the plight of the Stoic and of every 'virtuous man' who assumes a strength he cannot possess: 'perfect in himself ... Ignorant of themselves ... Degraded by himself.' These repetitions state the case against Stoicism succinctly; they also recall two crucial moments in book eight of *Paradise Lost*:

                    To attain
The height and depth of thy eternal ways
All human thoughts come short, supreme of things;
Thou in thyself art perfect, and in thee
Is no deficience found; not so is man,
But in degree, the cause of his desire
By conversation with his like to help,
Or solace his defects.   (*PL* 8.412–19)

I in thy persevering shall rejoice,
And all the blessed: stand fast; to stand or fall
Free in thine own arbitrament it lies.
Perfect within, no outward aid require;
And all temptation to transgress repel.   (*PL* 8.639–43)

Here, as in *Paradise Regained*, the nature of human perfection is at issue. In two encounters with heavenly beings, first as petitioner and then as pupil, Adam is used to articulate contrasting notions of self-sufficiency. As Adam asks for a mate, he argues that, unlike God, who is complete, 'Thou in thyself art perfect,' a solitary man is by nature deficient and requires a 'like' who may 'solace his defects.' (Adam is being literal: a mate will supplement him, and together they will perfect each other; Milton foreshadows at Adam's expense: Eve will 'solace his defects' in ways he cannot anticipate.) This argument is echoed at the end of the book when Raphael, in his parting admonition, maintains that Adam is 'perfect within,' able to resist 'all temptation' and 'no outward aid require.' While Adam sits silent, Raphael, who has heard the story of Adam's desire for a mate and his claims of incompletion, makes no allowance for any 'defects' in his human charge and argues instead for his essential sufficiency in the face of temptation.

With characteristic boldness, as part of the final preparation for the fall, Milton places enormous pressure on the question of the inherent perfection and deficiency of Adam. What Christ approaches through the medium of classical philosophy, as evidence of his mastery of the debate between Hebrew and Hellene, Adam must engage directly, as either an irresistible need built into his nature or an act of self-understanding urged on him by heavenly messenger. When Christ disparages the perfection of the Stoic, 'all possessing, / Equal to God,' we recall Adam's deference to the true perfection of his maker as well as the assurances of Raphael. Iteration inscribes that link, but the sequel forgoes the complexity of Adam's situation. The arrogance of pagan philosophers 'ignorant of themselves, of God much more' simplifies and displaces an Adam who spoke of perfection with God and Raphael in paradise. As in the implicit comparison of Belial to Adam, the subtlety of *Paradise Lost* is elided by the certainties of *Paradise Regained* and by the absolute sufficiency of Christ himself. In the iterative movement from Adam's 'Thou in thyself art perfect' and Raphael's 'perfect within' to the Stoic 'perfect in himself,' Milton implicates and orders the language of his epics.[5]

Through such iteration, the language of *Paradise Regained*, so often disparaged as austere, acquires a remarkable density apparent throughout the poem:

> And he still on was led, but with such thoughts
> Accompanied of things past and to come
> Lodged in his breast, as well might recommend
> Such solitude before choicest society.   (*PR* 1.299–302)

As Christ wanders alone into the desert, leaving Mary behind and preoccupied with thoughts 'of things past and to come,' Milton evokes the ancient *topos* of meditative solitude, and in so doing also recalls Adam's anxious words to Eve:

> For solitude sometimes is best society,
> And short retirement urges sweet return.
> But other doubt possesses me, lest harm
> Befall thee severed from me.   (*PL* 9.249–52)

Christ reprises the separation of Eve from Adam and, like Eve, will be tested in an encounter with the enemy. His very different success is already registered in Milton's subtle transformation of 'solitude.' Adam praises solitude in the midst of an emotional confusion: hoping to keep Eve by his side, fearing to offend by compelling her, and, in a neat proleptic irony, longing for her 'sweet return.' Where Adam's discourse is entangled in his relation to Eve – in ironic resistance to the *topos* he invents – the sequel, describing a meditative isolation where Christ seeks to purge his doubts and conceive his 'mission high,' affirms an ideal of self-ministering solitude bound to a sense of public duty.[6] The poems share an emotionally acute imagination of solitude, but the private struggle of Christ rectifies, even as it recalls, the confusion of Adam. Here, again, the sequel is marked by the polyvalence of its language, grounded in its power to cite the prior text and, in a word, multiply its effects.

The delicate renegotiation of solitude illuminates the ways in which iteration often serves to distinguish the psychic terrain of the epics and, in particular, the singular experience of Christ from the reciprocal subjectivity of Adam and Eve:

> Thus Mary pondering oft, and oft to mind
> Recalling what remarkably had passed
> Since first her salutation heard, with thoughts
> Meekly composed awaited the fulfilling:
> The while her son tracing the desert wild,
> Sole but with holiest meditations fed,
> Into himself descended, and at once
> All his great work to come before him set;
> How to begin, how to accomplish best
> His end of being on earth, and mission high.   (*PR* 2.105–14)

This passage marks the transition from the bittersweet disquisition of Mary on the destiny of her son to the 'holiest meditations' of Christ wandering 'the desert wild.' While Mary, 'pondering oft,' at last composes her thoughts, Christ's meditation is far more unsettled, its urgency communicated with a powerful metaphor: 'into himself descended.'

The metaphor recalls an equally dramatic descent near the end of *Paradise Lost*:

> He ended, and they both descend the hill;
> Descended, Adam to the bower where Eve
> Lay sleeping ran before, but found her waked;
> And thus with words not sad she him received.   (*PL* 12.606–9)

After enjoying a series of prophecies (that include the birth and death of Christ), Adam descends the hill with the archangel Michael to rejoin Eve. Their reunion precedes their exile from Paradise and foreshadows the separation of Mary and Christ, second Eve and Adam, that will prepare the way for the worldly career of her son. In a beautiful effect, Milton builds a slight delay into the descent of man and angel: 'they both descend the hill; / Descended, Adam ... ran before.' This internal echo, sutained by line break and caesura, revises the 'swift descent' (11.127) of Michael from heaven and completes the repeated 'ascends' – 'Ascend this hill ... Ascend, I will follow thee' (11.366, 371) – with which the episode of Michael's Vision began. The poetic manipulation of Adam's descent also corresponds to this particular moment of transition. Adam, vouchsafed a prophetic vision of history, returns to normal time, running before Michael to the bower in a poignantly temporal gesture of love. Here, he descends and is 'descended,' his physical action merging with his reduced, yet hopeful, spiritual state. In the sequel, however, all these descents will be profoundly transformed. As Christ descends 'into himself,' he supersedes the spectacle of angelic descent, forgoes a heavenly counsellor, and engages in an internal descent where he is the sole agent actively envisioning 'his great work to come.' Through the literal and metaphorical rendering of 'descended,' Milton mediates the transition from Adam to Christ; from a richly ambiguous signification at the close of one epic to a sharply defined act in the other, it measures the psychic space that lies between them.

Iterative Geographies

If repetition marks the transformation of psychic space, it also redefines the physical domains of the epics. So *Paradise Regained* begins with a recollection of *Paradise Lost* that limits its vast expanse:

> I who erewhile the happy garden sung,

By one man's disobedience lost, now sing
Recovered Paradise to all mankind,
By one man's firm obedience fully tried
Through all temptation, and the tempter foiled
In all his wiles, defeated and repulsed,
And Eden raised in the waste wilderness.
          Thou spirit who led'st this glorious eremite
Into the desert, his victorious field
Against the spiritual foe, and brought'st him thence
By proof the undoubted Son of God, inspire,
As thou art wont, my prompted song else mute.   (PR 1.1–12)

Iteration precedes inspiration as Milton delays the invocation of the spirit who will prompt his song in order to set his composition in the context of the epic sung 'erewhile.'[7] Yet, if sequel seems determined by precursor, Milton immediately disrupts this order. For even as these lines echo the prior poem,

Of man's first disobedience, and the fruit
Of that forbidden tree, whose mortal taste
Brought death into the world, and all our woe,
With loss of Eden, till one greater man
Restore us   (PL 1.1–5)

the sequel refines the symmetry between Adam and Christ, lesser and greater man. Through internal repetition and isocolon, Adam and Christ are brought into precise verbal and aural consonance. Where *Paradise Lost* describes a temporal process ('Of man's first disobedience ... *till* one greater man') bound by a remarkably involuted syntax, the sequel offers a simple iteration in metrical apposition ('By one man's ... By one man's') grounded in a radical transformation of the divine: Christ made man. As *Paradise Regained* echoes its predecessor, seeming to simplify its terms, it effects a transcendence.

Yet of all the echoes here, 'happy garden' epitomizes the iterative strategy of the sequel. Here it functions as trope: a synecdochic substitution of part for whole that reduces the prior epic to a *hortus conclusus* emblematically opposed to the desert that Christ's victory will re-create as an 'Eden raised in this waste wilderness.' The particular force of this tropic garden becomes clear when set against a crucial moment in the earlier epic:

About him all the sanctities of heaven
Stood thick as stars, and from his sight received
Beatitude past utterance; on his right
The radiant image of his glory sat,
His only son; on earth he first beheld
Our two first parents, yet the only two
Of mankind, in the happy garden placed,
Reaping immortal fruits of joy and love,
Uninterrupted joy, unrivalled love
In blissful solitude; he then surveyed
Hell and the gulf between, and Satan there
Coasting the wall of heaven on this side night
In the dun air sublime.   (*PL* 3.60–72)

The garden first appears in *Paradise Lost* embedded in a series of subtly
implicated scenes unfolded, as it were, by divine panopticon: 'sanctities'
blessed by the sight of God; the son reflecting the image of the Father;
Adam and Eve beheld in 'blissful solitude'; Satan spied as he himself
reconnoitres. Seen against this vast topography, the iterative garden of
Paradise Regained comes to signify a profound loss of context: a separation
from the realms that once enclosed it. In reducing *Paradise Lost* to a single
locus, Milton asserts the claims of mundane over cosmological epic and
prepares the way for an epic of diminished space.[8]

The elevation of mundane over cosmological perspectives is typical of
the iterative exchange between the poems and can assume several forms:

Before their eyes in sudden view appear
The secrets of the hoary deep, a dark
Illimitable ocean without bound,
Without dimension, where length, breadth, and height,
And time and place are lost; where eldest Night
And Chaos, ancestors of Nature, hold
Eternal anarchy, amidst the noise
Of endless wars, and by confusion stand.   (*PL* 2.890–7)

Yet he who reigns within himself, and rules
Passions, desires, and fears, is more a king;
Which every wise and virtuous man attains:
And who attains not, ill aspires to rule
Cities of men, or headstrong multitudes,

Subject himself to anarchy within,
Or lawless passions in him which he serves.   (*PR* 2.466–72)

In the first text, Satan has won through the gates of hell and, with Sin and Death, beholds the realm of Chaos described here for the first time. In the second, Christ has been tempted by Satan with wealth and responds, typically, with a discourse that extends the implications of the temptation beyond any articulated by Satan himself. 'Anarchy' binds them together and serves as the iterative core of complementary visions of rule that, in turn, reveal the sympathy of Milton's political and verbal imagination. In both texts 'anarchy' possesses a precise, paradoxical signification: disorder that constitutes a form of rule. In *Paradise Lost*, a personified 'Chaos,' elsewhere called the 'Anarch' (2.988), lies at the heart of an 'illimitable ocean' over which it still manages to preside.[9] In *Paradise Regained* the unworthy man who 'ill aspires to rule' is, in the language of political order, 'subject himself to anarchy within.' For Milton, 'anarchy' is a quintessentially 'complex word': subverting and embodying order in ways that allow him to construct contrary realms where lawlessness prevails but hierarchy and servitude, of a kind, still remain. The 'anarchy within' of the sequel is at once an echo and a transformation of the 'Eternal anarchy' of the epic. Milton dramatically shifts the site of anarchic disorder from a vast 'deep' governed by shadowy personifications to the individual who fails to 'reign within himself.' More than the mere accession of psychological realism, the translation of political realms is the fruit of the ongoing analysis of rule that binds the epics and divides them. As Christ internalizes anarchy in *Paradise Regained*, he recasts the question of rule in a form appropriate to a poem where the cultivation of inner space supplants the vistas of *Paradise Lost*.

If the renegotiation of space discloses the condition of wayward souls ruled by 'lawless passion,' it can also take more kinetic forms. When, near the end of *Paradise Regained*, Christ has finally triumphed over Satan, there is a sudden flurry of motion:

So Satan fell and straight a fiery globe
Of angels on full sail of wing flew nigh,
Who on their plumy vans received him soft
From his uneasy station, and upbore
As on a floating couch through the blithe air.   (*PR* 4.581–5)

For a moment the syntax is confusing as the angels seem to rescue Satan from falling, but 'uneasy station' clarifies the action: it is Satan who plummets unchecked while Christ, perched atop the Temple, is 'upbore' – opposed motions tracing the progress of defeat and victory. The lines also echo another dramatic flight, a moment in Satan's early career that, from a considerable distance of time and space, has led to Christ's triumph in the desert:

> At last his sail-broad vans
> He spreads for flight, and in the surging smoke
> Uplifted spurns the ground, thence many a league
> As in a cloudy chair ascending rides
> Audacious, but that seat soon failing, meets
> A vast vacuity: all unawares
> Fluttering his pennons vain plumb down he drops
> Ten thousand fathom deep.   (PL 2.927–34)

The angels 'on full sail of wing' hastening to receive Christ recall the 'sail-broad vans' of Satan, rising and falling as he begins his journey through Chaos, yet the conjunction of iterations around these episodes of ascent and descent also marks the imaginative divide between the epics. The 'Sail-broad vans' of *Paradise Lost* are disorienting, one of many images intended to dehumanize Satan and, in its vague intimations of his size and power, unsettle our imagination of him. In the sequel, Milton retains the image but transforms its effects. If the angels sent to retrieve Christ appear as a 'fiery globe ... on full sail of wing,' their 'vans,' on closer view, are 'plumy' – a 'couch' on which Christ will recline after his ordeal. The delightful domesticity of the images overturns the menace of Satan as thoroughly as did Christ's display of power. As elsewhere, the force of iteration lies in its economy: 'vans' bridges the gap between the Temple of Jerusalem and the Gates of Hell, between Christ and Satan poised on the brink of action.

The conjunction of angelic sightings, by turns horrific and comforting, re-minds us that angels often serve Milton as a potent iterative device in per-forming their limited but crucial repertoire of roles: messenger and tutor, guardian and worshipper. So angels mediate the most crucial set of iterations in the entire sequence as Michael's promise to Adam of a new paradise,

> then wilt thou not be loath
> To leave this Paradise, but shalt possess
> A paradise within thee, happier far   (PL 12.585–7),

is echoed by angelic choir at the end of *Paradise Regained*:

> Now thou hast avenged
> Supplanted Adam, and, by vanquishing
> Temptation, hast regained lost Paradise,
> And frustrated the conquest fraudulent:
> He never more henceforth will dare set foot
> In Paradise to tempt; his snares are broke:
> For though that seat of earthly bliss be failed,
> A fairer Paradise is founded now
> For Adam and his chosen sons, whom thou
> A saviour art come down to reinstall.   (PR 4.606–15)

This welter of 'paradises' presents a complex, problematical transition from epic to epic. If in words like 'anarchy' and 'descended' the sequel effects a process of abstraction, internalizing external actions, states, and spaces, 'paradise within' – the most potent abstraction of the prior poem – would seem to reverse this process. As physical paradise merges with psychic paradise in a marvellously economical union of matter and spirit, the conclusion of *Paradise Lost* prevents, even precludes, the iterative strategy of *Paradise Regained* and works its own transformation. Paradises proliferate once again in the sequel, but in a series of oddly shifting forms. The angels proclaim that Christ 'hast regained lost Paradise,' one in which Satan will 'never ... dare set foot,' and for a moment it would appear that Eden has indeed been 'raised in the waste wilderness.' Yet it quickly becomes clear that the original 'seat of earthly bliss' has not returned; that a 'fairer Paradise is founded now' – its foundations laid – where the children of Adam will one day dwell. The elegant metamorphosis of paradise at the end of *Paradise Lost* is obscured here by a succession of temporally and materially unstable repetitions.

As *Paradise Regained* echoes the transfigured spiritual paradise of the earlier epic, it struggles to occupy a verbal site already fully inhabited. In a striking reversal, *Paradise Lost* forestalls the characteristic verbal transformations of its offspring and reduces the sequel to *mere* repetition: a pleonastic paradise. As if in response to Ellwood's critique, Milton ends *Paradise Regained* insistently rehearsing the renewed foundation of paradise. Far from supplying what the earlier poem lacked, the poet strains to recollect the psychic plenitude of paradise in *Paradise Lost*. The iterative play of material and spiritual paradise leads to a difficult negotiation over epic territory that is nowhere better expressed than in the ungainly yoking of the two titles: 'thou ... hast regained lost Paradise.' The hint of this syntax, that the sequel has recapitulated the epic in its essence, reminds the reader of the pre-emptive claims of *Paradise Regained* at a moment when its powers of iterative transformation have finally failed.

Foregone Conclusions

In the third book of *Paradise Lost*, at another nexus of iterated words, sequence itself becomes the implicit subject of contemplation. Satan has come almost to the end of his long journey and landing on the sun spies the angel Uriel, who will direct him to paradise:

> His back was turned, but not his brightness hid;
> Of beaming sunny rays, a golden tiar
> Circled his head, nor less his locks behind
> Illustrious on his shoulders fledge with wings
> Lay waving round; on some great charge employed
> He seemed, or fixed in cogitation deep.
> Glad was the spirit impure; as now in hope
> To find who might direct his wandering flight
> To Paradise the happy seat of man,
> His journey's end and our beginning woe.   (*PL* 3.624–33)

In the final book of *Paradise Regained*, Satan, after failing in his temptation of Christ, assails him:

> Now contrary, if I read aught in heaven,
> Or heaven write aught of fate, by what the stars
> Voluminous, or single characters,
> In their conjunction met, give me to spell,
> Sorrows, and labours, opposition, hate,
> Attends thee, scorns, reproaches, injuries,
> Violence and stripes, and lastly cruel death,
> A kingdom they portend thee, but what kingdom,
> Real or allegoric I discern not,
> Nor when, eternal sure, as without end,
> Without beginning; for no date prefixed
> Directs me in the starry rubric set.   (*PR* 4.382–93)

In the movement from epic to sequel, there is a striking devolution, from the vital cosmology of *Paradise Lost*, where angels inhabit the spheres and guard the heavens, to a devilish astrology.[10] Satan is the focus in both passages, and his actions are complementary, his exploration of the heavens balanced against his reading of the heavens: 'what the stars ... give me to spell.' In each case Satan seeks heavenly direction, and direction, within limits, is given him. We are also aware that Satan's seeming mastery – he successfully deceives Uriel and his divination is accurate – is subverted by the cosmic framework that envelops him in *Paradise Lost* and that he himself evokes in *Paradise Regained*.

Yet the most potent iteration here is more temporal than cosmological. As Satan nears earth at last, Milton carefully notes the narrative and historical turning point: 'His journey's end and our beginning woe.' The crucial words recur in the angry discourse of Satan: 'eternal sure, as without end, / Without beginning.' In both instances, Milton echoes the Apocalyptic text: 'I am Alpha and Omega, the beginning and the end, the first and the last.'[11] So the 'journey's end' of Satan is the present goal of paradise and the conclusion of a narrative he cannot foresee even as he surveys the whole of creation. When Satan mocks the kingdom of Christ, 'eternal sure,' he falls into a temporal language that again reveals the limits of his sight: 'for no date prefixed / Directs me in the starry rubric set.' Through this apocalyptic iteration, that Satan speaks without fully understanding, Milton marks the limits of a narrative enclosed by the kingdom of Christ. In the union of beginning and end, the order of epic and sequel is consummated and consumed as the deep work of verbal iteration is strikingly revealed: to draw the poems together, not as sequence, but as sublimely coincident utterances.

Satan's inability to see the end of the story in which he is embroiled provides an ironic parallel to the reading of Thomas Ellwood. For both, the prospective restoration of paradise assumes a form they find elusive. Ellwood misses, or ignores, the vision of the 'paradise within' that sustains Adam and Eve, as well as Milton's modern critics, in their exile; Satan misconceives a saviour who will conquer the earth in unconventional ways. While Satan's misreading is the result of demonic perversity, Ellwood's carelessness is typically human: a critical misperception, perhaps, but also the demonstration of a need to have the terms of a vital bargain reiterated in the clearest fashion, a hedge against misunderstanding and shield against insecurity. As *Paradise Regained* echoes *Paradise Lost*, we are made aware that Milton fully understood the needs of his reader and pupil.

Notes

1 I am also indebted to the work of Schwartz; though she pays little attention to verbal

echo or *Paradise Regained*, her psychoanalytic study of recurring motifs of chaos and order, fall and creation, in *Paradise Lost* is wonderfully suggestive.

2 On passion in Milton's Paradise, see Turner 174–87. The best reading of the episode that begins with the lines cited here remains that of Fish 228–32.

3 There are other points of verbal comparison between Adam and Belial. Satan recounts how Belial and his crew 'cast wanton eyes on the daughters of men, / And coupled with them, and begot a race' (*PR* 2.180–1). 'Race' is a word powerfully associated with Adam and Eve, often by Satan, in *Paradise Lost*: 2.348, 2.382, 2.834, 3.679; similarly, the duty to propagate a 'race' is proper to Adam and Eve: 4.475; 4.732; 7.630.

4 This move to simplification for the sake of the reader or viewer appears to be a recurrent feature of the sequel, judging from the findings of other contributors to this volume; see Schellenberg (89–90) and Budra (194–5).

5 The debate surrounding the temptation of learning – how does the rejection of Greek philosophy accord with the classicism of Milton? – is relevant here. Read as part of a pattern of iteration in *Paradise Regained*, Christ's speech seems less a statement of Milton's views than a careful recollection of *Paradise Lost*. As the attack on the Stoic echoes earlier concerns with defining the terms of Adam's perfection, it clarifies the oblique engagement with Stoic philosophy in the prior poem. Satan's fall, in another perversion of self-sufficiency, is a crucial subtext here as well. See Samuel 122–9, and Fallon. In refining the debate on Milton and learning, Cable proposes that Christ's speech be read in the context of Milton's iconoclasm (5).

6 In this regard, Milton not only corrects Adamic solitude, but refines the classical ideal in his depiction of Christ. For a history of this *topos* in the Renaissance, see Røstvig 24–41. Budick discusses the complementary notion of 'redemptive retirement' (137–42).

7 Martz says of these opening lines: 'The allusion to *Paradise Lost* here asks us to recall that poem, and to note how different the new poem will be in its theme and hence in its style' (248). I argue the recollection of *Paradise Lost* blurs the boundary between the poems.

8 Milton anticipates the possibility of a mundane epic in the ambivalent engagements with cosmology that dot *Paradise Lost*: Adam's response to Eve's questions about the cosmos (4.660–88); their discussion in the wake of her dream (5.114–16); and Raphael's reply to Adam's cosmological questions (8.170–8).

9 For differing analyses of boundary in Chaos, see Schwartz, 11–24, and Rumrich 118–46.

10 Milton was ambivalent about judicial astrology: 'All study of the heavenly bodies, however, is not unlawful or unprofitable; as it appears from the journey of the wise men, and still more from the star itself, divinely appointed to announce the birth of Christ, Matt. ii 1,2' (*De doctrina Christiana*, 2.5, in *Complete Prose*, vol. 6). On Milton and astrology see Marjara 111–18; on the controversy surrounding astrology in this period see Capp.

11 This text echoes within the Book of Revelation: 1.8; 21.6; 22.13. On the temporal play of Alpha and Omega in Milton, see Tayler 105–22.

Works Cited

Budick, Sanford. *The Dividing Muse: Images of Sacred Disjunction in Milton's Poetry*. New Haven, CT: Yale UP, 1985.

Cable, Lana. *Carnal Rhetoric: Milton's Iconoclasm and the Poetics of Desire*. Durham, NC: Duke UP, 1995.

Capp, Bernard. *Astrology & the Popular Press: English Almanacs, 1500–1800*. London: Faber, 1979.

Fallon, Stephen. *Milton Among the Philosophers: Poetry and Materialism in Seventeenth-Century England*. Ithaca, NY: Cornell UP, 1991.

Fish, Stanley E. *Surprised by Sin: The Reader in* Paradise Lost. Berkeley: U of California P, 1967.

French, J. Milton, ed. *The Life Records of John Milton*. 5 vols. New Brunswick, NJ: Rutgers UP, 1949–58.

Marjara, Harinder Singh. *Contemplation of Created Things: Science in* Paradise Lost. Toronto: U of Toronto P, 1992.

Martz, Louis L. *Poet of Exile: A Study of Milton's Poetry*. New Haven, CT: Yale UP, 1980.

Milton, John. *The Complete Prose Works of John Milton*. 8 vols. Ed. Don M. Wolfe et al. New Haven, CT: Yale UP, 1953–82.

– *The Oxford Authors: John Milton*. Ed. Stephen Orgel and Jonathan Goldberg. Oxford: Oxford UP, 1991.

Parker, William Riley. *Milton: A Biography*. 2 vols. Oxford: Clarendon, 1968.

Røstvig, Maren-Sofie. *The Happy Man: Studies in the Metamorphoses of a Classical Ideal, 1600–1700*. Oxford: Blackwell, 1954.

Rumrich, John P. *Milton Unbound*. Cambridge: Cambridge UP, 1996.

Samuel, Irene. *Plato and Milton*. Ithaca, NY: Cornell UP, 1947.

Schwartz, Regina M. *Remembering and Repeating: On Milton's Theology and Poetics*. Chicago: U of Chicago P, 1988.

Tayler, Edward W. *Milton's Poetry: Its Development in Time*. Pittsburgh, PA: Duquesne UP, 1979.

Turner, James Grantham. *One Flesh: Paradisal Marriage and Sexual Relations in the Age of Milton*. Oxford: Clarendon, 1987.

Wilson, A.N. *The Life of John Milton*. Oxford: Oxford UP, 1983.

'To Renew Their Former Acquaintance': Print, Gender, and Some Eighteenth-Century Sequels

BETTY A. SCHELLENBERG

Historians generally locate the definitive moment in England's massive shift towards a print culture in the early eighteenth century. It was at this time that writers self-consciously lived out the implications of a gradual, but perceptible and inexorable, move away from an amateur, elitist, patronage system of authorship to a market system. Increasingly, success was measured by the ability of an author to sell copies and, essentially, to make of him- or herself an 'author function,' to establish a recognizable and saleable 'public literary signature' as 'The Author of ...'[1] As part of the same process, the successful author was leaving behind the image of the hack, attaining a more respectable social status as disinterested servant of the public good. This developing sense of identity based on a marketable skill, on supplying to a defined public a specialized service it was demanding, is what I am here calling the 'professionalization' of the author at this early modern stage.[2]

Interestingly, and I think not coincidentally, this historical moment also saw a proliferation of the sequel as a subform of prose narrative.[3] Terry Castle has noted this conjunction rather dismissively in her discussion of Samuel Richardson's 1741 sequel to *Pamela*:

At least since the early eighteenth century, when the economy of literary production began to take something of its modern capitalist form, the sequel has been an offshoot of the best-seller syndrome. It is an attempt to profit further from a previous work that has had exceptional commercial success: only charismatic texts, those with an unusually powerful effect on a large reading public, typically generate sequels.[4]

Even Castle finds the sequel, that ostensibly straightforward instance of the profit motive, puzzling in its Pamelian manifestation, however. The reader's desire for repetition is for some reason not catered to after all, and 'the novel is more than a disappointment. At times it seems almost to insult us, to affront our expectations, including our very desire for repetition.' 'Even for a sequel,' Castle concludes, 'it is exceptionally frustrating.'[5] This hint that some sequels, at least, may represent a movement more complicated than formulaic repetition, perhaps even a deliberate frustration of desire, suggests that the relation of author, reader, and originating text that produces the early English print sequel may in fact be a rather complex and various one. Thus the phenomenon of the sequel offers fertile ground for an examination of the dynamics governing the conjunction of author, book, and audience at this historic moment in textual production.[6]

Even further, the relations among female author, text, and audience in the mid-eighteenth century offer a particularly intriguing subset of the sequel phenomenon. As a culturally recognized force, these 'Amazons of the pen' were relatively new to the literary marketplace,[7] and the pressures against professionalization – through an increasingly rigid discourse of gender aligning women with the domestic, private, undereducated (or 'natural'), and non-capitalistic – were especially strong. In consequence, the disjunctions between anti-market and market values are particularly visible in the contrast between the rhetoric of these women and their actual practice and cultural position.[8] And again, these women showed a marked predilection for the sequel form. In a quick review of the best-known male and female mid-century authors, it seems significant that, while Samuel Richardson used the form only once, with *Pamela*, and adamantly resisted pressure to reopen his later narratives, while Henry Fielding quickly moved away from his *Pamela* parody, *Shamela*, towards novels whose intertextuality was more biographical than narrative, while Tobias Smollett had one set of characters make a cameo reappearance in his final novel but avoided any formal sequel, virtually all of their most prominent female contemporaries who wrote fiction used the sequel form, and at various points in their writing careers. This suggests a combination of external pressures towards the form, and some inherent generic appeal commonly felt by these women.

Therefore, although I will begin with a few generalizations about prose-narrative sequels, using John Bunyan, Daniel Defoe, and Samuel Richardson as my points of reference, my essay will ultimately focus on a more specific question: how might we read the frequent and successful use of the sequel by some of the most productive and acclaimed mid-century women writers of prose fiction – for example, Sarah Fielding's *Familiar Letters between the Principal Characters in 'David Simple'* (1747) and *David Simple, Volume the Last* (1753) following upon her *Adventures of David Simple* (1744); Frances Sheridan's 1767 sequel to *The Memoirs of Miss Sidney Bidulph* (1761); and Sarah Scott's *The History of Sir George Ellison* (1766) after *A Description of Millenium Hall* (1762)?[9] The career timing of these sequels refutes any hypothesis that they simply represent an immature, insecure writer's inability to imagine something new – Sheridan's sequel closely followed her first novel, but Fielding came back to her original story at intervals over nine years and between other successful publications, while Sarah Scott's pair of texts appeared in mid-career. Not only were these women using the sequel form consistently, but they were also exploring its entire range: one finds the typical continuation of a charismatic protagonist's story beyond its original closure (Fielding's *Volume the Last*), but also the second-generation narrative (Sheridan's *Sidney Bidulph*, Part Two), the 'prequel' (Scott's *Sir George Ellison*, whose first section fills in the period before the opening of *Millenium Hall*), and a popular eighteenth-century form, the collection of sentiments or letters purportedly written by characters from a novel (Fielding's *Familiar Letters*). In this essay I will examine both the external circumstances and the textual markers that accompany these sequels to support my claim that, for these writers, the sequel was a particularly congenial form. The sequel indeed performed a strategic career function, serving as a disguised bid for an expanded audience by ostensibly addressing 'old Friends'[10] while exploiting the widely known public identity of 'The Author of ...' But, at the same time, in portraying itself as written to please an already established readership, the sequel preserved the pretence of the modest woman's writing only for her intimate circle, while allowing the author a bold claim to moral and narrative authority as the established instructor of those readers. Thus the form offered women writers, in particular, an effective means of enhancing their professional status.

The ultimate effect of print for an author, according to Walter J. Ong, is unidirectional communication; unlike oral storytelling, 'printed narrative is not two-way, at least in the short run. Readers' reactions are remote and initially conjectural.'[11] While manuscript circulation dissociates author and reader temporally, but still limits audience scope to a relatively defined circle, print circulation offers neither an occasionally nor a socially defined audience. Thus early eighteenth-century writers who had known, or who inherited the model of, the select audience of the courtly amateur tended to resort to nostalgic backward looks or to the re-creation

of a facsimile in the form of an idealized reader or a subscription publication – one thinks here of Alexander Pope addressing the likes of
Bolingbroke, and of his highly successful use of subscription for his
translation of the *Iliad*. The early writer of prose fiction for publication, on
the other hand, generally had no claim to such a select, homogeneous,
and objectifiable audience – consider the socially ambivalent circumstances of John Bunyan, Daniel Defoe, and Samuel Richardson. And the
situations of the female authors I am focusing on might be called down-
right precarious – Sarah Fielding was an impoverished gentlewoman
spinster, Frances Sheridan the wife of an improvident and volatile Irish
theatre manager, Sarah Scott the estranged wife of a courtier and the
daughter of an avaricious man who cut her off financially. All three
therefore had to live the better part of their adult lives remote from the
expense of London, the centre of literary networks and sales.[12]

From such writers of prose narratives, dependent on the favourable
response of an anonymous and diverse readership, one can therefore expect techniques for realizing an audience within the text, techniques Ong
has characterized in the title phrase of his article 'The Writer's Audience
Is Always a Fiction.' Indeed, Defoe's Robinson Crusoe concludes that God
is the ideal reader of his narrative, and Richardson's Pamela deliberately
adopts a fiction of addressing her parents when the possibility of convey-
ing letters to them is gone. Among later eighteenth-century writers such
as Laurence Sterne and the novelists of sentiment, audience-creating techniques achieve considerable sophistication, with readers categorized into
groups according to gender, sensibility, or degree of moral hypocrisy.

One effect of writing a successful novel, conversely, was the establishment of an identifiable audience outside the fiction, an audience whose
various responses to the original text, for better or worse, replaced the
responses of this fictionalized readership. We know that Bunyan heard
complaints from readers about the bad example of Christian, the hero of
The Pilgrim's Progress, abandoning his family,[13] that Defoe was nettled at
those who attempted to 'reproach [*Robinson Crusoe*] with being a Romance, to search it for Errors in Geography, Inconsistency in the Relation,
and Contradictions in the Fact,' and that Richardson's detractors, most
famously Fielding, saw *Pamela* as instructing 'Servant-Maids ... To look
out for their Masters as sharp as they can.'[14] The preferred authorial
strategy for dealing with this newly defined readership seems to have
been an explicit sorting of the audience into the desirable and the unde-
sirable, excluding what Richardson called 'this hasty-judging world'
from the audience for whom the sequel was intended, and warmly

welcoming those who had shown themselves to be friends – that is, right interpreters – of the original text.[15] Having pleased a significant number of readers, in other words, the author now had the authority to write unwelcome readers out of the text. Thus, Bunyan instructs his sequel to *The Pilgrim's Progress* to leave 'to their choice' its dissatisfied readers, an arbitrary and antisocial minority who 'Love not their Friends nor their own House or home'; these antisocial few will suffer by their exclusion from the inner circle who are to be shown the mysteries that 'thou shalt keep close, shut up from the rest.'[16] As for the reader in that inner circle, the sequel welcomes her or him as an old friend, as an initiate, as precisely the one for whom this continuation is written.[17]

With respect to these friends, however, the early print sequel's impulses appear to be conservative, socializing, and didactic, as the work of a writer who is concerned with circumscribing desire rather than encouraging its potentially antisocial force.[18] As a result of his initial success, the previously anonymous (often literally so) writer has become an object of public scrutiny, in Roger Sharrock's phrase, 'the unknown explorer of a single personal theme finds himself a writer with a public.'[19] To use Richardson's case, while the sequel hopes 'to be judged not unworthy the *First* Part,' it is at least as preoccupied with proving not 'disproportioned to the more exalted condition in which PAMELA was destined to shine ...'[20] Just as all eyes are on the exemplary Pamela within the sequel's narrative, the public eye is now on the sequel and its author; the author is not an equal among friends, but rather the benevolent guide of a group gathered together under the authority of his public name. Ultimately, then, it is the tendency of such a sequel to become a 'safer' text, both in implicit response to the excluded audience (those who have criticized its predecessor) and in reflection of its author's heightened sense of responsibility to the social order of which he has become a representative.

I use the masculine pronoun deliberately here because, for Bunyan, Defoe, and Richardson, it appears that this self-consciousness about social responsibility is imaginatively allied to the position of the patriarch and the man of property.[21] All three of these authors respond the most strongly to a specific group of problem readers, those whose desires extend beyond misinterpretation to appropriation of the original text as property, through piracy and illegitimate sequels. In the publishing climate of the period, caught between a certain number of unscrupulous booksellers ready to invest in anything with a pre-established audience and the weakness of the law in controlling copyright violations, the author could hope to prove literary paternity only by producing a second offspring displaying irrefutable resemblances to the first. In these circumstances, it is not surprising that one of the most common functions of the early sequel seems to have been to strengthen an author's claim to his literary property.[22] Thus, Bunyan insists that those who 'Counterfeit the Pilgrim' in fact 'by their Features do declare / Themselves not mine to be,' while Richardson complains that he has been driven to write his sequel because the 'Plan' of 'my Pamela' has been 'basely Ravished out of my Hands,' raising the spectre of his legitimately descended characters being 'depreciated and debased.'[23] These authors were very deliberately engaged in creating Foucault's 'author function,' needing to establish some continuity of style, form, motive, or moral sentiment that would make of themselves 'a principle of unity in writing.'[24]

Neither author nor fictionalized audience of a sequel, then, is what it once was: each has taken on an elaborated identity, reflecting both its role as context of the original text and the socio-economic pressures arising from successful publication. For the male author in early print culture, as I have indicated, this identity appears to have been constructed primarily along the models of paternity and property ownership. Such models were easily absorbed by the developing marketplace and the public sphere which it helped to form, where the individual subject was understood to be, as Jürgen Habermas has argued, the man of property and head of a family.[25] For the woman writer, on the other hand, these models for constructing a professional identity were largely unavailable; they carried the risk, in fact, of marking such activity as transgressive. As a result, the woman writer's approach to the sequel is remarkably free from claims of proprietorship and of parentage, hence of the right to social or economic profit from her productions. In the absence of such claims, the image of an intimate community of select readers becomes the dominant figure for the shift from the first novel's mutual anonymity of writer and reader to the sequel's reunion of them. For the female author, the model of familiar acquaintances reunited to enjoy the mutual pleasures of conversation served as a means of associating her activity with a private, non-economic sphere. Paradoxically, however, this community existed for her only in the public sphere of letters, a sphere in which even the female writer could adopt the fiction of being 'one human being among others.'[26]

Despite its apparent contradiction of eighteenth-century English society's hierarchical, gendered view of the authoritative individual, the more egalitarian conversational model of sociable interaction was readily available in a culture whose discourse valued and theorized the private conversational gathering. Peter Stallybrass and Allon White have examined in detail the mechanisms by which emerging capitalist culture depended upon a 'network of discursive sites and institutions within which notions of the "public," the "author" and "constituencies"' could develop. The direction of this movement was towards 'the creation of a sublimated public body without smells, without coarse laughter, without organs, separate from the Court and the Church on the one hand and the market square, alehouse, street and fairground on the other' – in other words, a refined social space excluding physical difference, conflict between social strata, and individualistic profit motives.[27] The sequel's figure of a conversation between old friends in a kind of virtual reality points to a parallel, in this view, between the ideological direction of the novel sequel and that of the early periodical and the coffee-house.

For the female author, the figure of a refined, disembodied conversational community could allow even women, who were in general barred from actual coffee-houses, a legitimate cultural authority. Not only could the author and reader of a sequel use its space to overcome the anonymity of print, but the author could also use it to refine a now-established readerly community, correcting readings motivated by a desire for novelty or vicarious self-expression, for example, while dissociating herself from the vulgar greed of the bookseller's world. Moreover, the conversational ideal of the early eighteenth century celebrated the possibilities of heterosexual social exchange, emphasizing the contribution of women to the refinement of the public sphere.[28] Actual reading practice seems to have matched this conversational model of the public sphere of letters to some degree. Anecdotal evidence indicates that the early novel often 'happened' in a refined and intimate circle of acquaintance. Besides the famous Richardson circle, whose members read his novels to one another in the circle's embodied form and corresponded voluminously about them in its disembodied state, we have Frances Burney's gleeful accounts of eavesdropping at domestic readings of her novel *Evelina*, and numerous other references in eighteenth-century correspondence to the reading and discussion of novels as a communal activity. Thus, Patricia Howells Michaelson has argued convincingly that the orthodox critical image of the absorbed young reader devouring a forbidden text in the solitude of her closet (the image underlying Castle's description of the charismatic text with which I began) is a partial, if not misleading, one.[29] In fact, it can be argued that freedom from the male author's pressure to protect the paternal name and represent a stratified social structure enabled these women to elaborate upon a 'renewed acquaintance' model of the sequel, which drew upon the cultural value of conversation in order to produce more innovative – and hence more successful – sequels than did their male counterparts.[30]

The potential offered to the woman writer by a renewed acquaintance model can be illustrated with contrasting examples from two sequel prefaces. Daniel Defoe, in his preface to the *Farther Adventures of Robinson Crusoe*, is confident that the 'good Design' of his 'making [this Work] publick' will 'doubtless' render it 'every way as profitable and diverting' to 'the sober, as well as ingenious Reader' as its predecessor. Because he cannot ignore the marauding reader prowling outside the gates of his domain, however, he quickly turns from this high-minded image of concern only for the inner circle's moral profit to spend much more time identifying and threatening these thieving usurpers of his property, concluding:

> The Injury these Men do the Proprietor of this Work, is a Practice all honest Men abhor; and [the Author] believes he may challenge them to shew the Difference between that and Robbing on the Highway, or Breaking open a House.
> If they can't shew any Difference in the Crime, they will find it hard to shew why there should be any Difference in the Punishment: And he will answer for it, that nothing shall be wanting on his Part, to do them Justice.[31]

On the other hand, Sarah Fielding, in the 1753 preface to *David Simple Volume the Last*, remains in firm control of the image of a refined conversation between friends. This sequel's preface is presented as 'By a Female FRIEND of the AUTHOR'; the friend is thought to have been Jane Collier, co-author of a novel with Fielding, and indeed her close friend. The sense of Collier's intimate familiarity with Fielding's views of her sequel is reinforced by her speaking for the intentions of 'the Author of *David Simple*' throughout the preface. Unlike the voices of Sarah and her brother Henry in their respective introductory pieces to *David Simple*'s first and second editions, which apologize for the audacity and faults of the female writer, the 'Female Friend' as speaker serves less to distance a modest author from the act of publication than to reinforce the theme of loyal and sincere intimacy developed throughout the preface. Uninterested in pleasing

> 'Readers who seek for such Food [as Novelty] only,' our Author, who, no less than her own *David*, would on all Occasions chuse to pursue the unaffected Simplicity she has a Desire to recommend, and who detests all Fallacy and Imposture, is willing to introduce to her Readers their old Friends, with whom if

they were once pleased by them, they will undoubtedly not be displeased to renew their former Acquaintance.

A further sign of this author's sincerity and disinterestedness is her condemnation of exploitative sequels:

It is not the bringing known Characters again upon the Stage that is, or can be decried, if it is done with equal Humour and Spirit, as in their first Appearance; but it is building so much on public Approbation as to endeavour to put off a second-rate insipid Piece, void of the Spirit of the first, that ought to meet with universal Censure. A Character that once pleased must always please, if thrown into new and interesting Situations; for would any one complain of seeing Sir *John Falstaff* ever so often repeated, if he always appeared with the same Humour as in the *First Part of King Henry IV*?[32]

This sequel, then, uses the figure of a community of friends to dissociate itself from motives of profit as fully as does any poem by Pope. We may choose, of course, to read this stance as we do Pope's definition of himself against the Grub Street hack: as a revelation of just how unavoidable the marketplace has become for the eighteenth-century writer seeking an audience. 'Building on public Approbation,' though not 'put[ting] off a second-rate insipid Piece,' is precisely what Fielding and her female colleagues are doing, and they are doing it by offering readers a 'renew[al of] their former Acquaintance.' With the sequel form, these writers are choosing to capitalize upon a familiar work as the most immediate and efficient means of reproducing initial success.

Furthermore, despite her speaking through the voice of a friend and claiming only a desire to please her readers through this sequel, Fielding apparently finds that the mantle of authority sits as easily on her shoulders here as it did on those of Defoe. Like him, she declares the purity of her motives, and, like him, she knows that her sequel will 'undoubtedly' please those readers for whom it is intended. The rhetorical question about Shakespeare's reintroduction of Falstaff goes so far as to imply that this sequel will succeed where the master dramatist's failed. But where Defoe belligerently attacks inappropriate readers, Fielding simply excludes them from this community's intimacy as punishment enough: not only novelty seekers, but also readers who desire a happier conclusion to the story are implicitly invited to take their patronage elsewhere: 'And if any of her Readers approve not of her Manner of releasing [David] from his Difficulties, nothing that can be said by me has any Chance for altering such their Opinion.'[33]

A brief examination of changes in narrative form between original fictions and their continuations by Fielding, Sheridan, and Scott further marks a significant accession to authority between first and second work. This shift suggests that participation in literary production did indeed enable these authors to create for themselves public identities as economic producers, possessed of an earned professional autonomy and specialized in the moral guidance of vulnerable readers. In the *David Simple* of 1744, the narrative voice is tentative, at once self-deprecating and obtrusively self-conscious in chapter conclusions such as 'And there for some time I will leave him to his own private Sufferings, *lest it should be thought I am so ignorant of the World, as not to know the proper Time of forsaking People.*' *Volume the Last*, on the other hand, represents Fielding's first use of a Jane Austen–like narrator, unobtrusive, yet knowledgeable in the ways of the world and ironically distanced from those ways. Thus the simple word 'seems' in the opening paragraph deftly establishes a position of superior insight:

A Man, actuated by neither Avarice nor Ambition, his Mind moving on no other Axis but that of Love, having obtained a Wife his Judgment approves, and his Inclination delights in; seeing, at the same time, all his Friends chearful and pleased around him, *seems* to be in a State of Happiness, in comparison of which, every thing in this World is trifling.[34]

Although critics for many years saw Sarah Fielding's work as 'a rather pale yet delicate reflection of the master [her brother Henry],'[35] the very lack of elaborate self-portrayal which Jane Spencer sees as symptomatic of a need 'to keep masculine approval by disclaiming any intention to overturn the sexual hierarchy' is, I think, a much more successful means of keeping sympathy focused on the characters than anything in *Tom Jones*.[36] In *Volume the Last*, ironic detachment is never allied with moral ambiguity; when sympathy is called for, the narrator makes it very clear where those sympathies must lie: 'And here, ... I would detain my Reader by some Observations on the capricious Judgments that are shewn in passing Sentence on the Words and Actions of a Man, who is actuated by no other Motives than the simple Dictates of an honest Heart.'[37] One of the functions of the narrator of this sequel is clearly to challenge the reader to a more mature social ethic in the very act of reader response.

If there is something eminently professional about Fielding's later narrator, a similar argument might be constructed for the shift from a virtual epistolary monologue in Part One of Sheridan's *Miss Sidney Bidulph* to the sequel's use of multiple writers, and hence of multiple perspectives on the action, resulting in a more complex epistemology and moral structure. Again, Sheridan's male narrator shows increased detachment from 'his' story and a related deftness at invoking reader reflection; the text closes with an explicit challenge to the reader rather than the extensive moralizing of the first part: '[Mrs Askham] concludes her history with many serious reflections, which, though extremely pious and rational, the Editor chuses to omit, thinking it a compliment due to the judgment of his readers to leave them to make reflections for themselves.'[38] Significantly, both the shift to multiple letter-writers and the ultimate reference of a relatively open-ended text to the reader are techniques which have, in Richardson, been seen as signs of an increasingly sophisticated use of the epistolary form.[39]

In the case of Sarah Scott's *Millenium Hall* and *Sir George Ellison*, a heightened sense of authority is most unmistakably displayed in the shift of subject matter between the two parts. The women whose narratives comprise the text of *Millenium Hall* firmly circumscribe their charitable projects within the sphere of what is properly feminine: providing asylum for women, educating girls, caring for the local poor. As one of them puts it, '[w]e do not set up for reformers, ... we wish to regulate ourselves by the laws laid down to us, and as far as our influence can extend, endeavour to inforce them; beyond that small circle all is foreign to us; we have sufficient employment in improving ourselves; to mend the world requires much abler hands.'[40] By implication, Scott is composing women's stories as the most appropriate social contribution of the female writer. In *Sir George Ellison*, such rhetoric reappears even more explicitly when the women introduce to the hero their plan for a system of schools for girls; the narrator explains that '[t]he imprudent, and frequently vicious, course of life, into which too many fall, appeared to them evidently to proceed most commonly from a faulty education ... In regard to both sexes the case seemed much the same, but the education of boys was above their sphere; they aimed no further than to rectify some of the errors in female education.'[41] This disclaimer on the part of the characters, however, sheds an interesting light on the position of the author, who, in the role of a presumably male, third-person narrator, is telling the story of a male exemplar and his expansive sphere of influence. Thus without drawing attention to herself by explicitly defending her right to do so, this author moves 'above her sphere,' teaching independently wealthy men, Habermas's true individuals, how to conduct themselves.

More generally, the content of each of these sequels, in relation to its predecessor, shows an innovative freedom perhaps unavailable to the male author who views himself as producing more of the same in order to protect the patrimony. Fielding is in effect unwriting her first story, 'fully exploit[ing],' as her editor Malcolm Kelsall puts it, the 'ambiguities' of its sentimental morality.[42] Sheridan's sequel has been credited with being 'the first English novel to deal with the interlocking life of two generations,' and hence with influencing Emily Brontë's *Wuthering Heights*.[43] And Sarah Scott extends her Utopian project beyond a rural enclave, the setting of so much mid-eighteenth-century fiction, to all of England, and even to the slave plantations of Jamaica.

Nor was these writers' confidence in their earned authority misplaced, it seems. Fielding's subscription works won unusually strong and steady support after the initial publication of *David Simple*: Martin Battestin and Clive Probyn tell us that the *Familiar Letters* had five hundred subscribers, for example.[44] Contemporary readers greeted her later works with comments such as 'It were superfluous to compliment the Author of David Simple upon her merits as a Writer.'[45] Like the readers of Trollope and Montgomery, discussed by Lynette Felber and Carole Gerson in this volume, readers of Fielding and Sheridan, at least, do not seem to have felt cheated by these women's sequels, these ostensibly disappointing texts. Richardson, notorious for intending to read much more than he ever did, reread the *Familiar Letters* as an elderly man and wrote to Fielding that they revealed a 'knowledge of the human heart' exceeding that of her brother.[46] Lady Mary Wortley Montagu, embarrassed all along at the thought of her distant female relation's writing out of financial necessity, nevertheless grudgingly admitted of *Volume the Last*, 'Sally [Fielding] has mended her style in her last Volume of D[avid] Simple.'[47] The writer for the *Monthly Review* of September 1767 not only found Sheridan's sequel to *Miss Sidney Bidulph* consistent with the 'design' of the original, but also '*felt* that she wanted not power to effect her purpose' of reducing the reader to tears – despite some scepticism as to the moral efficacy of such a technique, whether in the original or in the sequel. Alicia LeFanu, Sheridan's granddaughter and biographer, reports in 1824 that, '[b]y many persons the second part of Sidney Biddulph [*sic*] was preferred to the first; as the production of a person who had acquired more extensive views of life, and a greater insight into character. Her talent for portrait-painting had certainly improved ...'; LeFanu adds several anecdotes testifying to the 'popularity with which the first and second parts of Sidney Biddulph were received both in France and England.'[48]

In sum, the rhetorical means by which these women eschew the marketplace in favour of an intimate conversation among a trustworthy author, familiar readers, and well-beloved characters indicate that the sequel was one strategy for dissociating oneself from the developing reality of literature-as-commodity, even while exploiting that reality. If experiences of piracy and unauthorized sequels taught writers such as Bunyan, Defoe, and Richardson that in such an environment they had much to lose, Fielding, Sheridan, and Scott showed that they, together with their male colleagues, had much to gain by winning a faceless audience over to the role of old friends. Writing sequels in such an environment allowed authors to create for themselves the fiction of an intimate, private readership, prepared by the first text to accept their moral prescriptions, thematic complexities, and formal innovations. For the female author, dissociation from the marketplace was further motivated by the impropriety of female claims to property, while drawing on the authority represented by a public literary signature as 'The Author of ...' was a professional necessity. As these writers exploited the sequel phenomenon to move out from under the protective cover of anonymity and self-deprecation, they thus not only recorded the gradual shift from an amateur-patronage to a market system of literary production, but also revealed the influence of successful publication on the woman writer's sense of identity. By giving readers what they wanted – their old friends – they built for themselves professional careers.

Notes

1 The 'author function' is Michel Foucault's term, in 'What Is an Author?' *Language, Counter-Memory, Practice*, ed. Donald F. Bouchard; trans. Donald F. Bouchard and Sherry Simon (Ithaca: Cornell UP, 1977) 113–38. Martin C. Battestin and Clive T. Probyn use the phrase 'public literary signature' to describe Sarah Fielding's reputation as 'the Author of *David Simple*' in the introduction to their edition of *The Correspondence of Henry and Sarah Fielding* (Oxford: Clarendon, 1993) xxvii. Historians have argued that, for England, the stage was set for the shift from an oral and scribal to a print culture in the seventeenth century, with the Civil War and the pamphleteering which fuelled that conflict. For histories of early English print culture see Bertrand H. Bronson, 'Strange Relations: The Author and His Audience,' *Facets of the Enlightenment, Studies in English Literature and Its Contexts* (Berkeley and Los Angeles: U of California P, 1968) 298–325, and Alvin Kernan, *Printing Technology, Letters and Samuel Johnson* (Princeton: Princeton UP, 1987). Dustin Griffin's *Literary Patronage in England, 1650–1800* (Cambridge: Cambridge UP, 1996) examines in detail a number of authors' careers, elaborating a profile of the period as 'characterized by overlapping "economies" of patronage *and* marketplace' (10).

2 This definition rests somewhere between a broad use of the designation 'professional

author' to refer to anyone earning money from writing (see, for example, Cheryl Turner, *Living by the Pen – Women Writers in the Eighteenth Century* [London: Routledge, 1992] 60) and the more narrow sociological sense of a vocation involving carefully structured training and a self-regulatory, generally hierarchical, corporate identity (see, for example, Geoffrey Holmes, *Augustan England: Professions, State and Society, 1680–1730* [London: Allen & Unwin, 1982] 7–11).

3 See note 11 of the introduction to this volume respecting the wide use of the term 'sequel' in titles of 1660–1800 publications of all generic types. Alexander Leggatt's essay in this collection demonstrates that the commercialization of drama and a concomitant professionalization of the playwright had earlier created a similar phenomenon in English theatre, while Mary Ann Gillies discusses a second stage of printing change bringing about a late nineteenth- and early twentieth-century proliferation of sequels.

4 Terry Castle, *Masquerade and Civilization: The Carnivalesque in Eighteenth-Century English Culture and Fiction* (Stanford: Standord UP, 1986) 133. Castle's discussion of the sequel, turning the 'attempt to profit' into an impersonal phenomenon of textuality and market forces, begs what are to me some of the most interesting questions about the form. See our introduction (5) for a further discussion of her argument. J. Paul Hunter has recently argued (in 'Serious Reflections on Further Adventures: Resistances to Closure in Eighteenth-Century English Novels,' *Augustan Subjects: Essays in Honor of Martin C. Battestin*, ed. Albert J. Rivero [Newark, DE: U of Delaware P, 1997] 276–94) that the 'habit' of sequelizing eighteenth-century novels (280) is one manifestation of a general resistance to closure. Hunter, like I do, sees the explanation of exploitation as 'too easy a social solution to complex aesthetic, cultural, and political problems' (281); he speculates more generally, however, about open-endedness as an expression of cultural shifts in paradigms of order and the resulting need to rethink conventional literary forms.

5 Castle, *Masquerade* 135.

6 Although some contributions to this collection, notably Samuel Glen Wong's on Milton and Mary Ann Gillies's on Bennett, have argued for their authors' responsiveness to readerly needs in their sequels, others, such as June Sturrock's examination of Charlotte Yonge and Thomas Carmichael's discussion of John Barth, note a deliberate use of the sequel to challenge reader expectations of repetition.

7 The phrase is Samuel Johnson's, *The Adventurer* 115, *The Yale Edition of the Works of Samuel Johnson*, vol. 2, ed. W.J. Bate, J.M. Bullitt, and L.F. Powell (New Haven: Yale UP, 1963) 458. Women were, of course, actively publishing for decades before their presence became remarkable to commentators such as Johnson.

8 For a helpful outline of these pressures and the disjunction between many women writers' practice and the models of femininity which they portrayed in their work, see Jane Spencer's *The Rise of the Woman Novelist: From Aphra Behn to Jane Austen* (Oxford: Blackwell, 1986) and Kathryn Shevelow's *Women and Print Culture: The Construction of Femininity in the Early Periodical* (London: Routledge, 1989) ch. 1.

9 Other cases include Mary Collyer's *Felicia to Charlotte* (1744 and 1749) and Frances Brooke's *Sir Charles Mandeville* (1790) as a belated sequel to her *History of Miss Julia Mandeville* (1763).

10 The phrase is Sarah Fielding's, and is discussed below.

11 Walter J. Ong, SJ, 'The Writer's Audience Is Always a Fiction,' *Interfaces of the Word: Studies in the Evolution of Consciousness and Culture* (Ithaca: Cornell UP, 1977) 69.

12 Sarah Fielding (1710–1768), a younger sister of Henry Fielding's, established a reputation as a scholar and novelist with the publication of at least nine 'unfailingly intelligent and ground-breaking works,' including the first English children's novel and a translation of Xenophon from the Greek: see *The Feminist Companion to Literature in English*, ed. Virginia Blain, Patricia Clements, and Isobel Grundy (New Haven, Yale UP, 1990) 371. Frances Sheridan (1724–1766), although admired in her day as author, playwright, and hostess of an intellectual circle, has been overshadowed in literary history by her husband, Thomas, and her son Richard Brinsley. Sarah Scott (1723–1795) wrote didactic fiction and biography after the break-up of her brief marriage; her best-known work, *Millenium Hall*, is modelled after a female community established by her and Lady Barbara Montagu, with which Sarah Fielding was marginally associated.

13 See Kathleen M. Swain, 'Christian's "Christian Behaviour" to His Family in *Pilgrim's Progress*,' *Religion and Literature* 21.3 (1989): 1.

14 Daniel Defoe, 'The Preface' [to *The Farther Adventures of Robinson Crusoe*], *Robinson Crusoe*, 3 vols. (Oxford: Blackwell, 1927) 1.viii–ix; Henry Fielding, *Shamela*, in *Joseph Andrews* and *Shamela*, ed. Douglas Brooks-Davies (Oxford: Oxford UP, 1970) 324.

15 Samuel Richardson to Lady Bradshaigh, in John Carroll, ed., *Selected Letters of Samuel Richardson* (Oxford: Clarendon, 1964) 289. See also Tom Keymer's detailed discussion of Richardson's theory of reading in *Richardson's 'Clarissa' and the Eighteenth-Century Reader* (Cambridge: Cambridge UP, 1992) 56–84.

16 John Bunyan, *The Pilgrim's Progress*, ed. James Blanton Wharey; rev. Roger Sharrock (Oxford: Clarendon, 1960) 171–2.

17 J. Paul Hunter, in *Before Novels: The Cultural Contexts of Eighteenth-Century English Fiction* (New York: Norton, 1990) 61–81, has examined the early-fiction phenomenon from the point of view of reception, using studies of early eighteenth-century demographics and literacy to imagine the desires of the readers who comprised the growing audience for romances, newspapers, periodicals, literature of self-improvement, and, emerging from these, the novel. According to Hunter's sketch, these readers were optimistic and ambitious, but socially isolated in a world that increasingly valued privacy while crowding itself into limited urban space. In this way, the writer's audience may have differed very little from the writer in the experience of anonymity and the desire to find familiar faces in print. If such a reader were drawn to a Christian's or a Robinson Crusoe's or a Pamela's charismatic story of alienation followed by wish-fulfilling success, she or he might be equally attracted to a sequel elaborating on that success and setting it in an affirming communal frame.

18 In this response to audience pressure the eighteenth-century sequel writer seems little different from the late twentieth-century film producer who rehabilitates the action film's hero and thereby pays lip-service to social concerns while leaving fundamental power structures intact: see McLarty, this volume 206.

19 Roger Sharrock, *John Bunyan: 'The Pilgrim's Progress'* (London: Arnold, 1966) 43–4.

20 Samuel Richardson, *Pamela*, 2 vols., ed. Mark Kinkead-Weekes (London: Dent, 1962) 2.v.

21 Mark Rose, among others, has noted the prominence in the early modern period of the figure of 'paternity: the author as begetter and the book as child,' in *Authors and Owners: The Invention of Copyright* (Cambridge, MA: Harvard UP, 1993) 38. Rose goes on to note the adaptation of this figure 'to the discourse of proprietory authorship' in the early eighteenth century (39–41).

22 For a helpful overview of this situation, see John Feather, *A History of British Publishing* (London: Croom Helm, 1988), chs. 6 and 8. Using French publishing history as his basis, Foucault locates the claim to literary discourse as an author's property, as 'a thing, a product, or a possession,' later in the eighteenth century, with the establishment of strict copyright rules and a compensatory restoration of a sense of literature as transgressive (124–5). The argument for such a view of copyright, however, was a constant and increasingly vocal theme in the eighteenth-century English publishing world, as Rose has made clear.

23 Bunyan, *Pilgrim's Progress* 168; Richardson to James Leake, *Selected Letters* 43. Elsewhere in this collection, Alexander Leggatt's argument that the playwright ultimately feels a sense of competition with his successful progeny and is therefore forced to reassert his authority by killing his offspring points to an intriguing shadow image of this paternal motif. And Michael Zeitlin's discussion of Barthelme's *The Dead Father* as the 'refractive postmodern sequel of some of the foundational narratives of Freudian psychoanalysis' (160) identifies the passing of this patriarchal model of author, text, and sequel.

24 Foucault, 'What Is an Author?' 128. Thus the disjunction between the actual producer of the text and the author function becomes visible not only in Bunyan's and Richardson's self-conscious presentation of their sequels, but also in the criticism of such sequels for not fulfilling expectations.

25 Jürgen Habermas, *The Structural Transformation of the Public Sphere: An Inquiry into a Category of Bourgeois Society*, trans. Thomas Burger with Frederick Lawrence (Cambridge: Polity, 1989) ch. 2.

26 Habermas, *The Structural Transformation* 55–6.

27 Peter Stallybrass and Allon White, *The Politics and Poetics of Transgression* (London: Methuen, 1986) 82, 93–4.

28 See Lawrence E. Klein, 'Gender, Conversation and the Public Sphere in Early Eighteenth-Century England,' *Textuality and Sexuality: Reading Theories and Practices*, ed. Judith Still and Michael Worton (Manchester: Manchester UP, 1993) 100–15. Klein's view of public discourse as inclusive of women through an ideal of polite conversation that required the contribution of both sexes has been challenged by Kathleen Wilson ('Citizenship, Empire, and Modernity in the English Provinces, c. 1720–1790,' *Eighteenth-Century Studies* 29 [1995]: 69–96), who notes the inevitable contingency of a woman's role in such discourse.

29 Patricia Howells Michaelson, 'Women in the Reading Circle,' *Eighteenth-Century Life* 13 n.s. 3 (1989): 59–69.

30 The 'renewed acquaintance' phrase is Sarah Fielding's, and is discussed below. Like Wilson, Michaelson notes the at least potentially unequal realities of such reading circles: 'In the extreme, family reading became a form of censorship, controlling access to books, censoring offensive passages, and interrupting the text with moralistic commentary' ('Women' 59).

31 Defoe, *Farther Adventures*, ix.

32 Sarah Fielding, *The Adventures of David Simple*, ed. Malcolm Kelsall (Oxford: Oxford UP, 1987) 310.

33 Fielding, *David Simple* 311

34 Fielding, *David Simple* 20 (italics in original); 313 (italics mine)

35 Wilbur L. Cross, *The History of Henry Fielding*, 3 vols. (1918, rpt. New York: Russell, 1963) 2.7.

36 Spencer, *The Rise* 94.

37 Fielding, *David Simple*, 324.

38 Frances Sheridan, *Conclusion of the Memoirs of Miss Sidney Bidulph* (London: Dodsley, 1767) 402.

39 The former observation is a commonplace of Richardson criticism; for the relevance of open-endedness to Richardson's theory of reading see Keymer, *Richardson's 'Clarissa'* 71–6.

40 Sarah Scott, *A Description of Millenium Hall*, ed. Gary Kelly (Peterborough, ON: Broadview, 1995) 166.

41 Sarah Scott, *The History of Sir George Ellison*, ed. Betty Rizzo (Lexington: UP of Kentucky, 1996) 90.

42 Kelsall, introduction to *David Simple*, xv.

43 Margaret Anne Doody, 'Frances Sheridan: Morality and Annihilated Time,' *Fetter'd or Free? British Women Novelists, 1670–1815*, ed. Mary Anne Schofield and Cecilia Macheski (Athens: Ohio UP, 1986) 346.

44 Battestin and Probyn, 'Introduction,' *The Correspondence* xli.

45 *The Monthly Review*, July 1757. Such comments suggest that Fielding had succeeded in establishing a market for her literary signature as much as for any characters she had created; this selling of an authorial name rather than a story is prevoyant of the more developed early twentieth-century marketplace described by Carole Gerson in this volume, in which Montgomery's name was seen by her agent as the saleable commodity (149–50).

46 Richardson to Fielding, *Selected Letters* 330.

47 Lady Mary Wortley Montagu, *The Complete Letters of Lady Mary Wortley Montagu*, 3 vols., ed. Robert Halsband (Oxford: Clarendon, 1967) 3.66–7.

48 Alicia LeFanu, *Memoirs of the Life and Writings of Mrs. Frances Sheridan* (London: Whittaker, 1824) 290, 297.

Sequels, Series, and Sensation Novels: Charlotte Yonge and the Popular-Fiction Market of the 1850s and 1860s

JUNE STURROCK

Times change: inevitably any sequel or series underlines this truism. Whether the narrative of any succeeding text itself precedes or continues that of the originating text, whether it is 'prequel' or sequel, it is produced under different and subsequent conditions which affect its particular version of the interplay between recognition and variation that is essential to an effective sequel. This essay comments on the relation between sequel and originating text in connection with the changes in cultural contexts involved. The particular change to be examined is the dramatic and rapid shift in the British market for popular fiction between the 1850s and the 1860s, while the specific instance is the relation of two novels by Charlotte Mary Yonge (1823–1901) dating from the period of her greatest success as a popular religious novelist.

Yonge probably devoted as many words to series fiction as did any of her prolific contemporaries. Her last novel, *Modern Broods* (1900), recycles at least forty characters, who make their original appearances in at least ten separate previous novels,[1] the earliest of which was first published fifty-three years before. Some characters had already featured in six or more novels, for after 1870[2] about half of Yonge's many novels of contemporary middle-class life were series novels. Yonge, that is, exploited in the latter part of her career the market for series novels proved by the success of Anthony Trollope's Barset (1855–67) and Palliser (1864–80) series and Margaret Oliphant's Chronicles of Carlingford series (1861–76).[3] Her production of series also accorded with the known preferences of her established readership – 'hardly a week passed without a letter from some old reader begging [Yonge] for more news of old favourites.'[4] Moreover, her own continuing interest in her characters (which parallels Trollope's liking for 'old friends,' discussed by Lynette Felber elsewhere in this collection) is well documented. Yonge's series novels, then, can be seen in the context of a specific mid-to-late nineteenth-century literary market, of a loyal readership, and of her own concept of fiction.

However, my focus here is not directly on the huge bulk of Yonge's series novels, but on a related phenomenon – her solitary sequel, *The Trial* (1864). I will discuss the series briefly, in part in order to assess the different kinds of continuation, but only after examining how *The Trial* relates to changes in the literary market immediately after the publication of its originating text, *The Daisy Chain* (1856).[5] In the eight intervening years,[6] domestic fiction, which dominated in the fiction market in the 1850s, was notoriously overtaken by the sensation novel. Accordingly, Yonge rewrites a prototypically domestic novel, centred on church and home, as a quasi-sensation novel, centred on a bloody murder. *The Daisy Chain* vindicates its heroine, Ethel May, through her activity within the domestic sphere. *The Trial*, through its generic modification, allows Ethel to be vindicated beyond the confines of the domestic, indeed beyond the confines of England, not through independent action, but through her power over a male protagonist, Leonard Ward, who eventually as a missionary carries her message – her feminized and domesticated Christianity – to the Antipodes. At the same time, in the sequel the ahistoric and private domestic world of *The Daisy Chain* is firmly placed in contemporary history through the role of public events, such as the 1859–60 invasion scare in England and the consequent volunteer movement, the American Civil War, and the settlement of the Midwest. Yonge's work moves with trends of the time from the tranquillity of the domestic novel to the excitement of the plot-driven novel.

The Daisy Chain announces on its title page both its moral pretensions and its literary subgenre: its full title is *The Daisy Chain or Aspirations: A Family Chronicle*. Yonge attempts to divert possible hostility to such a narrative in the preface to its first edition:

No one can be more sensible than is the Author that the present is an overgrown book of a nondescript class, neither the 'tale' for the young, nor the novel for their elders, but a mixture of both ... It would beg to be considered merely as what it calls itself, *a Family Chronicle – a domestic record of home events, large and small* ... For those who may deem the story too long, and the characters too numerous, the Author can only beg their pardon for any tedium that they may have undergone before giving it up.[7]

The Daisy Chain, that is, proclaims itself as more domestic than the domestic novel, as purely 'a domestic record of home events,' and thus as the quintessence of the most popular genre of its period; it is arguably more domestic (and certainly more static) even than Yonge's earlier successes, the two immediately preceding novels, *The Heir of Redclyffe* (1853) and *Heartsease* (1854). The Victorian chronicle – as the word is used in *The Last Chronicle of Barset* and *The Chronicles of Carlingford*, for instance – including the family chronicle, tends to sidestep closure and to foreground continuity because it involves the narratives of a large group of characters of different generations. Indeed, George Levine argues that not just the chronicle, but Victorian realism as a whole, is imbued with 'a sense that there are no endings, only constant shiftings and developments in time';[8] elsewhere in this collection Lynette Felber discusses realism and continuation in the context of Trollope's work. Nevertheless, *The Daisy Chain*, despite the 'too numerous' characters to which Yonge refers, like other chronicles does move towards a kind of closure; its last twenty-five pages include a death, a long-awaited birth, a marriage, emigration, a church consecrated, and a soul saved. When its central character, Ethel May, in the last paragraphs of the novel contemplates her future, trying to 'realize what her lonely life might be' (667), the effect is a sense of finality, the marking of the end of her youth, rather than a promise of continuity.[9] There is no sense of a need for an ongoing narrative. Nevertheless, *The Trial* begins with Ethel, five years older, making tea for her brothers and sisters, once again in the May family drawing room, catching up once again with May family gossip; it has already announced itself on the title page as *The Trial: or, More Links in The Daisy Chain* (the 'Daisy Chain' being formed by the May children). So *The Trial* proclaims itself immediately as a sequel, and not until almost halfway through the novel does it become apparent that the sequel is generically different from its originating text, or that its narrative focus is not on the various quiet histories of the May family but rather on the more dramatic life of their young friend Leonard Ward. In chapter 12, Leonard disappears; his old uncle is found dead, with his head battered in; and Leonard's rifle is discovered with blood and white hairs on its stock. From this point onwards, the novel centres on the murder and its consequences – Leonard's arrest; his trial, conviction, and imprisonment; the search for further evidence; and his eventual vindication when the real murderer is discovered, dying horribly after a Parisian brawl, with 'fearful shrieks of despair':[10] 'Whoso sheddeth man's blood by man shall his blood be shed' (*Trial* 297; Genesis 9.6). After chapter 12, that is, *The Trial* moves beyond the quiet realm of the domestic novel to take on many of the horrific, extreme, and mysterious trappings of the sensation novel, the new vogue in popular fiction.

The completeness and rapidity of the conversion of the novel-reading public to the sensation novel was already evident in 1862, the year when *The Trial* began publication in serial form: Margaret Oliphant observed that year in *Blackwood's Magazine* that domestic novels, 'the virtuous chronicles which have lately furnished the larger part of our light literature,' were quite superseded by 'a new school in fiction.'[11] The periodical press of the 1860s rapidly produced a barrage of enjoyably disparaging comments on the new trend; 'the wrathful cry of sensationalism, "that Cry of cries" for the 1860s, made the rounds of the critical journals.'[12] *Punch* lampooned the trend in 1863 with a mock-advertisement for the 'Sensation Times, and Chronicle of Excitement,'[13] and the Archbishop of York devoted a sermon to attacking it in 1864, the year of *The Trial's* publication in book form.[14] Wilkie Collins, in promoting the sensation novel – his own brand of fiction, after all – suggests one reason for its superseding the domestic novel; in his 1859 novel, *The Queen of Hearts*, a young woman complains bitterly of being

sick to death of novels with an earnest purpose ... Good gracious me! isn't the original intention or purpose or whatever you call it, of a work of fiction to set out distinctly by telling a story? And how many of these books [domestic novels], I should like to know, do that? Why so far as telling a story is concerned, the greater part of them might as well be sermons as novels. Oh dear me! what I want is something that seizes hold of my interest and makes me forget when it is time to dress for dinner; something that keeps me reading, reading, reading, in a breathless state, to find out the end.[15]

Oliphant also comments on the comparative novelty of fictional suspense, complimenting Collins 'on being the first novelist since Scott to keep readers up all night over a novel.'[16] Certainly such plot-driven novels as Collins's *The Woman in White* (1859), Ellen Wood's *East Lynne* (1861), and Mary Elizabeth Braddon's *Lady Audley's Secret* (1862) and *Aurora Floyd* (1863) kept large sections of the British public in the 1860s 'reading, reading, reading'; their popularity was rapidly perceived as related to increasing literacy and leisure and to their suitability for marketing as 'railway novels,'[17] although this brand of fiction certainly existed before the era of the sensation novel, as is apparent in *The Daisy Chain* (409).

Yonge responded promptly to current trends in fiction throughout her career: for instance, her first adult historical novel, *The Dove in the Eagle's Nest* (1866), follows the literary vogue established by *Henry Esmond* (1852), *Hypatia* (1853), *Westward Ho!* (1855), *Romola* (1862–3), and *The*

Cloister and the Hearth (1861),[18] and, as shown above, she leans heavily on the popularity of series novels at the end of her career. So it is not surprising that already in 1860, in *Hopes and Fears*, the novel immediately preceding *The Trial*,[19] she is employing such elements of the new sensation fiction as elopements, robbery with violence – and a trial. Like other writers of the realist tradition, she both deplores and exploits the sensational vein.[20] She suggests that to read Scott 'after any of our present school of fiction [i.e., the sensation novel] is like getting up a mountain side after a feverish drawing-room or an offensive street' (*The Trial*, 52).

The Trial uses many of the essential elements of the sensation novel – but definitely not all. Certain common ingredients of this genre were virtually debarred to Yonge, a writer who saw herself as 'a sort of instrument for popularizing Church Views'[21] and who identified John Keble, the Anglo-Catholic poet and priest, as 'the greatest influence of my life.'[22] The bigamy, fornication, and adultery that were staples of many sensation novels were not viable plot elements for one schooled by Keble in 'delicacy and reverence.'[23] Unable to deal with sexual crime, Yonge turns to violent crime, and keeps herself in the current market with a brutal murder, since, according to *Fraser's Magazine* in 1863, 'no novel in the present day can be reckoned complete without one.'[24]

Yonge, then, employs features of the new subgenre – violence, injustice, and mystery, set against a carefully contemporary background – to write a sequel that, like other sequels, can be seen as rewriting its originating text. The novelty of the sensation school of fiction, that is, allows for the expansion and variation on the familiar text necessary for such a sequel. As Yonge moves from the domestic novel to the novel of plot, she rewrites and expands the story of Ethel May, the heroine of *The Daisy Chain*, and reconfirms that novel's exploration of appropriate forms of

feminine behaviour. Ethel, at the beginning of *The Daisy Chain*, is fifteen, intellectual, vigorous, plain, clumsy, tactless, indifferent both to her personal appearance and to household details – unfeminine, in short. However, her painfully and conscientiously acquired gender identity and apparently spontaneous Christian virtues in combination finally make her the centre of the household, where she takes her dead mother's place as her father's beloved companion and the teacher and protector of the younger children, over the claims of her more commonplace and traditionally feminine sisters.

Ethel's considerable energies are by no means entirely confined to the home – she turns a wild and desolate settlement into a village with an air of civilization (*Daisy Chain* 631), starting a school there and instigating the building of a church. However, as a woman she is still necessarily and essentially confined to the private sphere, and any public acknowledgment of her achievement is avoided as being either 'very painful, or very hurtful to her' (643). For all her remarkable qualities, she must remain at home and without a formal public role.

In *The Trial*, Ethel retains a central position, but she functions through Leonard. In the earlier domestic novel, her achievements result from her own actions but are unacknowledged because of her gender, whereas here, in the later novel of plot, she achieves a more dramatic vindication, but through precept rather than through action. It is her power over Leonard, his 'chivalrous devotion' (302) to her, which provides her with a field for action in this novel. It motivates him to survive prison, heavy labour, and near-madness, and to succeed in his dream (implanted by her) of becoming a missionary. He claims that she 'taught me what bore me through it all' (345); his last words in the novel are addressed to her: 'If ever I come to any good, I owe it to you' (372). Leonard is ten years her junior, but is strongly attracted to her warmth and energy, complying with all her suggestions and adopting all her tastes and beliefs. Early in the novel, when he makes the winning catch at a cricket match, he tells Ethel, 'I couldn't fail with you looking on. *You did it* by coming' (64; my emphasis). Such vicarious success in masculine fields – prowess by proxy – allowing feminine passivity credit for achievement as the inspiration for male activity is foregrounded throughout this novel. When Ethel's brother teases her about her 'conquest,' she responds in terms of ambition and achievement (but modestly uses the passive voice): 'If it were not nonsense to build upon people's generous visions at seventeen, I should sometimes hope a spark had been lit [in Leonard] that would shine some day in [Melanesia]' (87). The narrative comment at this point draws attention to Ethel's earlier triumphs: 'Going up that hill [towards the village she has evangelized] was not the place for Etheldred May to talk of the futility of youthful aspirations' (87). Ethel's youthful aspirations in *The Daisy Chain* bring Christianity to the desolate village, as in the later novel (through Leonard) they bring Christianity to the South Seas.

Moreover, Leonard's ability to survive prison and to retain an unquestioning faith in a benevolent providence, despite the temptations to doubt caused by his three years of wrongful punishment and the suffering brought on his family, is presented as largely Ethel's doing. This is the 'trial' of the title, as much as the lengthy legal trial (Yonge enjoyed such word-play). *The Trial* re-presents Ethel as Christian hero; her version of feminine Christianity is vindicated here publicly as in *The Daisy Chain* it is vindicated privately. Thus, rather like Samuel Richardson in *Pamela* Part Two, Yonge in *The Trial* provides a sequel to a story of *Virtue Rewarded* in which feminine virtue is further rewarded and the moral standards of the heroine further vindicated through her emotional power over a male character. This continuation is dramatic and public, in keeping with the new school of fiction, and - because of Yonge's hierarchical Anglo-Catholic views of family and gender roles – in order to be acceptable, dramatic and public action (a 'sensation' plot) necessarily involves a male rather than a female protagonist.

Throughout *The Trial* the shift from the private realm associated with the feminine to the public realm associated with the masculine is foregrounded. Structurally the very contrast between the earlier and purely domestic chapters and the later focus on crime and punishment has this effect, and so does the central role of the murder trial. The O.J. Simpson trials have highlighted the role of the law courts in the late twentieth century as a branch of the entertainment industry, but this is no new phenomenon. In Victorian London, the Old Bailey trials provided a series of amusing spectacles, while in the provinces the assizes, with their accompanying dinner parties and balls, were an important part of the social calendar.[25] As Pykett suggests, the divorce courts (first constituted in 1857) offered novelty, while murder trials of women were especially piquant.[26] In Yonge's novel the protracted description of Leonard's trial, with its crowds of spectators occasionally reduced *en masse* to 'a universal weeping and sobbing' (181) and individually to fainting and hysterics, shows the private realm of family tensions brought into full public view. In the courtroom, the conscientious Leonard confesses to violent outbreaks against his dominating elder brother that deepen the case against Leonard himself. The public nature of Leonard's ordeal is underlined not only by the treatment of the trial as a spectacle, but also by the references to ghoulish souvenir hunters (193), and especially to the throng of crime reporters brought in by the notorious murder. The journalists turn the local spectacle of the trial into national entertainment: '"Murder of an Uncle by his Nephew" ... figured everywhere in the largest type; newsboys on the railway shouted "To-day's paper – account of inquest"; and the illustrated press sent down artists, whose three-legged cameras stared in all directions' (166). Crime journalism itself was becoming increasingly notorious at the time through the detailed immediacy of accounts in such journals as *The Times*, *The Daily Telegraph*, and *The Illustrated Police News*. Contemporaries rapidly perceived the connection between sensational crime reporting and the sensation novel itself,[27] for fiction and newspapers alike combined dramatic and grotesque events with an emphatically contemporary background, just as Yonge does here.

The sense of the uneasy intermeshing of public and private is further seen in the careful historical placing of *The Trial*. In *The Daisy Chain*, Yonge creates not just a family chronicle, but a timeless domestic idyll with few overt signs of its period. While, like other domestic realist writers, she works carefully with the contemporary details that establish verisimilitude, the sense of period in her novels of the early 1850s is general rather than particular. *The Trial*, however, like a contemporary newspaper, juxtaposes sensational crime with both domestic trivia and the national and international events of the day, so that virtually all its events can be precisely dated. Its plot is carefully linked to external and contemporary elements. The murder weapon itself, Leonard's rifle, is acquired in order to enable him to join the local Volunteer Corps, a fictitious branch of an actual organization that was set up in 1859–60 all over the country in response to a scare over a possible French invasion. After the murder trial, Leonard's family, in order to escape public humiliation, leave England for the United States and become directly involved in both the hardships and dangers of the settler's life in Indiana and the anguish of the American Civil War, which was being fought as Yonge wrote (Leonard's brother serves as a surgeon to the Northern armies). The novel constantly insists on the ways in which public events, affect private lives: the provincial town where the action is set finally acquires public baths as a memorial to the Prince Consort (who died in 1861), and its drainage system is laid down by funds raised in celebration of the Prince of Wales's marriage in 1863, so that fever outbreaks like the one that triggers the plot by killing Leonard's parents become less likely (*The Trial* 280). Moreover, the novel is placed as contemporary not only through public events, but also through repeated references to current fashions in dress, to the crinolines spread over 'a mountain of mohair and scarlet petticoat … upborne by an over-grown steel mouse-trap' (21–2) which constantly encumber the female characters, the hanging sleeves that knock everything over (Leonard's fashionable sister is a perfect nuisance in the sickroom). Current pastimes like illuminating and fossil-collecting also touch on the plot: Leonard throws a pointed belemnite at his brother. Even the weather is dated: 'though it was the year 1860,' a year notorious for its bad weather, the sun shines for the Volunteers' parade (97).[28] The idyllic and generalized domesticity of *The Daisy Chain*, against which the first part of Ethel's story is played out, has become emphatically and disturbingly the here and the now.[29]

This combination of dramatic action ('romance') and contemporary detail ('realism') again suggests Yonge's movement away from the more aesthetically homogeneous domestic novels of the 1850s and towards the more heterogeneous form of the sensation novel.[30] The disparity between the extremity of events and the quotidian nature of setting in sensation novels distressed some contemporaries both aesthetically and morally. Such diversity appeared both unseemly and dangerous, as Hughes suggests: 'For the critics, the supreme absurdity of the sensation novel lies in its implausible mixture of the contrary modes of perception: romance and realism. According to their rules, fantasy should be labeled as such; it should stay comfortably remote from ordinary concerns; it should not be allowed to impinge on the "real" world, as the Victorians have defined it.'[31] Yet such a mixture by force of contrast increased the impact of a plot, as Henry James recognized, observing of *Lady Audley's Secret*, that epitome of the sensation novel, that its 'novelty lay in the heroine being, not a picturesque Italian of the fourteenth century, but an English gentlewoman of the current year, familiar with the use of the railway and the telegraph. The intense probability of the story is constantly reiterated. Modern England – the England of today's newspaper – crops up at every step.'[32] Yonge, like both the sensation novelists and the journalists, exploits the heightened effect of the juxtaposition of realism and romance, apparently recognizing the dramatic not as fantasy, but as possibility. Accordingly, the domestic and the sensational run parallel in her novel, with Leonard's prison life, for instance, juxtaposed with a May family marriage. The uniform tranquillity which appealed in the 1850s seemed less viable in the 1860s. Oliphant sees the domestic novel as the product of an age 'lost in self admiration,' and explains the sensation vogue by reference to contemporary political catastrophes: 'it is only natural that art and literature should, in an age which has turned out to be one of events, attempt a kindred depth of effect and shock of incident.'[33]

Yonge, then, exploits many features of the sensation novel for both didactic and market purposes; indeed, as a committed Anglo-Catholic propagandist, she might hardly distinguish between these two purposes. However, she resists other features of the sensation novel, and presumably for similar reasons. As I have suggested, the gender politics of sensation novelists like Mary Elizabeth Braddon and Rhoda Broughton, with their dissatisfied daughters and murderous wives, presented problems to a woman writer who, in identifying herself as an Anglo-Catholic, also identified with established authority, family hierarchy, and patriarchal control. The anxieties about women's roles which Pykett sees as underlying the gender interactions of the women's sensation novel[34] appear in Yonge's work but are more evident in novels later than *The Trial*, especially in the explicit anti-feminism and conservatism of *The Clever Woman of the Family* (1865) and *The Three Brides* (1876). Feminine roles in the family are as unchallenged in *The Trial* as in *The Daisy Chain* – the murderer and the suspected murderer are both male, and anxieties about insanity are connected with men not women, in contrast to such contemporary novels as *Lady Audley's Secret*.

However, the 'household tensions' that Anthea Trodd sees as central to the sensation novel[35] certainly play their part in Yonge's murder mystery, which depends on the 'crime within the family, the apparently respectable middle or upper class English family,' that Kathleen Tillotson regards as characteristic of the form.[36] Leonard's violent rejection of his elder brother's patriarchal authority after the family is orphaned causes him to be sent away to live with the old uncle who is the murder victim and doubly strengthens the case against him, while the actual murderer is another nephew also living with the uncle, resentful of his authority and anxious to inherit. Father figures are threatened and killed in this novel. However, despite its presentation of the relation between family hierarchy and family violence, and the reliance of its plot on a failure of the justice system, *The Trial* overtly argues for traditional power relations both in social institutions and in the family. Policemen, lawyers, and prison officers are all presented as sympathetic and helpful, and Leonard, his sisters, and the May family all come to regard the murder and its consequences in part as a lesson in the necessity for being 'submissive and yielding' (237) to patriarchal figures.

For religious reasons, Yonge resists accepting the family interactions of sensation fiction, and for similar reasons she also resists its concept of free will and destiny. Such novels of plot necessarily represent characters as caught up in events over which they have little control, and *The Trial* is no exception. But, whereas in typical sensation novels, characters live in an irrational world and are 'played upon by forces outside [their] control,'[37] forces that are vaguely invoked as destiny, Yonge's novel accounts for the involuntary nature of human life not through destiny, but through divine providence. Like other popular novelists of her generation, that is, Yonge necessarily engages with the questions about providence and mortality that Tennyson had more tentatively raised a dozen years earlier in *In Memoriam*.[38] Early in *The Trial*, Ethel teaches Leonard through a reading of both Scott's *Marmion* and the Book of Job that 'Divine Justice is longer-sighted than human justice' and that 'human injustice at its worst may be working for the sufferer an exceeding weight of glory or preparing him for some high commission below' (53). This teaching allows Leonard to maintain his sanity through a long course of human injustice and to prepare for his own 'high commission' of life as a missionary. Again Yonge uses the characteristics of that genre to provide a critique of the genre and its social and religious implications. The obsession with domestic tension in sensation fiction allows her to voice her own conservative version of these tensions; its insistence on human impotence enables her to glorify divine providence. Just as she had adapted the domestic novel to the purposes of Anglo-Catholic propaganda, so she adapts the apparently less tractable form of the sensation novel to the same ends.

The Trial shows Yonge as a sequel writer responsive to shifts in popular taste. This responsiveness enabled her to reiterate the related concepts of gender, class, and religion on which her domestic fiction depended in different and more forcible terms through an apparently antipathetic development in popular fiction. *The Trial* is her solitary sequel, but, as I have indicated, it is by no means the only manifestation of her leaning towards continuations. Besides the linked novels that absorbed much of her energy after 1870, a few shorter continuations were published, apparently to satisfy her friends' and correspondents' wish to know what happened after the end of the story.[39] Like the eighteenth-century women writers whose work Betty Schellenberg discusses in this volume, Yonge could rely on a community of habitual readers to whom her characters were like 'old friends.' Indeed, one of these pieces, 'Last Heartsease Leaves,' a continuation of *Heartsease*, counts among the earliest manifestations of the nineteenth-century preoccupation with ongoing narratives, as it either predates or is contemporary with Trollope's Barset series.[40] Yonge's own continuing interest in her characters, like that of Trollope and Austen,[41] is well documented: her friend Elizabeth Wordsworth, later the first principal of Lady Margaret Hall, Oxford, said Yonge spoke of her characters 'exactly as if she was explaining the involutions of some *real* piece of history, and she was quite as much in earnest ... she *liked* talking over her people.'[42] Yonge's letters record the flow of gossip about her characters before, during, and after the narratives in which they feature, to which she treated (or subjected) her friends.[43] Her greatest success, *The Heir of Redclyffe*, is one of the very few among her novels whose characters never appear in print again; but even here further developments were apparently once available to the curious, though they were never written up completely.[44] Moreover, this novel in itself

I like June

operates almost as originating text and sequel within one cover. The central narrative ends when Guy, the hero, dies on a three-star, three-hankie, VicFic deathbed a hundred-odd pages before the end, but the novel continues, and Guy's brand of domestic Christianity continues, to ennoble all the surviving characters. He remains the chief agent, though dead, much as Ethel remains the chief agent in *The Trial*, though female, femininity and death presenting similarly severe but not insurmountable blocks to action for Anglo-Catholics in the mid-nineteenth century. Guy and Ethel are glorified not only for their own actions, but also – even more so – for their effect on the actions of others, and so they can continue to be rewarded with success and approval no matter what their physical or social condition of passivity.

Here perhaps is some indication of one basis for the appeal of the continuation to writers such as Yonge. Rewards and punishments become in her hands not just the matter for the last chapter, but a pleasure that can be extended almost indefinitely. When Guy is dead he can receive posthumous tributes, and his wife and child can be sanctified in his name, while Leonard and Ethel can be praised by the truly discerning characters in novel after novel. In the same way, the penance of the less saintly is unending: the boredom and fatigue of the life of Ethel's sister Flora, who makes a worldly marriage, are constantly reiterated, while the 'unreasonable extent' of the expiation of Guy's adversaries in the *Heir of Redclyffe* continuation is noted by Yonge's biographer Christabel Coleridge.[45] Yonge as a critic acknowledges, in writing about children's novels, that the didactic power of a novel can be vitiated by exaggerated rewards and punishments, but nevertheless as a novelist she is extremely generous in her own fictional allocation of just deserts.[46] Not only in its steady popularity, but also in its capacity to foreground both commendation and condemnation, the continuation was neatly fitted to Yonge's propagandist needs. Her one sequel shows in concise form her capacity to exploit for her own purposes the popular form of the moment.

Notes

1 The Mohun family first appear in *Scenes and Characters* (1847); Mother Constance (Lady Herbert Somerville) in *The Castle Builders* (1854); the Mays in *The Daisy Chain* (1856); Robert Fulmort in *Hopes and Fears* (1860); the Merrifields in *The Stokesley Secret* (1861); the Audleys, Vanderkists, and Underwoods in *The Pillars of the House* (1873); the Brownlows in *Magnum Bonum* (1879); the younger Merrifields and Dolores Mohun in *Two Sides of the Shield* (1885); the Hendersons and Whites in *Beechcroft at Rockstone*

Lady Phyllis's ... lord ... inspires ...

(1888); the little Hendersons in *The Long Vacation* (1895). The dates refer to publication in book form, not to serialization.

2 In 1870 the serialization of *The Pillars of the House* began in *The Monthly Packet*, which Yonge edited.

3 Oliphant says that her series 'made a considerable stir at the time, and *almost* made me one of the popularities of literature. *Almost*, never quite, though "Salem Chapel" really went very near it, I believe' (*The Autobiography of Margaret Oliphant*, ed. Elisabeth Jay [Oxford: Clarendon, 1991] 91). *Salem Chapel* is the novel of Oliphant's that most closely approaches sensation fiction; it was produced at the same time as *The Trial*.

4 Christabel Coleridge, *Charlotte Mary Yonge: Her Life and Letters* (London: Macmillan, 1903) 274.

5 I largely agree with Mary Ann Gillies's argument (in her essay in this volume) against distinguishing sequel and series. I see the differentiation as proceeding through a spectrum rather than as involving rigid categories. However, the two words have different connotations and I proceed here on the basis of an 'intuitive' definition.

6 Although eight years intervened between the publication of *The Daisy Chain* and *The Trial* as books, in fact the interval between the two novels was rather less, for *The Trial* began serialization in *The Monthly Packet* in January 1862.

7 Charlotte Mary Yonge, *The Daisy Chain or Aspirations: A Family Chronicle* (London: Virago, 1988) xi–xii; my emphasis. All further references to this work are to this edition and are made parenthetically.

8 George Levine, 'Can You Forgive Him?: Trollope's *Can You Forgive Her?* and the Myth of Realism,' *Victorian Studies* 18 (1974): 19.

9 Yonge, *The Daisy Chain* 667. In my comments on this passage, I differ from Catherine Sandbach-Dahlstrom, who argues that 'although the story of one sibling ends in the conventional device of marriage, the final pages point to developments to come in the lives of other members of the family. In the last scene Ethel May looks back over what has been, at the same time as she ponders her own future and looks forward to the continuation of family life and prospects for her younger brothers and sisters' (*Be Good Sweet Maid: Charlotte Yonge's Domestic Fiction , A Study in Dogmatic Purpose and Fictional Form* [Stockholm: Almqvist & Wicksell, 1984] 61). What Ethel thinks about is the end of the more eventful part of her life; moreover, several other siblings' narratives are completed in the last chapters of *The Daisy Chain*, one through death, one through bearing a second child as a consolation for the death of the first, another through the consecration of the church for which he is the curate, and yet another through marriage and emigration.

10 Charlotte M. Yonge, *The Trial* (Stroud: Alan Sutton, 1996) 299. All subsequent references to this novel are to this edition and made parenthetically.

11 Margaret Oliphant 'Sensation Novels,' *Blackwood's Magazine* (1862): 565. *The Woman in White*, arguably the first sensation novel, was published in 1859. Lyn Pykett, in *The Sensation Novel: From The Woman in White to The Moonstone* (Plymouth: Northcote House, 1994), says that its 'sensational success ... inaugurated the sensation decade' (14). Jonathan Loesberg, however, regards the sensation novel as being inaugurated largely by the reviewers who grouped this novel together with *East Lynne* and *Lady Audley's Secret* ('The Ideology of Narrative Form in Sensation Fiction,' *Representations* 13 [1986]: 116).

12 According to Winifred Hughes, quoting the *Belgravia* magazine in 1868; see *The Maniac in the Cellar: Sensation Novels of the 1860s* (Princeton: Princeton UP, 1980) 166.

13 Hughes, *The Maniac* 3.

14 Patrick Brantlinger, 'What Is "Sensational" about the "Sensation" Novel?' *Nineteenth Century Fiction* 37 (1982): 7.

15 Quoted by Kate Flint in *The Woman Reader, 1837–1914* (Oxford: Clarendon, 1993) 274.

16 Nicholas Rance, *Wilkie Collins and Other Sensation Novelists: 'Walking the Moral Hospital'* (London: Macmillan, 1991) 37.

17 Pykett, *Sensation Novel* 9.

18 Margaret Mare and Alicia Percival make this point in *Victorian Best-Seller: The World of Charlotte Mary Yonge* (London: Harrap, 1947) 207.

19 Generally, in this essay I refer only to Yonge's novels of contemporary life and not to the many tales intended for Sunday school pupils or to the historical fiction.

20 Hughes says that, while 'in theory sensationalism was routinely denounced, "the realist writers," even Trollope and Eliot, began to incorporate recognizably sensational elements into their own portrayals of everyday life' (*The Maniac* 70). She sees in Trollope's *The Eustace Diamonds* a parody of *The Moonstone* (168) and points out the elements of sensation in Mrs Transome's story in Eliot's *Felix Holt*. Pykett makes the same point (*Sensation Novel* 69–70).

21 Georgina Battiscombe, *Charlotte Mary Yonge: The Story of an Uneventful Life* (London: Constable, 1944) 14.

22 Charlotte Yonge, *Musings over 'The Christian Year' and 'Lyra Innocentium' Together with a Few Gleanings of Recollections of the Rev. J. Keble* (London 1871) iii.

23 Battiscombe, *Charlotte Mary Yonge* 72. By 1895 Yonge bases the plot of *The Long Vacation* on the question of whether or not her hero was the product of bigamy or adultery or conceived in wedlock. As he is the hero, he turns out to be legitimate, of course.

24 Hughes, *The Maniac* 31. Oliphant in 1862 describes the sensation novel as 'a kind of literature which must, more or less, make the criminal its hero' ('Sensation Fiction' 568).

25 Wesley Pue's unpublished paper 'The Quest for Law as Popular Discourse,' given at the conference of the Victorian Studies Association of Western Canada in October 1994 in Vancouver, includes interesting comments on the Victorian trial as public spectacle.

26 Pykett, *Sensation Novel* 2. Yonge was especially concerned with the accuracy of the legal details, and commented, 'there ought to be a novelist's lawyer. Sir John Coleridge [a distinguished judge] looked over all the law in *The Trial* for me. He took me to the Portland Prison [where Leonard is incarcerated], and made all sorts of enquiries in my presence as if for his own edification': see Ethel Romanes, *Charlotte Mary Yonge: An Appreciation* (London: Mowbray, 1908) 143.

27 Thomas Boyle writes of sensation novels and crime reporting in *Black Swine in the Sewers of Hampstead: Beneath the Surface of Victorian Sensationalism* (New York: Viking, 1989) 129.

28 A *Punch* cartoon of 15 September 1860 shows a crinolined lady about to step into a gondola in a London street. The caption reads: 'What it must have come to if the rain had continued much longer' (101).

29 The first of Yonge's novels to historicize its action in this way is *Dynevor Terrace* (1859), in which the French Revolution of 1848 and the opening to Atlantic–Pacific traffic of the Isthmus of Panama both play an important role.

30 Domestic novels such as *The Heir of Redclyffe* frequently use romantic elements. See Sandbach Dalhlstrom's discussion (28–58) and my own rather different treatment of

this combination of elements in the conclusion of *Heaven and Home: Charlotte Yonge, Tractarianism, and the Nineteenth Century Women's Movement* (Victoria: U of Victoria English Literary Studies, 1995).

31   Hughes, *The Maniac* 66.

32   Quoted by Flint, *Woman Reader* 277.

33   Oliphant, 'Sensation Novels' 564-5. Oliphant also writes: 'We who once did, and made, and declared ourselves masters of all things, have relapsed into the natural size of humanity, before the great events which have given a new character to the age' (quoted by Rance, *Wilkie Collins* 27). The 'great events' are the Crimean War; the American Civil War; and the uprisings in Greece, Italy, and Poland. However, by the same reckoning, the 'self-admiration' ('Sensation Novels' 564) that Oliphant regards as typical of the 1850s should have been seriously affected by the European uprisings in 1848, the distress and disaffection in the industrial North of England, the Chartist movement, and the famine in Ireland.

34   Pykett, *Sensation Novels* 40–67.

35   Anthea Trodd, *Domestic Crime in the Victorian Novel* (London: Macmillan, 1989) 11.

36   Kathleen Tillotson, 'The Lighter Reading of the Eighteen-Sixties,' introduction to *The Woman in White* by Wilkie Collins (New York: Houghton Mifflin, 1969) xvi.

37   Hughes, *The Maniac* 57.

38   Alfred, Lord Tennyson, *In Memoriam*: 'Oh yet we trust that somehow good / Will be the final goal of ill' (53.1–2).

39   Yonge wrote in the introduction to one of her series novels that '[i]t is sometimes treated as an impertinence to revive the personages of one story in another, even though it is after the example of Shakespeare ... Yet many a letter in youthful hands has begged for further information on the fate of the beings who had become favourites in the schoolroom; and this has induced me to believe that the following out of my own notions as to the careers of former heroes and heroines might not be unwelcome; while I have tried to make the story stand independently' (*Two Sides of the Shield* [London 1885] v). An anonymous correspondent wrote to Yonge: 'People say that continuations of a story are never successful, but my feeling is this: the Underwoods and many more of your brain-children are just like old friends, whom we meet again after a long separation. They may be less beautiful than they were; they may say little that is striking or amusing, but they are themselves; we see and hear them again and that is sufficient pleasure' (Coleridge, *Yonge* 352).

40   This piece is difficult to date. It must have been written some time between 1854, when *Heartsease* was first published, and February 1862, the date of the first known reference to 'Last Heartsease Leaves' in *The Monthly Packet*: see Georgina Battiscombe and Marghanita Laski, *A Chaplet for Charlotte Yonge: Papers by Georgina Battiscombe [and Others]* (London: Cresset, 1965) 207.

41   Trollope writes that he resented adverse criticism of *The Prime Minister*, 'so much do I love the man whose character I had endeavoured to portray,' namely Plantagenet Palliser (*An Autobiography* [Oxford: Oxford UP, 1982] 360. Austen's involvement with her characters is suggested by her pleasure at finding a portrait which she sees as being a likeness of her own Jane Bennet (Park Honan, *Jane Austen: Her Life* [New York: Fawcett Columbine, 1987] 321).

42   Romanes, *Yonge* 147.

43   See, for instance, the facsimile of a letter dated 1895 (after the publication of *The Long Vacation*) in Mare and Percival, *Victorian Best-Seller* 208.

44 According to her biographer, Christabel Coleridge, after the publication of *The Heir of Redclyffe* Yonge worked on 'a whole second part of the Morville story, following the characters to their life's end. This sketch was never, I think, really written and though the facts were always at the service of eager admirers who wanted to know more of their old friends, she always said that the public would not stand anything so melancholy, and her literary judgment told her that its publication would be unwise. The idea of expiation of, and retribution for, the faults of youth in Philip and Laura was certainly carried to an unreasonable extent, and it is enough to know that Guy's daughter was all she ought to have been, and a sort of guardian angel to the rest of the family' (*Yonge* 168).

45 Coleridge, *Yonge* 168.

46 Yonge, 'Children's Literature of the Last Century: Didactic Fiction,' *Macmillan's Magazine* (1869) 310.

Trollope's Phineas Diptych as Sequel and Sequence Novel

LYNETTE FELBER

The idea that 'sequels are always disappointing'[1] suggests that both a reader's failure to repeat an original reading experience and the inferiority of a work produced merely to capitalize on a previous success are inevitable. The assertion that sequels disappoint is, however, an aesthetic judgment, not a narrative law. Sequential genres – that is, sequels, serials, and sequence novels – may be appraised more favourably and generated by less mercenary motives. Anthony Trollope's Palliser novels (1864–80), for example, were motivated less by the success of one particularly popular novel than by the author's desire to extend his relationship with characters he found congenial. The Pallisers, sometimes called 'the Parliamentary novels' because of their cast of politicians, focus on a group of upper-middle-class and aristocratic characters, central among them Plantagenet Palliser and his ambitious wife, Glencora.[2] This sequence novel exceeds the usual sequel by repeating the 'follow-up' pattern of publication through six volumes. Whereas sequels may entice readers with the promise of repeating the experience, the multivolume sequence novel Trollope developed along the Balzacian model offers to *prolong* the reading experience. The subtle differentiation between the workings of the sequel and the sequence novel (also called the *roman-fleuve*) may perhaps best be illustrated by examining a text which is both at once.[3] Within Trollope's Pallisers are two novels which also comprise a sequel: *Phineas Finn* and *Phineas Redux* (second and fourth in the sequence), separated by the intervening publication of *The Eustace Diamonds*. Despite Trollope's use of the two subgenres in the Pallisers, I will argue that he preferred the sequence novel to the sequel as better suited to meet certain aesthetic and psychological needs of writers and readers.

The diptych structure of the Phineas novels, the second identified as a 'sequel' by Trollope himself,[4] at first seems to contribute to the idea that sequels repeat their predecessors. Juliet McMaster calls the second novel a 'complement': 'the events, though literally different, closely parallel those in the first novel, so that Phineas seems to be going through it all again; only it has all turned sour.'[5] In the first novel the titular Irish barrister, barely finished with his education, is quickly and effortlessly elected to parliamentary seats, first of Loughshane, then of Loughton. In the sequel, he finds it much more difficult to acquire the seat of Tankerville, and even the politically savvy Glencora Palliser cannot procure him a Cabinet seat. Similarly, his former romantic success with heiresses – Lady Laura Standish and Madame Max Goestler fall in love with him, and Violet Effingham briefly considers him a suitor before Phineas decides to marry his Irish sweetheart – is not repeated in *Phineas Redux*. Here, his Irish wife having died in the interval between the two novels, he passively receives the tedious attentions of the now married Laura Standish Kennedy and is shot at by her husband after the marriage breaks down. In a sort of revision or corrective action, Phineas ends up marrying Madame Max Goesler, the widow-heiress whose proposal he refused at the end of *Phineas Finn*. The political and romantic content of the novels is clearly parallel: taken together they suggest a movement from innocence to experience, or the rise and fall of Phineas's expectations. Examined more closely, however, the second novel deepens and builds on the first rather than repeating it.

Moreover, while the desire to repeat the original experience may motivate readers of sequential genres, it is literally impossible for narrative to satisfy their desire. Readers' supposed disappointment is not so much characteristic of the sequel as of narrative itself. Inherently generated by difference, narrative is a *series* of events; a series is built on related items rather than those which are identical: a-a-a does not comprise a narrative; a-b-c or b-a-c or a^1-a^2-a^3 does. As Wallace Martin explains, 'no matter how exactly an event repeats one that occurred earlier, they are separated by time, context, and probably by their consequences ... Since narrative is based on the estranging distance that time puts between events that appear similar, it can always undercut the meaning we find in "repetition of the same" by showing that it is really repetition with a difference.'[6] Trollope is aware of this developmental quality of repetition; in his *Autobiography* and in the novels themselves, he and his narrator emphasize the objective of delineating change in characters over time, a goal for which sequential genres are ideally suited. Phineas explains to his mentor Mr Low that his experiences have rendered him 'like a man who has had his knees broken, or his arms cut off ... I cannot be the same afterwards as I was before,'[7] underscoring the function of the sequel to depict change over time.

While the first novel offers more exciting love stories, the sequel provides an intriguing detective plot (challenging platitudes about the disappointment of sequels) in Phineas's trial for the murder of Mr Bonteen, president of the Board of Trade.[8] In the sequel, a falsely accused Phineas retraces the steps of the naïve youth, suggesting, as he matures, the *Bildungsroman* pattern so prevalent in the Victorian novel. Only after Madame Max travels to Prague and procures evidence to implicate the real killer is Phineas acquitted and released from prison. Phineas in adversity is a far more interesting character than the young 'child of fortune' who effortlessly achieved a parliamentary seat in the first novel. As *Phineas Redux* unfolds, its protagonist is increasingly disillusioned, even after he is exonerated: 'I shall hate to go back to the House, and have somehow learned to dislike and distrust all those things that used to be so fine and lively to me. I don't think that I believe any more in the party; – or rather in the men who lead it. I used to have a faith that now seems to me to be marvelous' (2.277). The sequel provokes a re-evaluation of the values and experiences of *Phineas Finn* which renders much of the original, viewed retrospectively, as exposition. The diptych structure bestows closure, the privilege of the last word, on the second volume, the sequel that undermines the finality of the first. Furthermore, *Phineas Redux* actually was more popular with reviewers (critical readers) than was its predecessor,[9] again discrediting the assertion that sequels will always disappoint or be aesthetically inferior.

The Phineas novels have a dual function, as sequels in themselves and as individual components of the Palliser sequence. John Halperin comments on the way *Phineas Finn* 'develops themes more mutely present in *Can You Forgive Her?* [first in the sequence] and introduces us, in its examination of the beginnings of a political career, to a number of motifs that are to be threaded throughout its successors.'[10] As part of the sequence, the Phineas novels provide, in the character of the Irish MP, a political and personal counterpoint to Plantagenet Palliser. The rise and fall of Phineas's career anticipates Palliser's resignation and subsequent diminished position as Chancellor of the Exchequer to Gresham. The death of Phineas's Irish wife, Mary Flood Jones, in the interval between the original novel and its sequel, foreshadows Glencora's death in the gap between the penultimate and last novels in the sequence, *The Prime Minister* and *The Duke's Children*. Phineas is initially drawn to Marie as Palliser is drawn to Glencora, because of the woman's fortune, although both marriages end up being complex and nuanced love matches. Ironically, while both women are enthusiastic politicians' wives, Marie fosters Phineas's relatively modest political career, while Glencora proves ultimately to be a hindrance to Palliser as prime minister.

In both the Phineas sequel and the larger Palliser sequence, then, Trollope uses variation (or repetition with a difference) to develop a contrapuntal narrative. Closely related through the use of such technique, the sequel and the sequence, as subgenres of the novel, often differ more in degree than in kind.[11] For example, both the sequel and the sequence novel emphasize process and continuation; they de-emphasize closure. Linda Hughes and Michael Lund generalize that 'Victorians, in fact, looked forward in their reading toward endings that only provided jumping off places to more and other stories.'[12] Trollope's Pallisers comprise an early, experimental form of the sequence-novel genre that links the Victorian preference for extended narratives (often serials) to the modernist inclination towards encyclopedic development in such forms as purportedly comprehensive novels (e.g., *Ulysses*) or treatises on the history of man. The sequence novel was subsequently refined by twentieth-century writers such as Marcel Proust (*Remembrance of Things Past*), Dorothy Richardson (*Pilgrimage*), and Anthony Powell (*A Dance to the Music of Time*) into something much closer to a huge meganovel.

There are, nevertheless, several significant distinctions between the sequel and the sequence novel. One important distinction is that the sequel is often more linear. The two volumes which are necessary for a sequel are differentiated from each other in that the initial novel is the foundational one: it can generally stand by itself, unless the two were conceived as interdependent. (This process works in reverse for the prequel, where exposition is supplied after the fact, making foundational what initially had seemed to be extraneous or was only implied.) As a sequel, *Phineas Redux* uses much more explicit connections to *Phineas Finn* than do other volumes of the larger sequence novel of which it is a part. Whereas sequels are generally published in the order of narrative chronology, this is less often the case with sequence novels. The novels in the popular Jalna series, for example, were neither written nor published in the order suggested by the chronological unfolding of the family saga. Instead, the first volume published, *Jalna* (1927), ended up being the seventh in the chronological series, as Mazo de la Roche filled in the antecedents to the story, composed retrospectively, patchwork style.

Narrative linearity is correspondingly less evident in the multivolume sequence novel, where exposition is often repeated in each new volume.

Because of this feature, novels within a sequence may be read in isolation or out of order, although they are ideally read in narrative sequence and as a whole. Readers of Proust's *Remembrance of Things Past* or Powell's *A Dance to the Music of Time* often worked backward, reading from the final to the initial novels, or from the two ends to meet in the middle.[13] Other more subtle distinctions are contained in the beginnings and endings of the narrative in the two subgenres. The first novel in a sequence often begins with a more complex oblique or multiple exposition, introducing not only the individual novel, but the entire multiplotted series. Because of the repeated 'follow-up' pattern of publication, the individual novels within a sequence also tend to be more anticlimactic; after a certain point, the reader learns no longer to expect an ending, having come to believe that ending is always provisional.[14]

Because the sequence novel inevitably exceeds the sequel in quantitative complexity, it is also more likely to contain abortive subplots, plots which reach the end of their development before the end of the text. In the Palliser sequence, only the story of Plantagenet Palliser carries through all the six volumes, but even so this plot is subordinated in some of the novels as the stories of minor characters temporarily predominate. Thus, Phineas Finn is the major character in the two novels that comprise a sequel; but in subsequent novels he becomes an extra, appearing only briefly at political parties and social events where the Pallisers are central. The Phineas plot that predominates in the sequel is eventually phased out in the continuing sequence. Readers never learn the intimate details of his marriage to Marie Goesler, although she plays an important role as a friend to the Palliser family in the final volume, *The Duke's Children*, after Glencora's death. Plantagenet Palliser and his family, secondary to Phineas in the sequel and merely an audience for Lizzie Eustace's adventures in *The Eustace Diamonds*, again take centre stage in the later novels. Length however, or the number of volumes, is the primary distinction between the sequel and the sequence novel: when sequels multiply – as, for example, in the case of the Jalna books – the sequel may evolve into a sequence novel, particularly if the author develops strong links with previous volumes and an overall sense of unity. Although both the sequel and the sequence novel are natural vehicles for process-oriented themes, because of the difference in their length, the sequel is more likely to focus on an individual's process (i.e., the *Bildungsroman*), whereas the sequence novel more appropriately depicts a family saga or societal change. Thus, Trollope's Phineas novels comprise a sort of *Bildungsroman*, while the encompassing Palliser sequence not only includes many individual stories (of Glencora and Plantagenet Palliser, for example), but also includes the evolution of British society during the latter part of the Reform era (*Phineas Finn* is set in the 1860s; *Phineas Redux* in 1868–71).[15]

Despite his work in both subgenres, Trollope clearly prefers the sequence novel; even within his sequel, the two Phineas books, he employs features of the larger, encompassing subgenre. His conception of sequential novels differs from that of writers introducing sequels to charismatic texts, who assume that readers will know the original novel, which is, after all, the source of their attraction. Trollope is painfully aware that readers of the sequel may not have read *Phineas Finn* – or perhaps he fears that the intervening *Eustace Diamonds* dilutes readers' memories of the first half of the sequel. Thus, Trollope often supplies rather repetitious exposition (often essential in the sequence novel) to enlighten out-of-sequence readers or to refresh the memories of those who have forgotten. Such awkward devices as Phineas's 'audible' memories and letters, for example, provide supplemental exposition really needed only by new readers. Thus, Laura Kennedy writes to Phineas, reminding him that her father and husband were Cabinet members (*Phineas Redux* 1:58) or tells him about events of two years ago that he, as a participant, could hardly have forgotten. As an *aide-mémoire*, speeches such as Violet Chiltern's exclamation to Phineas – 'Why should you be altered? It's only two years' (*Phineas Redux* 1.21) – stress the obvious passage of time.

In another difference from the usual sequel publication process, where success of a charismatic narrative begets a sequel, Trollope is aware of the fact that the sequence novel exacerbates difficulties for less than ideal readers, those who pick up a sequential volume in isolation. He notes despairingly in his autobiography: 'Who will read *Can You Forgive Her?*, *Phineas Finn*, *Phineas Redux* and *The Prime Minister* consecutively, in order that he may understand the characters of the Duke of Omnium, of Plantagenet Palliser, and Lady Glencora? Who will even know that they should be so read?' (159). Trollope articulates doubts about his readers' commitment – in contrast to the self-confident assumptions of writers of sequels to charismatic texts – and formulates self-imposed rules to accommodate his readers:

The writer of this chronicle is not allowed to imagine that any of his readers have read the wonderful and vexatious adventures of Lady Eustace, a lady of good birth, of high rank, and of large fortune, who, but a year or two since, became almost a martyr to a diamond necklace which was stolen from her. With her history the present reader has but small concern, but it may be necessary that he should know that the lady in question, who had been a widow with many suitors, at last gave her hand and her fortune to a clergyman whose name was Joseph Emilius. (*Phineas Redux* 2.38)[16]

In another difference from the usual sequel publication pattern, where success of a charismatic narrative begets a sequel, Trollope preconceived his successor novel and described the Phineas novels as 'in fact, but one novel' (*Autobiography* 274). As early as the first pages of *Phineas Finn*, Trollope lays groundwork for the sequel by foreshadowing the protagonist's fall in the second part: 'Where should [Phineas] dine if Loughshaners elected him to Parliament? And then he painted to himself a not untrue picture of the probable miseries of a man who begins life too high up on the ladder, – who succeeds in mounting before he has learned how to hold on when he is aloft.'[17] While the texts themselves illustrate his preconception, Trollope himself confesses to poor authorial judgment when the larger, intertextual relationship of the novels is considered: 'As I fully intended to bring my hero again into the world, I was wrong to marry him to a simple pretty Irish girl, who could only be felt as an encumbrance on such return' (*Autobiography* 273). His preference for beginning serial publication only when he had finished writing the novel[18] – in contrast to Dickens's practice – also suggests his holistic conception of sequential subgenres of the novel. For Trollope, the sequel or novel which follows is simply another chapter of the story; his conception of ideal narrative extension is realized in the meganovel.

Trollope's vast conception of narrative expansion, exceeding the sequel, is shown in the unique construction of the Phineas books: the diptych structure of the two parts of the sequel is interrupted – and extended – by *The Eustace Diamonds*. The usual function of a diptych is, when folded together, to hide and protect an inner surface. In the Palliser sequence, the 'inner surface' bulwarked by the two Phineas novels is *The Eustace Diamonds*, the novel devoted to the basest characters and impulses of the series. When this inner surface is exposed, its parallels to the Phineas novels reveal the corrupt, darker side of the major characters; the novel also functions as a dark complement to the other Palliser novels, extending the sequel through a sort of narrative doubling. Just as Lizzie Eustace is a shadow character or dark double to Glencora Palliser in *The Eustace Diamonds*, in *Phineas Redux* she functions as a foil and double to other female characters. The parallels between Lady Laura's and Lizzie's marital difficulties, for example, are striking, despite the enormous gap in quality between the women's inherent natures. Both are married to dominating husbands; Emilius 'subject[s] his young wife [Lizzie] to marital authority' (*Phineas Redux* 2.39), just as the tyrant Kennedy does to Laura. While Emilius is a clergyman, Kennedy is a religious zealot who insists that his wife attend two Sunday services and forgo any company on the Sabbath. Both women initially sacrifice their fortunes to rid themselves of their husbands, and after their wives leave them, both husbands try to force them to return. Laura recovers her fortune and inherits her husband's estate after his death, while Emilius's claim to Lizzie's wealth is invalidated when his bigamy is discovered.

Even more illuminating is the function of Lizzie as both a double and a foil to Marie Goesler, one of Trollope's finest female characters and an apparent study of integrity. Both women are married to Jews, and each is involved with one of the two men accused of Bonteen's murder. Lizzie is married to the actual murderer, Emilius; Madame Goesler is romantically tied to the accused, Phineas, although her interest is not reciprocated until the end of *Phineas Redux*. The parallels between Lizzie and Madame Max nevertheless suggest a less flattering cast to Marie's integrity than would otherwise be evident. Marie, for example, has earned Glencora's (and the reader's) respect in *Phineas Finn* by turning down an opportunity for social mobility: the proposal of marriage by the old Duke of Omnium. Her subsequent refusal of his legacy of jewels and money in *Phineas Redux* furthers that positive impression. While Lizzie appropriates the Eustace jewels, Marie refuses the Duke of Omnium's costly collection and 20,000 pounds even though, as Glencora tells her, '[e]verybody takes what anybody leaves them by will' (*Phineas Redux* 1.232). Yet Marie is not selfless in her decision: she deliberately weighs the social cost of acceptance both in public gossip and in the inevitable loss of Glencora's friendship. The statement made of Lizzie, then, that she 'knew well how to ingratiate herself with the friend of the hour' (*Phineas Redux* 2.163), also applies to Marie.

At the same time, Lizzie is a foil to Marie, creating an illuminating contrast between a woman who is merely a base social schemer and one who studies the social implications of her actions. While the narrator implies that Lizzie 'know[s] how to keep her own life and her own pocket separate from her romance' (*Phineas Redux* 2: 167), this mercenary calculation is not present in Marie's offer (repeated in both the initial novel and its sequel) to save the man she loves by placing her fortune at his disposal. At the same time, it must be mentioned that Marie can act so beneficently in regard to Phineas only because her first, loveless marriage has endowed her with this fortune. Marie's first marriage is described so minimally in the text that it is never clear whether she married for money or whether it was an arranged marriage (or something else). Thus, the parallels with Lizzie expose an element of ambiguity, possibly a taint, in Marie's character.

The contrapuntal structure illustrated above suggests a further advantage of the sequence novel over the sequel. The number of novels in a sequence prolongs the reading time and narrative expanse (Martin's 'estranging distance that time puts between events'); any impression of repetitiousness is avoided. In the sequel, repetition occurs in a smaller expanse, at closer proximity – a problem Trollope forestalls in the Phineas sequel by interposing *The Eustace Diamonds*. Thus, the sequence novel is better able to satisfy readers' desire for repetition, *without actually repeating or seeming to repeat*. Castle notes the paradoxical desire which motivates sequel readers: 'Unconsciously [readers] persist in demanding the impossible: that the sequel be different, but also *exactly the same*. Their secret mad hope is to find in the sequel a paradoxical kind of textual doubling – a repetition that does not look like one, the old story in a new and unexpected guise. They wish to read the "unforgettable" text once more, yet as if they had forgotten it.'[19] In contrast to the sequel, the greater length of the sequence novel provides writers with a larger canvas on which to vary their stories, inscribing tales of the same and the different, and thereby permits readers to 'forget' between repetitions. The sequence novel, in other words, is ideally suited to satisfy this deep-seated, contradictory psychological need of readers.

Extending the same story and relying upon familiar characters were means for Trollope to achieve both personal engagement and psychological realism, a manifestation of his nineteenth-century world-view: 'In writing *Phineas Finn* I had constantly before me the necessity of progression in character, – of marking the changes in men and women which would naturally be produced by the lapse of years. In most novels the writer can have no such duty, as the period occupied is not long enough to allow of the change of which I speak ... But I do not think that novelists have often set before themselves the state of progressive change, – nor should I have done it, had I not found myself so frequently allured back to my old friends' (*Autobiography* 273–4). By interrupting the Phineas story with *The Eustace Diamonds*, Trollope created the impression of a realistic passage of time: a gap in the reading suggests that considerable time has passed in Phineas's life. But the return to Phineas also represents the desire for a continuing relationship with characters, an impulse shared by Trollope's readers. Betty Schellenberg argues in this collection that sequels establish a 'readerly community,' a figurative space which, like the eighteenth-century periodical or coffee-house, offers an opportunity for 'a conversation between old friends in a kind of virtual reality.'[20] Through his sequence novels, Trollope re-creates the temporal reach and plenitude of real life – and populates his world with company of his own creation.

Recent cultural studies subordinate the writer's motivation to the role of the marketplace in fuelling genre formation. Castle, for example, views the sequel from the eighteenth century onward as 'an offshoot of the bestseller syndrome.'[21] The origination of the sequence novel in the nineteenth century[22] is clearly indebted to the proliferation of serial publications, a significant market factor. In their book-length study of the Victorian serial, Lund and Hughes emphasize the connections between economic and generic features of fiction: 'the confident capitalist framework during the booming years of nineteenth-century economic expansion had a kind of literary analogue in the serial form. The assumption of continuing growth and the confidence that an investment (whether of time or money) in the present would reap greater rewards in the future were shared features of middle-class capitalism and of serial reading.'[23] Such emphases privilege cultural forces evident when a text is viewed in its historical context.

Biography, the history of an individual, should also be considered as part of the wealth of cultural factors that stimulate textual and generic production. In the massive Palliser novels, Trollope created for himself, and not just for his readers, a community, expanding on an objective already evident in Victorian three-decker novels which dramatize the interconnections of characters in various social strata, linked by the exigencies of setting, plot, and subplot. Trollope reveals that his extended relationship with characters met psychological needs he could not satisfy in real life: 'By no amount of description or asseveration could I succeed in making any reader understand how much these characters with their belongings have been to me in my latter life' (*Autobiography* 155). It is interesting to note that Trollope's popularity experienced a resurgence in England during the Second World War, a time when alienation, insecurity, and separation of family members contributed to the same sense of personal alienation Trollope himself experienced because of his father's financial failure and the resultant break up of his family.[24]

Trollope also seemingly compensated for his own failure to enter politics by his creation of a semi-fictional political realm. His disastrous defeat in the election for the parliamentary seat of Beverley occurred, significantly enough, in the period between his composition of *Phineas*

Finn and *Phineas Redux*, and his preoccupation with the campaign recurs in *Ralph the Heir* (1871), composed during the interim. In his autobiography he claims, 'As I was debarred from expressing my opinions in the House of Commons, I took this method of declaring myself' (272). Although critics of the autobiography suggest that we should regard sceptically his statements about his writing, since autobiography may be a kind of 'fiction,' or 'self-production,' and 'Trollope's chief occupation was making things up,'[25] it is difficult to attribute any but the most benign motives to such innocuous self-creation. Phineas Finn and Plantagenet Palliser are fictional agents who achieve (for a time) Trollope's own much coveted political success: 'how frequently I have used them for the expression of my political and social convictions. They have been as real to me as free trade was to Mr Cobden, or the dominion of a party to Mr Disraeli' (*Autobiography* 155).

It may be productive to re-examine authorial intention (albeit sceptically) as part of the cultural context that produces genres.[26] If New Critics were too quick to dismiss the author as irrelevant to the text, practitioners of cultural studies, focused on broad socio-economic factors, have similarly ignored the actual living individual through whom cultural forces are mediated and translated into text. Trollope is not alone, as other essays in this collection demonstrate, in desiring a continuing relation with characters and their fictional worlds. His creation of sequence novels takes the attraction to continuing narratives – the sequel impulse – to its most extreme nineteenth-century expression. In a recent series on writers and works 'ripe for rediscovery,' Cynthia Ozick recommends Trollope's longest novel (*The Way We Live Now*) because of its very length. 'What disappoints in any novel by Trollope is the visible approach of its end: when more has been read than remains to be read,' she asserts.[27] The attractions of sequential genres, the satisfactions they offer to readers and writers, are illuminated by Trollope's self-described motives, today as in the nineteenth century.

Notes

1 Terry Castle, *Masquerade and Civilization: The Carnivalesque in Eighteenth-Century Culture and Fiction* (Stanford: Stanford UP, 1986) 133.
2 The titles of the six Palliser novels, in order of publication, are: *Can You Forgive Her?* (1864–5), *Phineas Finn* (1869), *The Eustace Diamonds* (1873), *Phineas Redux* (1874), *The Prime Minister* (1876), *The Duke's Children* (1880).
3 The term 'sequel' is inherently ambiguous, suggesting at the same time the second

volume of a pair of novels and, in the relationship between the two volumes, a genre (or subgenre). While I have used the term in both senses, the context clarifies which meaning is intended.

4 Anthony Trollope, *An Autobiography*, introd. Michael Sadleir, (London: Oxford UP, 1950, rpt. 1974) 274. All subsequent references to this work are to this edition and made parenthetically.

5 Juliet McMaster, *Trollope's Palliser Novels: Theme and Pattern* (New York: Oxford UP, 1979) 60.

6 Wallace Martin, *Recent Theories of Narrative* (Ithaca, NY: Cornell UP, 1986) 168.

7 Anthony Trollope, *Phineas Redux*, introd. F.S.L. Lyons, 2 vols. (Oxford: Oxford UP, 1983) 2.293. All subsequent references to this work are to this edition and made parenthetically.

8 Trollope thus exploits the entertainment potential of the trial as 'public spectacle'; as June Sturrock points out elsewhere in this collection, the O.J. Simpson phenomenon of trial-as-entertainment has historical British precedents (108).

9 John Halperin, *Trollope and Politics: A Study of the Pallisers and Others* (London: Macmillan, 1977) 165.

10 Halperin, *Trollope and Politics* 87.

11 Mary Ann Gillies's reluctance to distinguish among sequels, series, and sequence novels is a logical consequence of her emphasis on cultural and market forces (see her essay in this collection). It is nevertheless important to consider the difference between *modes of production* (e.g., the serial instalment) and *genre* as defined by particular formal or structural features, to differentiate between forces that *produce* and characteristics that *define* genres. Market forces may generate certain kinds of texts, and the features within these texts may then be used to classify and define them by genre (or subgenre). A novel published in nineteenth-century serial instalments will, of course, be perceived differently when it is released in book form, but it is a novel nonetheless. Cliff-hangers, for example, are emphasized as a feature of instalment fiction, but they are rendered identically *as words on a page* in the text subsequently published as a book (presuming no textual revision is made). Though I acknowledge the significance of cultural forces that produce genres (as my conclusion makes clear), my focus is on genre as defined by textual features.

12 Linda Hughes and Michael Lund, 'Studying Victorian Serials,' *Literary Research* 11 (1986): 236.

13 Paul Gaston, '"This Question of Discipline": An Interview with Anthony Powell,' *The Virginia Quarterly Review* 61 (1985): 644; Lynette Felber, *Gender and Genre in Novels Without End: The British Roman-Fleuve* (Gainesville: UP of Florida, 1995) 20–1.

14 For a more extended definition of the narrative dynamics of the sequence novel or *roman-fleuve* see Felber, *Gender and Genre* 11–19.

15 Halperin, *Trollope and Politics* 166.

16 This sort of intrusive narratorial metacommentary may be characteristic of sequential genres, in which the time between reading or viewing the sequel – or the volumes of a sequence novel – gives the audience time to reflect, and in which the cumulative length gives the author space to comment on the repeated experience. Alexander Leggatt and Lianne McLarty note that theatrical and film sequels, for example, tend to be metatheatrical and self-referential (see essays in this volume, 62–4 and 200, respectively).

17 Anthony Trollope, *Phineas Finn* (Oxford: Oxford UP, 1982) 8.

18 Kathleen Tillotson, *Novels of the Eighteen-Forties* (Oxford: Clarendon, 1954) 40.
19 Castle, *Masquerade* 134.
20 Schellenberg, 91, this volume.
21 Castle, *Masquerade* 133.
22 Elizabeth Kerr, 'The Twentieth-Century Sequence Novel,' diss., U of Minnesota, 1941, 27.
23 Linda Hughes and Michael Lund, *The Victorian Serial*, Victorian Literature and Culture Series, Gen. eds. Karen Chase, Jerome McGann, and Herbert Tucker (Charlottesville: UP of Virginia, 1991) 4.
24 Phillip Holcomb, 'A Study of the Critical Responses to Anthony Trollope's Novels with an Annotated Bibliography (1920–68),' diss., U of Colorado, 1971, 17. The low point of his popularity, from which Trollope's reputation recovered during the Second World War, was from his death in 1882 until the 1930s (17, 1).
25 See, respectively, James R. Kincaid, 'Trollope's Fictional Autobiography,' *Nineteenth Century Fiction* 37 (1982): 340–9; Sarah Gilread, 'Trollope's *Autobiography*: The Strategies of Self-Production,' *Modern Language Quarterly* 47 (1986): 272–90; and John Halperin, 'Trollope's *Phineas Finn* and History,' *English Studies* 59 (1978): 122.
26 An even more obvious example than the sequel or sequence novel is what has recently been termed 'creative non-fiction.' While some texts may be more convincingly 'true' than others, ultimately it is the author's or the biographer's profession that the narrative really happened that defines a text within this genre.
27 Cynthia Ozick, 'More Than Just a Victorian,' *New York Times Book Review*, 1 January 1995, 7.1.

The Literary Agent and the Sequel

MARY ANN GILLIES

In this essay I want to explore the notion of the sequel[1] in a different manner from many of the authors in this book. Indeed, I will question the collection's working definition of the sequel as a *single* continuation of an original text which initially appeared to invoke closure and to stand alone, and as existing in some precise chronological relation to the originating work. I wish to propose an alternative definition, less restrictive in its terms, that emerges from Pierre Bourdieu's theories about cultural production. I will suggest that cultural and material forces come into play both in the production of the original text and in any text which is written in response to it; and I argue that these forces are in many ways responsible for the writing of texts that we call sequels. To make my concept of the sequel concrete, I draw on the work of the Edwardian writer Arnold Bennett and on his relationship with J.B. Pinker, his literary agent, who was instrumental in Bennett's creation of sequels to his popular novel *Anna of the Five Towns*.

I recognize that a broader definition of the sequel carries the danger of eliminating any real distinction between a sequel in its relation to its originary text and any work which responds to an existing text. As well, a definition risks the charge of being ahistorical if it claims a universal applicability. With these two potential difficulties in mind, I want to construct a carefully circumscribed definition.

My definition is grounded in the last decade of the nineteenth century and the first few decades of the twentieth century. The material conditions of publishing in this period – a rise in the market demand for literature (both in Britain and abroad), rapid change in printing technology and distribution systems, and the professional literary agent's intervention in the power dynamics between writers and publishers – provided fertile soil for the growth of the sequel as a literary product. While it is true that literary sequels existed long before this time, I suggest that the unique cultural and material conditions of this period brought about an unprecedented proliferation of sequels.

To define those elements that make up the sequel, it is necessary first to take a step back from textual concerns or qualities and to ask the basic question: why write/publish/read a sequel? Each of these three acts is subject to similar cultural and material forces, but each is also motivated by unique desires, so I turn first to the importance of this triumvirate in the production and consumption of literature.

Readers desire to re-create the pleasures fostered by their experience of the original work. Yet it would be underestimating them to suggest that a repetition of the original work, in all its particulars, would be satisfactory. In fact, readers want a new story that satisfies their desires for further engagement with the world, or characters, or writing that they found so stimulating in the original text. Carole Gerson addresses this issue in commenting on the supposed disappointment readers must feel when reading sequels to *Anne of Green Gables*: 'According to a recent analysis of [L.M.] Montgomery's readers, the sequels substantially reinforce the value of the originating book because they "tell ... what happened later" and prolong the pleasure of inhabiting the "alternative world" of Montgomery's fiction.'[2] It is a desire for more and *new* that often leads readers to clamour for sequels.[3] Although many authors, including Montgomery, have rued the day their work became a best-seller for forcing them to revisit places and characters they have outgrown or in which they have lost interest, equally as many are happy to continue exploring the territory defined by the original text.[4] The motivations for doing this are complex; they include the author's need to fulfil his or her own internal desires, which may be separate from the cultural and material forces prompting composition of a sequel. A fascination with a character, a storyline, or a world which has been created, or even a desire to rewrite a story that has proven unsatisfactory, may all be internal motivations for authors. However, unless there is some sort of external demand for the new work, the publication of a sequel written because the author desires a further treatment of the original text is not at all certain. Publishers' motivations for commissioning sequels are much more clear-cut, arising primarily from the desire to capitalize on the market created by the success of the original text. Yet they, too, are concerned with more than economic success; a desire to define cultural value plays a role in some publishers' decisions to publish sequels. Sequels become almost inevitable when the desires of all three – reader, writer, publisher – intersect.

Cultural forces often contribute to this intersection of desires that influence the production of sequels. Bourdieu's *The Field of Cultural Production* provides me with two central concepts that help to explain the forces at work here. Bourdieu distinguishes between symbolic and cultural capital. Symbolic capital 'refers to degree of accumulated prestige, celebrity, consecration or honour and is founded on a dialectic of knowledge (*connaissance*) and recognition (*reconnaissance*),' while cultural capital 'concerns forms of cultural knowledge, competences or dispositions.'[5] A text may win an award or be placed on a critic's top-ten list or be studied in school or university, thereby acquiring both symbolic capital – because of the reader's knowledge of the prestige acquired by the text – and cultural capital – because of the assumed cultural competency of critics and teachers. A text that accumulates this sort of capital may well create a market for subsequent texts; in effect the critical apparatus attached to the text may well generate the desire for sequels in readers and authors, which, in turn, generates it in publishers.

Terry Castle identifies the workings of the material forces at play in sequel production when she says that the sequel is 'an offshoot of the best-seller syndrome,' a work produced 'to profit further from a previous work that has had exceptional commercial success.'[6] The disdain evident here for the commercial aspect of publishing unfairly belittles the very real market conditions that affect the decision to publish any work. Publishing is a business, and it makes good economic sense to capitalize on the success of a text by producing a follow-up one. Most publishing houses survive on the profits generated by their backlists – this was certainly the case at the turn of the century, and it is broadly true today. The work that goes into creating even a moderate success with a first book is often justified by the argument that future books will be easier to sell, and will generate larger profits, because the market will be familiar with the writer's work from that first book. In essence, publishers create a market for a particular writer; they nurse the market, and risk this effort on the expectation that through the course of a relationship with an author their investment will pay off.[7] Capitalizing on the success of one text by suggesting, or even demanding, that the writer's next work re-create characters, storylines, or the world of that text is one way of achieving a return on this investment.[8]

Castle's comments also reflect a cardinal error in conceiving of the sequel, for she asserts that economics is the sole motivating force behind the sequel. In fact, as I have outlined above, the decision to compose a sequel results from a complex interaction of cultural and material forces in which reader, writer, and publisher are involved. Indeed, as Bourdieu argues, 'the literary or artistic field is at all times the site of a struggle between the two principles of hierarchization: the heteronomous principle, favourable to those who dominate the field economically and politically (e.g. "bourgeois art") and the autonomous principle (e.g. "art for art's sake").'[9]

Having answered the question of why we have sequels in terms of the forces which are factors in the desire to produce them, I wish now to suggest a broader definition of the sequel. First, a sequel arises from what Castle calls a 'charismatic text,'[10] although I define 'charismatic' differently, suggesting that such a text has a powerful effect on its readership because it supplies them with enormous reading pleasure.[11] Second, a sequel need not be restricted by number or genre. The distinctions among sequel, sequence, and series strike me as arbitrary and do not reflect the reality of the late nineteenth-century publishing world. The commercialization of literature often dictated the format in which a story was published – a work conceived as a novel was often also serialized, sometimes before publication as a volume (as had been customary throughout the nineteenth century), and sometimes afterwards (as was the case when publishers sought to squeeze more money from the multiple sales of a text). In addition, the charismatic text might well have been of a different genre from its sequels – a short story written for a journal might well have struck a responsive chord in its readers, who then demanded a more extensive treatment of the characters, plot, or themes, thereby encouraging the publisher and author to produce a sequel in the form of a novel. In other words, by restricting the form or number of a sequel, we ignore the material conditions in which it and the originary text were produced. Third, there need to be clear links to the originary text in terms of character, storyline, and the world created by the author. The sequel need not have all three elements, but it usually contains at least two of them. Again, this condition reflects the writing practices of the time, where writers often carried characters from one story to another and grounded the whole in an imaginative world that remained similar from sequel to sequel. The novels of Thomas Hardy, by contrast, would not be seen as sequels because, although they work within his imaginatively constructed Wessex, there is little or no continuity between characters and storylines.

I now turn to a case study of the relationship between J.B. Pinker, literary agent, and Arnold Bennett, writer, which will illustrate my definition of the sequel.

Arnold Bennett, who today is often best remembered as one of the three realist writers attacked by Virginia Woolf in her famous essay 'Mr Bennett and Mrs Brown,' was a leading figure in Edwardian letters; his route to success was closely monitored and copied by aspiring writers. He was also directly influenced by the commercialization of literature, and as such not only was acutely aware of the markets he was writing for, but also was willing to see himself as a professional author who depended on knowledge of the market for his livelihood. While Bennett did want cultural acclaim for his work – indeed, he craved acknowledgment of its artistic or aesthetic qualities – he nonetheless was practical about the need to meet market demand.

James Brand Pinker belongs to what I call the second wave of professional literary agents. A.P. Watt is generally recognized as the founder of British literary agencies, having established himself as an agent in London in the late 1870s. Pinker opened his London agency in 1896 and very rapidly established himself as a force to be reckoned with. Unlike Watt, Pinker was not part of the publishing establishment; he came from relatively humble circumstances, his formal education was not extensive, and his previous literary experience was largely in the newspaper field and then in literary journals – notably with *Black & White* and *Pearson's Magazine*. These two very different publications – the former appealed to a more literary audience and the latter to a broader public – provided him with an almost encyclopedic knowledge of the literary-journal market. Pinker's work as an editor had brought him into almost daily contact with book publishers, from whom he acquired an insider's knowledge of the material forces at work in this branch of the literary marketplace. When Pinker opened his agency, he was almost uniquely qualified to serve the needs of his clients: he understood the cultural and material forces that dominated the production of literature and he knew the inner workings of the three major outlets for literature; he was well positioned to guide writers to the appropriate publishers or editors; and he was also well qualified to advise his clients on how to establish a professional career. It was an added bonus that he seemed to have an uncanny sense of the quality of materials submitted to him; and although his formal education was inferior to that of many of his clients, his editorial suggestions frequently improved the literary quality of their work.[12]

From the beginning, Pinker exploited the full possibilities afforded by the literary marketplace. He often took the work of a so-called literary writer – someone whose work had an excess of symbolic or cultural capital and a deficiency of economic capital – and placed it in a journal with a popular audience, thereby creating a much larger market for writers who might well have failed to reach such an audience on their own. In contrast to many agents, including Watt, Pinker was willing to take on clients who were unlikely to make much money for him initially, gambling that over the long run, and with his own effort and knowledge of the market, they would succeed and he would then see his investment pay off.[13] He participated in the creation and nurturing of markets as well – assessing the works of new writers, placing them in carefully chosen periodicals or with publishers, participating in drawing up advertising campaigns, and then advising the writers on what works would capitalize on the newly developed market. By performing these services, Pinker acquired more than a substantial income; he became a powerful force in the process of literary production. His interventions on behalf of a client helped shape the market, thereby influencing the decisions made by producers of literature, writers and publishers alike. With this type of influence, it is not surprising that he often guided his clients towards the composition of sequels to successful texts.

Pinker became Arnold Bennett's literary agent in 1901.[14] Bennett had worked for a number of years as a literary journalist before turning to fiction as his primary means of earning a living in September 1898.[15] Over the course of their almost twenty-year relationship, Bennett rose to the status of the wealthiest author of his period. But he also craved, and achieved, a degree of critical acclaim, although his star has slipped in the latter half of the twentieth century.[16] His working arrangement with Pinker was also unusual, given Bennett's own interest in, and aptitude for, all business matters. The correspondence which remains as a testament to their relationship indicates that Bennett was forthright about his opinions and that he had a distinct sense of how to shape his career; nonetheless, it also reveals that he frequently bowed to Pinker's wishes. Their partnership enabled Bennett to achieve his success; without Pinker's expertise, and particularly his early financial support, Bennett may well not have risen to the heights he did.

Bennett's creation of the distinctive world of the Five Towns, or Potteries, as they are still called, and his subsequent return to it at various points during his collaboration with Pinker exemplify the ways in which cultural and material forces shape the production of sequels. Bennett's initial elaboration of this distinctive literary landscape occurs in 'an anonymous article on the Potteries ... in the 12 March 1898 issue of *Black & White*' (*Letters* 1.20), and his first major critical success – *Anna of the Five Towns* (1902) – is also his first extended fictional treatment of this world. As well as a number of novels, three subsequent volumes of short stories – *Tales of the Five Towns* (1905), *The Grim Smile of the Five Towns* (1907), and *The Mata-*

dor of the Five Towns (1912) – also explore this landscape.[17] Bennett clearly saw Anna and Tales as closely related texts, writing to Pinker in 1904, 'I regard it as very important that the book of "Five Towns" stories should appear in the autumn, because they are serious work ... What with A Great Man, Loot of Cities, & Hugo[18] the public would stand a good chance of losing sight completely of the author of Leonora.[19] This must not be ... It is Leonora & Anna which will be talked of 20 years hence' (Letters 1.49). The autumn season was generally reserved for publishing works of significant literary merit, and Bennett's insistence on publishing the short stories then, as well as his explicit linking of them with Anna through their titles, illustrates that he saw them as companion pieces. He viewed them as serious works (distinct from the light works he churned out primarily to earn immediate financial rewards) that explored the same physical and psychological landscape and also had some links in terms of common characters. The Grim Smile of the Five Towns is also envisioned in the same way: the short stories are 'artistic work, some of my best' (Letters 1.87), wrote Bennett in 1907. Again, the reference to the Five Towns alerts the reader to this volume's link to the previous work, thereby capitalizing on the existing market. He says little about the collection of stories in Matador, but he does write to Pinker about the quality of the work in the volume he proposes for Methuen in 1911: 'The principal story in the new volume would be "The Matador of the 5 Towns" ... quite as good as "Simon Fuge"'; he regarded "The Death of Simon Fuge" as 'one of the best things I have done' (Letters 1.152), so this is high praise indeed. While space constraints prevent a thorough examination of the conditions surrounding the production of these linked works, I wish to look now at how both Pinker's role in the process and the texts themselves reflect my definition of the sequel.

In Anna of the Five Towns, Bennett creates a world every bit as real as Hardy's Wessex or Dickens's London. The Five Towns were loosely fictionalized portraits of the industrialized county of Staffordshire in which he was born. He drew his landscape from the actual towns, changing only names; characters were often based on people Bennett knew personally, or at least knew about; and the social and economic subtexts accurately reflected contemporary concerns. This distinctive world becomes the focal point of much his fiction until 1915; it also fills the third criterion of my definition of a sequel – that is, that the linked works explore and develop the author's unique world. Bennett's own sense of the world he creates in Anna, 'the grim and original beauty of certain aspects of the Potteries,'[20] anticipates the reaction of critics who recognized the originality of his vision: 'The outstanding merit of the story is its intimate and not unpoetic understanding of the life of the Five Towns. [It is] a drama set under a smoke-pall, filled with portraiture of petty chapel life, and dominated by the harsh and miserly character of Ephraim Tellwright' (*Heritage* 162–3). This is the world to which Bennett returns in many of the short stories. One reviewer of *Tales of the Five Towns* expresses his sense of Bennett's unique creation when he comments, '[Bennett] has the gift of seeing how diversified are the mental and moral attributes of humanity in these parts [the Potteries] as elsewhere, and how varied and with what comprehensiveness of pain and happiness are the beatings of the human heart. He has a strong eye for local colour ... North Staffordshire has a strongly-marked individuality of its own, ... and Mr Bennett's local books sketch and develop that individuality to the life' (*Heritage* 181–2).

While the plot linkages visible in the later *Clayhanger* trilogy are not necessarily present in *Anna* and the three volumes of stories, Bennett nonetheless manages to unite them by returning again and again to various moral parables. For instance, his Five Towns are steeped in Wesleyan Methodism. 'One of [Methodism's] most puzzling features,' according to Bennett's biographer Margaret Drabble, is 'its strange combination of emotionalism, enthusiasm, even fervour, and extreme dourness and repression.'[21] It is the hypocrisy of this world which becomes the focus of Bennett's moral lessons.[22] Exposing the hypocrisy of Anna's father, Ephraim, is one of the central focuses of the novel. Bennett's increasing skill as a writer permits him to treat this topic with greater subtlety in his short stories. The sensitive and moving account of Loring's encounter with the Potteries in 'The Death of Simon Fuge'[23] brings into question, not the specific behaviour of one individual, but the underlying cultural constructs of the town. By repeating the underlying structures of the texts – social and moral lessons learned through dint of experience which transforms, or fails to transform in some cases – Bennett creates the appearance, if not the reality, of one story often told.

An unsigned review of *Anna* in *The Times Literary Supplement* sketches out the method Bennett was to return to time and again in both his novels and short stories: 'At the first page ... we make the acquaintance, just outside Sunday school, of a child who, though she has little or nothing to do with the story, should stand to the author's credit for an excellently natural little-girl study. She serves to convey us into the religious (Wesleyan-Methodistic) and social (solid manufacturing) atmosphere of the five (Staffordshire Pottery) towns, and also to introduce to each other the young man and woman round whom the love interest of the story centres' (*Her-*

itage 165). The girl here functions as both an archetypal figure – she is the 'natural little-girl' – and as an essential plot device. It is her archetypal function that is a paradigm for the recurring characters in Bennett's Five Towns texts. He does not necessarily take the same character and move him or her from one text to another, though he does this in the *Clayhanger* trilogy. Rather, he populates his works with stock characters: the miserly minister, the gossipy old women, the shopkeeper, and so on. The repetition, and I might add almost interchangeability, of these characters creates a resonance that serves to link the texts. They may have different names, but we know them when we see them pop up in yet another story.

Links of world, character, and plot, the three recurring elements in my definition of sequel, are clearly present in these works. Pinker's role in the production and marketing of these texts remains to be explored.

Bennett brought his as yet unsold *Anna* with him to Pinker's agency in January 1902.[24] Pinker assisted him in placing the text and in the sale of its American rights. This was the start of Bennett's successful exploitation of his Potteries landscape; Pinker also helped Bennett by guiding him towards markets for the short stories. This involved three distinct services: placing individual stories with appropriate periodicals, thereby expanding the market for the material; advising Bennett on when and how to issue collections of stories, thereby profiting on the primed market without oversaturating it; editing the material as it came in, thereby tailoring Bennett's work for the market Pinker had identified.

Because Bennett's output was varied in subject and style, Pinker had to use all of his contacts to find appropriate outlets. The letters Bennett wrote to Pinker reveal the effort to which the agent went in order to carry out his task. For example, Pinker helped Bennett place some of the stories which later were gathered together in *The Grim Smile*; he then negotiated with two presses – Chatto & Windus and Chapman & Hall – over the British publication of the volume, placing it with the latter on extremely good terms;[25] and then he placed individual stories from this collection in American magazines, thereby gaining Bennett three separate sales, and payments, for the stories. At the same time, each publication went to a separate market – British periodicals, British books, American periodicals – so that Pinker was all the time broadening Bennett's audience and thereby creating new markets to exploit.

One of Pinker's greatest difficulties as Bennett's representative was to convince the writer that it was important to space out the publication of his works. Bennett was prolific, claiming, 'I could take long holidays & still produce as much as you would require from me' (*Letters* 1.50). But

Pinker insisted that flooding the market with too much work would lead to a diminishing of Bennett's readership, and thus to a decline in Bennett's asking price, possibly even to the demise of his career. Bennett eventually saw Pinker's wisdom, writing, 'It is absurd to pay an expert for advice & then only to take the advice when it agrees with your own views' (*Letters* 1.50–1). Pinker's advice in this instance was to hold back *Tales* until 1905 so that Bennett did not overload the market with Five Towns stories; this strategy paid off, since the collection was sold to Chatto & Windus on favourable terms.

Finally, Pinker's editorial advice helped to shape the work Bennett produced. In 1904, Bennett wrote to Pinker: 'Shortly I am going to do some purely humorous stories with a view to magazines ... What magazines had I better keep in my mind's eye while writing? And do you prefer "Five Towns" stuff or more general stuff?' (*Letters* 1.55). Bennett often wrote to order, and he relied on Pinker to tell him what would sell. In fact, Pinker often provided detailed feedback, indicating style, plot, character, and even word changes that should be made.[26] Pinker was also involved in the packaging of Bennett's material for best effect. For example, Bennett's letter of 9 May 1903 appears to respond to a Pinker suggestion. 'I should like to do a series of stories in the vein of "Nocturne at the Majestic,"' he writes (*Letters* 1.37). Bennett had thought about writing a collection of stories in 1902, but had been unable to sell the concept to a publisher. It was Pinker's insistence that *Anna* appear first, his advice about what stories should go into *Tales*, and his persistence in convincing Bennett as to when to publish it that led to the book's appearance in 1905. Pinker was to perform this service over and over for Bennett and for his other clients. In this way he exerted considerable influence on the early twentieth-century literary marketplace.

If we rely on an overly narrow definition of the sequel, we do not get a clear picture of some of the factors that led to Arnold Bennett's success. His Five Towns stories were seen as continuations of the first immensely popular novel *Anna of the Five Towns*. In effect, the volumes of stories capitalized on both market conditions – readerly desire for more about the Potts and its inhabitants; writer's and publisher's desires to capitalize economically on an established market for anything to do with the Five Towns – and cultural capital – Bennett basked in the glowing reviews accorded *Anna* and sought to enhance his status as writer by returning again and again to the world of his first triumph. Pinker's interventions on behalf of Bennett – placing material in the right place at the right time, guiding Bennett in terms of what material to produce and how often to publish – contributed to the development and maintenance of a readership that demanded more Five Towns stories. Bennett's marginal position in English literary studies today may well be explained by the propensity of critics to overvalue what Bourdieu calls symbolic and cultural capital, which in its manifestations in critics' judgments, writers' circles, or the academy is often ahistorical, ignoring the crucial material conditions of publication. A broader definition of sequel not only more closely approximates Bennett's actual output – his novels and short stories exploited the world, characters, and plots that he had created – but also demonstrates the way in which he generated cultural and economic capital, thereby explaining his position as one of the foremost British authors in the first fifteen years of this century.

Notes

1 I find the term 'sequel' to be almost hopelessly ambiguous, given that its very definition is the subject of the essays in this volume. I am nonetheless obliged to employ the word in order to derive a usage which is workable for the type of literary production I outline in my essay. I will use the word in two ways. In the first portion of the essay, it refers to texts composed as continuations of an originary text, although I do not restrict the term to one continuation text since I find the distinction made between sequel and sequence somewhat arbitrary (despite Lynette Felber's fine argument in this volume for a subtle distinction). In the remainder of the essay, I use the word as I define it in specific relation to the publishing practices of the late nineteenth century.

2 Gerson 145, this volume, quoting Ross.

3 June Sturrock makes just this point when she writes about the fact that 'the known preferences of [Charlotte Yonge's] established readership' (102 in this volume) were taken into account when she sat down to write. Felber has commented as well on the complex nature of repetition-with-variation in sequential forms (119–21).

4 See Gerson 152–6, on Montgomery's assessment of her own situation. Sturrock says that Charlotte Yonge's 'continuing interest in her characters ... is well-documented' (102); Felber makes a similar assertion about Anthony Trollope, who, she says, 'was motivated less by the success of one particularly popular novel than by [his] desire to extend his relationship with characters he found congenial' (118).

5 Pierre Bourdieu, *The Field of Cultural Production* (New York: Columbia UP, 1993) 7.

6 Terry Castle, *Masquerade and Civilization: The Carnivalesque in Eighteenth-Century English Literature and Fiction* (Stanford: Stanford UP, 1986) 133.

7 This is clearly a simplification of a very complex issue, and my assumptions are based on a capitalistic model. It is true, however, that, by and large, the British publishing world has operated on a model of this sort at least since the mid-nineteenth century, when writing became explicitly commercialized, if not from the eighteenth century, when the transition from the old patronage system to the developing capitalist one began.

8 The later twentieth century is marked by the breakdown of author–publisher loyalty. Publishers now cannot rely on holding an author, though they may be more likely to do so in sequels of a generic kind such as mystery novels, science fiction, or romance novels.

9 Bourdieu, *Field* 40.

10 Castle, *Masquerade* 133.

11 Castle's assertion that this power derives 'from deep collective sources' (*Masquerade* 133) ignores the heterogeneity of any readership. By insisting on readerly pleasure as the source of the power, I make room for the various reasons for this pleasure that one finds in a disparate readership. We may read *Pamela* today and derive a great deal of pleasure from it, but I would argue that today's reader may well gain that pleasure for reasons different from those of an eighteenth-century reader, and that a reader in Britain may well gain that pleasure for reasons different from those of a reader in the United States, for example.

12 Pinker's relationship with Joseph Conrad is well known and is clearly revealed in their published correspondence. Pinker often edited Conrad's material, and Conrad was grateful for his input, though he sometimes ignored it: see *The Collected Letters of Joseph Conrad*, ed. Frederick R. Karl and Laurence Davies (Cambridge: Cambridge UP, 1983).

13 His client roster included James Joyce, D.H. Lawrence, and T.S. Eliot. None of them made money for Pinker, though he worked as hard for them as he did for other, more profitable clients, and the latter two parted company with Pinker after relatively short relationships. Eliot left amicably, but Lawrence's departure was marked by a series of angry letters in which the writer attacked Pinker's efforts and judgment – this was most likely the result of both Lawrence's embarrassment over Pinker's loans to him, which Lawrence apparently failed to repay, and his resentment that as a producer of literature he was unable to generate an income, while Pinker made a very good living without writing anything.

14 The earliest letter from Bennett to Pinker that James Hepburn was able to uncover is dated 5 January 1901: see *Letters of Arnold Bennett*, vol. 1, ed. James Hepburn (London: Oxford UP, 1966) 31. Subsequent citations of this source appear parenthetically in the text as *Letters* 1.

15 Bennett himself identifies this date as the moment in his life when he committed himself to writing full time: see Margaret Drabble, *Arnold Bennett* (London: Weidenfeld & Nicolson, 1974) 78.

16 Bennett has been marginalized in this century because his work did not conform to the theoretical paradigms first posited by modernists such as Virginia Woolf and subsequently adopted by the next generation of literary critics and scholars. I believe that Bennett's work merits serious reassessment, particularly in light of recent reassessments of modernism itself.

17 This group also includes the first play he had produced, *Cupid and Commonsense* (1907), which is an adaptation of *Anna*. I will not deal with it in this essay, in part because of space constraints and in part because Bennett did not hold it as one of his best works (nor did critics) and I'm particularly concerned here with tracing the double path of economic and cultural success which Bennett carved out. I am also excluding other works which are set in the Potteries – *The Old Wives' Tale* (1908), for example, and the critically and financially successful Clayhanger trilogy, *Clayhanger* (1910), *Hilda Lessways* (1911), *These Twain* (1915) – which Bennett conceived as linked

works. While many of his texts delve into the same world as the texts I look at, they were not necessarily marketed as a group. The volumes of stories, however, deliberately built on the success of the novel by using 'Five Towns' in their title. They also provide an example of cross-genre sequels.

18 These are earlier novels that do not focus on the Five Town world. Bennett saw them as potboilers, written primarily for economic reasons.

19 Bennett considered this novel to be the first of his 'literary' works. But it does not focus on the world he draws in the Five Towns stories.

20 James Hepburn, ed., *Arnold Bennett: The Critical Heritage* (London: Routledge & Kegan Paul 1981) 20. Subsequent citations of this source appear parenthetically in the text as *Heritage*.

21 Drabble, *Bennett* 13.

22 Interestingly, Bennett does not focus as much, and frequently not at all, on religious hypocrisy in his non–Five Towns works.

23 The story appears in the English edition of *A Grim Smile* and the American edition of *The Matador*.

24 See his letter to Pinker in *Letters* 1.31.

25 Bennett's royalty was 20 per cent, much more than Chatto had offered.

26 Many of Pinker's clients relied on him for such service. This brings into question the whole concept of the single author figure: with how much should we credit Pinker and how much his client in the composition of a text? However, this is a question for another time and place.

'Dragged at Anne's Chariot Wheels': L.M. Montgomery and the Sequels to *Anne of Green Gables*

CAROLE GERSON

'Elderly couple apply to orphan asylum for a boy. By mistake a girl is sent to them.'[1] As later recounted in Montgomery's revised journals, this 1895 notebook jotting eventually resulted in a 1906 manuscript that was rejected by four major American fiction publishers before being accepted by the Boston firm of L.C. Page in 1907. Issued the following year as *Anne of Green Gables*, the book soon achieved worldwide recognition as a classic novel of girlhood and adolescence. 'They took it and asked me to write a sequel to it,' Montgomery wrote in her journal:

I don't know what kind of a publisher I've got. I know absolutely nothing of the Page Co. They have given me a royalty of ten percent on the *wholesale* price, which is not generous even for a new writer, and they have bound me to give them all my books on the same terms for five years. I don't altogether like this but I was afraid to protest, lest they might not take the book, and I am so anxious to get it before the public. It will be a start, even if it is no great success. (*Journals* 1.331)

Success indeed it was. Classed as an 'overall bestseller' by Frank Mott, who states that *Anne of Green Gables* had sold between 800,000 and 900,000 copies by 1947 (312), the book had earned Montgomery over $22,000 for more than 300,000 copies by the time a bitter lawsuit resulted in the sale of her copyright to Page in 1919 (Rubio 67).

Before recounting Montgomery's long and troubled connection with her publisher and her equally problematic relationship with her most famous character, I would like to explore the implications of Page's terms by situating Montgomery at the intersection of several specific issues. These are the contested literary and cultural value of the sequel; the publication of Canadian-authored books at the turn of the century, in particular series or sequels and writing for children (two formulations which sometimes coincide); and the international commodification of children's literature in children's periodicals and series. As a case study of one author's generation of sequels, this essay enlarges upon the material conditions of literary production that are briefly described in the preceeding essays on Sarah Fielding, Charlotte Yonge, and Anthony Trollope, whose experiences with the expanding literary marketplace in turn present a historical context for L.M. Montgomery's career. The latter contrasts markedly with that of her British contemporary Arnold Bennett, outlined in Mary Ann Gillies's preceding study, for whom a deliberate and felicitous production of sequels was expertly orchestrated by his literary agent, J.B. Pinker, to bring him maximum profits. Montgomery felt trapped by a domineering, exploitive publisher into writing books about a character in whom she quickly lost interest. Yet, at the end of her life, her return to the Anne books would provide surprising solace, restoring confidence and the comfort of nostalgia to an ageing author otherwise overwhelmed by personal difficulties and the spectacle of a world marching once again towards war.

Positing that the sequel originates in a 'charismatic text' that has had 'an unusually powerful effect on a large reading public,' Terry Castle opens her discussion of *Pamela* Part Two by asserting the 'commonplace' that 'sequels are always disappointing' (133–5). The same generalization is applied more specifically to *Anne of Green Gables* in an article by Gillian Thomas that begins, 'It is a cliché of popular literature that sequels tend to be disappointing, and students of children's literature are all too sadly familiar with the decline of writers who turn themselves into human factories on the basis of a successful first book' (23). Disappointing for whom? one might ask. For the general reading public, the audience and consumers of sequels, who not only have always been eager to buy additional Anne books, but more recently have been gobbling up associated texts such as the edited volumes of Montgomery's journals and newly issued collections of her scattered magazine stories?[2] According to a recent analysis of Montgomery's readers, the sequels substantially reinforce the value of the originating book because they 'tell ... what happened later' and prolong the pleasure of inhabiting the 'alternative world' of Montgomery's fiction (Ross 30). Indeed, the very name L.M. Montgomery signals the combination of familiarity with novelty that Liane McLarty identifies in her opening discussion (this volume 204–6) as intrinsic to the resilience of sequels in many genres of popular culture. Disappointing, then, for the publishers and marketers who realize sizeable profits from such spin-off products as cookbooks, address books, birthday books, diaries, colouring books, and abridged and rewritten versions of the texts, as well as Anne dolls and girl-sized souvenir wigs with red braids? For the artists who produce and perform in television, ballet, and musical versions of Montgomery's works?[3] For the province of Prince Edward Island, and especially the residents of Charlottetown and Cavendish, whose economy benefits enormously from the tourist industry generated by the popularity of Anne in North America and Japan?[4] As if to emblematize the material value of Montgomery's book to Canada as a whole, in 1994 the Royal Canadian Mint issued a 22-karat gold coin commemorating Anne, featuring (in the words of the brochure) 'a young girl under a gazebo, daydreaming about the adventures of Anne of Green Gables.' With a face value of $200 but selling for $399.95, this was the most expensive item in the Mint's Christmas brochure – more highly priced than coins commemorating other national cultural icons.[5] Clearly, the charisma of *Anne of Green Gables* spills far beyond the notions of value constructed by the traditional literary critic, into a dense web of cultural activity that includes romance and popular culture, national identity, provincial and international economics, and social history. Full analysis of these concerns would con stitute an intriguing cultural-studies project for a collaborative interdisciplinary team; the intention of this essay is to discuss some of the earlier historical events and contexts that underpin the later commodification of L.M. Montgomery and her works.

At the turn of the century, Maud Montgomery was an unmarried woman in her late twenties, single-mindedly forging a commercially viable literary career by working her way upward from occasional newspaper poems and stories to larger commissions and serials in popular American periodicals such as *Outing* and *The Boys' World*. Trapped in the rural community of Cavendish, Prince Edward Island, as the sole caretaker of her ageing grandmother, even if she had so desired she could not have followed the route taken by Janet Royal, a secondary character in her 1925 novel *Emily Climbs*, who moves to New York to pursue a successful career as a literary journalist.[6] Nonetheless, like her Canadian-born predecessor Sara Jeannette Duncan, Montgomery well knew that 'the market for Canadian literary wares of all sorts is self-evidently New York' (Duncan 518). Although Duncan herself would later develop a substantial British readership, as would other Canadian authors with Imperial connections and concerns, such as Gilbert Parker and Stephen Leacock, her 1887 comment foretold the career orientation of the majority of ambitious Canadian authors around the turn of the century. A canny businesswoman,

Montgomery recorded in her letters her preference for selling her work to American publications as they could pay substantially better than Canadian magazines. Regardless of her personal patriotism and her subsequent difficulties with Page, she declared she 'wouldn't give [a] MS. to a Canadian firm. It is much better financially to have it published in the United States' (*Green Gables Letters* 80). Her comments on the selection of publishers to whom she first sent the manuscript of *Anne of Green Gables* demonstrate her pragmatic assessment of the publishing industry. She began with Bobbs-Merrill as a new firm just establishing its list, then 'went to the other extreme and sent it to the MacMillan Co. of New York,' then tried Lothrop, Lee and Shepard, 'a sort of "betwixt and between" firm' specializing in juvenile series (including the series of boys' books written three decades earlier by fellow Maritimer James De Mille), then approached Henry Holt, and finally turned to L.C. Page (*Journals* 1.331).

American publishers cater to American readers, whose interest in Canada has historically been rather slight. However, these limitations appear to have been less stringent around the turn of the century, when Montgomery first broke into print. According to Pierre Berton, during the period before the Great War the American film industry was fascinated with Canada: 'the country, to most Americans, was almost unknown and therefore exotic' (*Hollywood's Canada* 18). In the realm of popular fiction, the situation was more complex. First of all, virtually no Canadian authors attempting to support themselves by writing could afford to publish only in Canada, with a population (and book market) one-tenth of that of the United States. Second, prevailing market and copyright conditions prevented Canadian publishers from gaining easy access to American markets. Our grasp of the situation is hindered by the fact that co-publishing arrangements are seldom indicated on title pages, which therefore may imply that a book was solely a Canadian product when it was actually issued in arrangement with an American firm. From my archival research on a number of Canadian authors, I think it likely that during Montgomery's lifetime (1874–1942) no Canadian-authored popular series appeared that was *not* co-published in the United States. For Montgomery, one of Page's initial attractions was the firm's recent production of books by Charles G.D. Roberts and Bliss Carman (*Green Gables Letters* 52), two major Canadian literary figures of Maritime origin who successfully established visible identities in the United States – although they both had to move there in order to do so, and both would later have their own troubles with Page.

If the primary market was the United States, how appealing was fiction set in Canada? On the one hand, a number of American publishers successfully promoted Canadian-authored popular and juvenile fiction series (sometimes comprising sequels) with distinctively Canadian settings. These include James De Mille's B.O.W.C. series set in the Grand Pré area of Nova Scotia, first issued in 1869–73 and still in print with the Boston firm of Lee & Shepard in the early 1900s; Norman Duncan's Billy Topsail books (1906–16) set in a Newfoundland not yet part of Canada; Ralph Connor's Glengarry series set in rural Ontario and the West (1901–33); Scribners' twenty-three-volume edition of *The Works of Gilbert Parker* (1912–23); and, somewhat later, Mazo de la Roche's Ontario-based *Jalna* books (1927–54) and Muriel Dennison's Western 'Susannah of the Mounties' series (1936–40). On the other hand, it is known that several Canadian authors working in the market area of juvenile and popular fiction, such as Marshall Saunders for *Beautiful Joe* (1894) and Elsie Bell Gardner for her Maxie series of girls' adventure stories (1932–9), were required to change their Canadian settings to American locations in order to secure publication.[7]

While it is necessary to keep in mind the often precarious position of identifiably Canadian texts within the larger world of British and American publishing, more significant with regard to the development of Montgomery's career was the late nineteenth-century explosion in commercial publishing aimed at children, particularly through the production of series. Series production, according to Norman Feltes, expanded along with the capitalist system's mode of controlling and profiting from commodity-texts by producing both the audience (i.e., the market) and the wares purchased and consumed by that market (*Modes* 9–12). In the realm of juvenile literature, this development took place in conjunction with the rapid expansion of children's periodicals in the second half of the nineteenth century, in both Britain and the United States, many originating as Sunday-school publications. Faye Kensinger, whose *Children of the Series* documents the production of juvenile serial literature in the United States, explains that series issued under the name of the American Tract Society gave the imprimatur of respectability to the often suspect genre of fiction (19). Kensinger also reports two specific findings important for our understanding of the atmosphere into which Montgomery launched herself as an author: series aimed specifically at girls were especially likely to follow the maturation of the main character, that is, to be sequels rather than chronologically static series of vacation adventures; and series production peaked during the second decade of the twentieth century, the decade when Montgomery wrote most of the Anne books.

Our full understanding of the production of Montgomery's books is seriously hampered by the lack of surviving archival material. Lewis Page's personal and business papers seem to have vanished, as has Montgomery's correspondence with her publishers. Although she states in her journal that she is saving her business papers for her biographer, that package has since gone astray.[8]

Available evidence, however, suggests that Lewis Page was an exploitive publisher who grew increasingly difficult over the years, owing to his volatile temperament and his costly recreations of gambling and philandering, neither of which endeared him to an author who in 1911 became the wife of a Presbyterian clergyman.[9] Intersecting with this personal antagonism were conflicts stemming from the changes in practices and attitudes analysed by Norman Feltes in his two books on the evolving structure of publishing in the nineteenth and earlier twentieth centuries. While Montgomery wanted to make money, like most authors she also aspired to literary respectability and thought of herself as an artist who should control the terms of her work. Page, however, as a commercial entrepreneur, regarded her as the producer of raw material for a process of book production over which he had absolute control (Feltes, *Literary Capital* 15). From the time he established his company in 1896, his staple was juvenile series, beginning with Annie Fellows Johnston's twelve-volume Little Colonel series that eventually sold more than a million copies (Becket and Mills). In Feltes's terms, Page was a 'speculative' publisher (*Literary Capital* 18) whose acceptance of *Anne of Green Gables* was a gamble on the value of 'future texts' (25) to be produced by Montgomery. Hence, while Montgomery seemed surprised and pleased that Page requested a sequel upon his acceptance of *Anne of Green Gables*, to Page, who inevitably viewed the first Anne book as the beginning of a series, there was nothing unusual about requesting a 'second story dealing with the same character'[10] long before the originating text had been produced and tested in the market. In other words, the second Anne book, *Anne of Avonlea*, was generated not by the clamour of enchanted readers but by the current practices of market publishing (discussed as well in Gillies's essay on Bennett, this volume); the charismatic quality of *Anne of Green Gables* was not substantive to the production of its initial sequels, but rather an incidental surprise. In fact, in the spring of 1909, Page decided to delay the appearance of *Anne of Avonlea* until the following autumn to avoid competition with the unexpectedly brisk sales of *Anne of Green Gables* (*Green Gables Letters* 85). Moreover, Page's contracts did not distinguish between sequels and series; his reiterated demand for all Montgomery's books for the next five years, whatever they happened to be, indicates that he saw his product as commodity-texts, whose selling point was Montgomery's name, rather than as the ongoing story of a character named Anne.[11] This interpretation is borne out by the uniform appearance of all Montgomery's books issued by Page (*Journals* 2.134), and by his insistence on symmetrical titles.[12]

In light of the publishing structure of her era, the interesting question is whether or not Montgomery at some level expected to write a sequel to *Anne of Green Gables*: was it a text originally envisioned as closed and complete? On 10 September 1908, while she was struggling with *Anne of Avonlea*, Montgomery wrote to a friend that she agreed with reviewers of *Anne of Green Gables* that 'the ending was too conventional.' She then added, 'If I had known I was to be asked to write a second Anne book I wouldn't have "ended" it at all but just "stopped"' (*Green Gables Letters* 70–1). *Anne of Green Gables* concludes with Anne relinquishing a university scholarship in order to teach in the local school and support her beloved, aging adoptive mother. In the book's social context, this decision represents a mature choice to assume responsibility and conform to community norms with regard to both class and gender, teaching being one of the few respectable paid occupations for impecunious young women of Montgomery's own social class. Yet, deliberately or not, Montgomery left open a number of subsequent narrative possibilities. First of all, while she initially resisted the conventional closure of marriage (it takes three books to marry off Anne, as it would later take three books to marry off Emily), the reader would not likely expect Anne to remain unmarried permanently, since one would be hard put to name a contemporary female fictional character who does not eventually marry – unless she dies young. Furthermore, in Montgomery's romance world, which permits surprise legacies and other delightful turns of fortune, there is no irrevocable reason why Anne should not get a later chance at university (as transpires in *Anne of the Island*). In the meantime, her impending experiences as a teacher provide ample opportunity for Montgomery to further develop what will become her usual episodic narrative mode, composed of relatively discrete sequential stories and events unified by theme and character rather than by plot. Indeed, many earlier and contemporary authors turned the novel of adolescence into a narrative sequence on family life, beginning with Louisa May Alcott's novels and continuing with sequential series like the *What Katy Did* books by 'Susan Coolidge' (Sarah Chauncey Woolsey) and Harriet M. Lothrop's stories of the 'Five Little Peppers.' In other words, while Montgomery might not have openly acknowledged (even to herself) the possibility of writing a sequel, she had nonetheless prepared the way. Once she got started, sequels and sequences proved her natural mode, only five of her eventual twenty-two volumes of fiction being unattached narratives.[13]

In support of this interpretation, Montgomery's journals, novels and letters offer ample evidence of her familiarity with the practices of series publication outlined above. She frequently refers not only to Louisa May Alcott, whose books she knew well, but also to more ephemeral series such as the Pansy books (*Journals* 1.37) and Marietta Holley's Samantha books (*Journals* 1.282). As well, her familiarity with periodical publishing for children necessarily brought her into contact with the interconnections between the publishing of children's periodicals and the production of series of children's books (see Kensinger 16–17).

Montgomery's complex relationship with the fictional Anne Shirley is entangled with her equally complex relationship with the very real Lewis Page, thus demonstrating the impossibility of disengaging the single term 'sequel' from the complicated experiences of the people affected by sequels in real life. The picture is further complicated by the lack of surviving primary sources other than Montgomery's journals. Her biographers suggest that she shaped her life to fit the narrative of her journals (Rubio and Waterston 36). In view of her later preparation of the earlier volumes of these personal writings for public view, with ample opportunity to adjust her wording while she copied the text and added numerous photographs, I think it more probable that this professional storyteller shaped her own story retrospectively. In a sense, the journals can be seen as an ongoing sequel to her experiences and her published books. Thus, when upon first meeting Page in November 1910, she records in her revised journal 'I do not trust him' (*Journals* 2.25), we cannot know if this was her actual impression at that time or a later reinterpretation, since she recopied these portions of her original diaries in late 1920 and through 1921, while in the throes of lawsuits and countersuits with Page. According to notes from her now destroyed correspondence with John McClelland, it was only in early 1916 that she began seriously to doubt Page: 'Three months ago, I had no real distrust of Mr Page in any way. Since then I have heard so much against him and his methods from different quarters that I am distrustful; but the fact of his threatening me with "the courts" is the one thing that has really turned my former loyalty into suspicion.'[14] Similarly, we cannot know whether the quotation that opens this essay represents her actual thoughts in August 1907, or if her words have been recast as the beginning of a rather gothic tale about an innocent female writer's struggle to escape the magnetism and power of a wily publisher determined to extract sequels from her for the rest of her days. Certainly her letter to Ephraim Weber of 2 May 1907, announcing the acceptance of *Anne of Green Gables*, is less apprehensive. Here she describes Page as 'a good company' that 'has published several successful books by well-known authors, including Charles G.D. Roberts and Bliss Carman.' She mentions nothing about her stingy royalty agreement, and although a little uneasy about being committed for the next five years, she takes the binding clause as 'rather complimentary' (*Green Gables Letters* 52).

When Montgomery commenced her second Anne book, her journals describe how her initial pleasure in returning to her fictional character – '*Anne* is as real to me as if I had given her birth – as real and as dear' (*Journals* 1.332) – soon yielded to frustration: 'My publishers are hurrying me now for the sequel. I'm working at it but will not make it as good as *Green Gables*. It doesn't *come* as easily. I have to force it' (*Journals* 1.336). In Montgomery's case, the disappointment supposedly generated by sequels includes the plight of the author, now fearing she is 'to be dragged at Anne's chariot wheels the rest of my life' (*Green Gables Letters* 74). Trapped in Lewis Page's ongoing binding contracts, she produced *Anne of Avonlea* (1909), *Chronicles of Avonlea* (1912), and *Anne of the Island* (1915), as well as three unrelated books: *Kilmeny of the Orchard* (1910), *The Story Girl* (1911), and *The Golden Road* (1912). Her journal records that in September 1913, 'I began work on a third "Anne" book. I did not want to do it. But Page gave me no peace and every week brought a letter from some reader pleading "for another Anne book." So I have yielded for peace sake. It's like marrying a man to get rid of him' (*Journals* 2.133).

This troubling, ironic image (suggesting a dynamic that we now associate with battered-wife syndrome) adumbrates the gendered subtext of Montgomery's narrated relationship with Page, in which her gratitude to him for having launched her career conflicted with her anger at the knowledge that his royalty arrangements paid her less than half of what she should have received (*Journals* 2.171). After signing two contracts promising him all her books for the next five years, she determined to break what threatened to become an eternal commitment. But in November 1910, Page cunningly invited her to Boston for a fortnight, during which visit he wined and dined her so graciously that, as his guest, despite her 'disgust' with the 'binding clause' (*Journals* 2.25), she once again signed away her books for the next five years.

This would, however, be the last such contract. Montgomery does not seem to have considered seeking professional assistance until 1916, when she joined the Authors' League of America. That year she gained some control over her lucrative Anne sequels by selecting John McClelland as her Canadian publisher and literary agent, to whom she assigned the task of negotiating a better deal with an American firm. Out of good will, she insisted on giving first refusal to Page, who instead responded aggressively, with a threat to sue for the rights to *Anne's House of Dreams*. When McClelland concluded an agreement with Frederick Stokes for the American publication of Montgomery's books, there ensued a legal war with Lewis Page and his brother George, paralleling in intensity the narrative of the First World War that dominates her journal at this time. Further complicating the picture was her view that 'the Page firm are the best bookmakers in America. Everybody admits that' (*Journals* 2.188) – a detail that would explain why Page seemed to thrive, despite the complaints of booksellers (*Journals* 2.176), authors (*Journals* 2.188, 193), and former employees (*Journals* 2.182). Montgomery's suit against Page for unpaid royalties (*Journals* 2.284) ended with his firm buying out the rights to her earlier books for $18,000 – 'nothing like the value of my books,' she fumed. 'But with a pair of scoundrels like the Pages, a bird in the hand is worth half a dozen in the bush' (*Journals* 2.285). Page then countered with the unauthorized publication of the only known text that could be described as a 'false sequel' to *Anne*. *Further Chronicles of Avonlea*, cobbled together in Page's office from discards from *Chronicles of Avonlea*, was manufactured uniformly with the earlier *Anne* books. Montgomery sued again, he threatened countersuits, and then dealt the greatest blow of all by selling the film rights to *Anne of Green Gables* for $40,000.

Montgomery's disputatious relationship with Page placed her in good company, insofar as his dealings with other Canadian authors can be determined. In 1908, Charles G.D. Roberts complained bitterly that Page had 'acted abominably' by attempting to force him into 'new & disadvantageous contracts' and later had great difficulty reclaiming rights to poems that had been published by Page. Bliss Carman ran into similar copyright altercations, as did John Garvin when compiling *Canadian Poems of the Great War* (1918).[15] The experiences of Marshall Saunders, author of the best-selling *Beautiful Joe* and other turn-of-the-century animal stories, corroborated Montgomery's view that 'the man must simply have an obsession of dishonesty' (*Journals* 2.313).

For Montgomery, extricating herself from Page did not, however, mean extricating herself from Anne. She seems never to have contemplated the irrevocable step of killing off her star character, in imitation of Shakespeare's and Marlowe's resolutions of their conflicts with their heroes.[16]

Anne's House of Dreams (1917), the first Anne book issued under her new terms with McClelland and Stokes, was followed by *Rainbow Valley* (1919) and *Rilla of Ingleside* (1921). Indeed, it was the continuing appeal of the Anne books that produced terms with Stokes so good that, she wrote, they 'rather frighten me. Can I continue to write up to them? I am always haunted by the fear that I shall find myself "written out"' (*Journals* 2.198). Upon completing *Rainbow Valley* she complained, 'I want to do something different. But my publishers keep me at this sort of stuff because it sells and because they claim the public, having become used to this from my pen, would not tolerate a change' (*Journals* 2.278). Finally, in August 1920, she declared, 'To-day I wrote the last chapter of "Rilla of Ingleside." I don't like the title. It is the choice of my publishers ... The book is fairly good. It is the last of the *Anne* series. I am done with *Anne* forever – I swear it as a dark and deadly vow' (*Journals* 2.390).

Montgomery may have been done with Anne, but Anne was scarcely done with Montgomery. Still to come were *Anne of Windy Poplars* (1936) and *Anne of Ingleside* (1939), as well as a manuscript of previously written stories linked by Anne, 'The Blythes are Quoted,' which was eventually edited by Montgomery's son and issued posthumously as *The Road to Yesterday* (1974). The production of these last books presents a poignant conclusion to the story of Montgomery's sequels.

The first six Anne books form a classic *Bildungsroman* sequence, following the major character through girlhood to maturity as the captivating, iconoclastic child fades into a sedate doctor's wife. Once married, Anne slips to the margins of her books, becoming incidental to the major story – a point discussed by Gillian Thomas. Displaced as the centre of interest by her children and assorted members of the community, she presides over her household as the idealized good mother (reminiscent of Alcott's Marmee) that Montgomery, orphaned at the age of two, missed in her own life and proved unable to enact with her own children. Despite her complaints about the expectations of her publishers and public, the continued production of Anne books allowed Montgomery to have her cake and eat it too: to profit from the insatiable market for Anne books while using them as an opportunity to tell other stories, such as the experiences of women and children less fortunate than Anne,[17] as well as to depict daily life on the home front during the First World War through the maturation of Anne's youngest daughter in *Rilla of Ingleside*.[18] In Lynette Felber's terms in the preceding essay in this volume, this shift from Anne as centre to Anne as frame can be described as an evolution from the sequel to the sequence novel, a shift most clearly manifested in the way the last two books disrupt the chronology, returning to the happiest periods of Anne's life: as a teacher before her marriage, and then as a busy, satisfied young mother. Because the previous texts had not presented a continuous narrative, but, rather, discrete portions of Anne's story, there were chronological gaps into which Montgomery could later insert new texts. Thus the last books, set around the beginning of the twentieth century, coincide chronologically with Montgomery's own halcyon years, before the upheavals of the First World War, lawsuits, the 1919 death of her best friend, and the onset of her husband's mental illness.

Montgomery's decision to write again about Anne in these last two books derives from many factors: her economic precariousness brought on by the Depression, the purchase of a new home, and a switch in her English publisher (from Hodder and Stoughton to Harrap); her publishers' and readers' continuing requests for more Anne books; and, above all, the popular success of the 1934 talking-film version of *Anne of Green Gables*. An avid movie-goer, Montgomery enjoyed the film despite its altered ending, and although she found little connection between what she saw on the screen and her own notion of her characters.

In March 1935, ill, and depressed as a result of difficulties with her husband and sons, Montgomery approached her return to the world of Anne with mixed feelings. She was at a transition point in her own life, planning to move to Toronto after having resided in the manses of two small Ontario towns (Leaskdale, then Norval) following her 1911 marriage to the Reverend Ewan Macdonald. On the one hand, she wondered if she would be able to '"get back into the past" far enough to do a good book'; on the other, she found the work therapeutic: 'I had a strange feeling when I sat down to my work. Some interest seemed to return to life. The discovery that I may still be able to work heartens me, so often lately I have been afraid I never could again.'[19] The writing of a chapter of *Anne of Windy Poplars*, she recorded six months later, 'seemed like escaping back into the past. I am feeling so much better – have begun to sleep normally again.'[20] Similar dynamics, intensified by her ever-increasing distress at the deterioration of her husband's condition, of her own health, and of the European political situation, accompanied the composition of her last Anne book three years later. At the age of sixty-three, less than four years before her death, she wrote:

On this cool dark and muggy day I sat me down and began to write 'Anne of Ingleside.' It is a year and nine months since I wrote a single line of creative work. But I can *still* write. I wrote a chapter. A burden rolled from my spirit. And I was suddenly *back in my own world* with all my dear Avonlea and S ... [Summerside] friends again. It was like going home.[21]

Sequels were a determining factor in Montgomery's literary and personal life, producing the launch of her first book and her financial well-being, as well as decades of bitter dispute with her publisher and a problematic relationship with an intrusive, adoring readership. In her last years, sequels provided a refuge from an increasingly troubled world; they had ceased to be disappointing, even for their author. For her publishers and other beneficiaries of the Anne industry, the sequels and spin-offs of *Anne of Green Gables* continue to produce tremendous profits. And for her public, who today still eagerly welcome every new text written by or associated with Montgomery, there can never be enough of Anne.

Notes

I would like to thank Professor Mary Rubio of the English Department at the University of Guelph for sharing some of her research materials on L.M. Montgomery; and both Dr Rubio and Nancy Sadek, former Head of Archival and Special Collections at the University of Guelph Library, for facilitating my access to Montgomery's unpublished journals. Anne Goddard at the National Archives of Canada, and Carl Spadoni and Renu Barrett at the Wilson Ready Division of Archives and Research Collections, McMaster University, provided valuable assistance with material relating to the publishing history of the *Anne* books. An early version of this essay was presented at the third annual conference of SHARP (Society for the History of Authorship, Reading and Publishing) in Edinburgh, in July 1995. A somewhat different version appears in the *Papers of the Bibliographical Society of Canada* 35.2 (Fall 1997).

1 Mary Rubio and Elizabeth Waterston, eds., *The Selected Journals of L.M. Montgomery, Volume 1 (1889–1910); Volume 2 (1910–1921); Volume 3 (1921–1929)* (Toronto: Oxford UP, 1985, 1987, 1992) 1.330. Text citations of this source are identified as *Journals*, followed by volume and page numbers.
2 These are (to date) *The Doctor's Sweetheart and Other Stories*, ed. Catherine McLay (Toronto: McGraw, 1979), and *Akin to Anne* (1988), *Along the Shore* (1989), *Among the Shadows* (1990), *After Many Days: Tales of Times Past* (1991), *Against the Odds: Tales of Achievement* (1993), *At the Altar: Matrimonial Tales* (1994), *Across the Miles: Tales of Correspondence* (1995), *Christmas with Anne and Other Holiday Stories* (1995), all edited by Rea Wilmshurst and published in Toronto by McClelland & Stewart.
3 Mavis Reimer claims that a ballet version of *Anne of Green Gables* is regularly performed at Christmas in her home town (2). The musical version is a ritual component of the Charlottetown Festival held every summer in Prince Edward Island. For a discussion of the televised version, see Susan Drain, '"Too Much Love-making": *Anne of Green Gables* on Television,' *The Lion and the Unicorn* 11.2 (1987): 63–72. Another spin-off is critiqued by Virginia Careless in 'The Hijacking of Anne,' *Canadian Children's Literature* 67 (1992): 48–56.

4 See Douglas Baldwin, 'L.M. Montgomery's *Anne of Green Gables*: The Japanese Connection,' *Journal of Canadian Studies* 28.3 (1993): 123–33; Diane Tye, 'Mutiple Meanings Called Cavendish: The Interaction of Tourism with Traditional Culture,' *Journal of Canadian Studies* 29.1 (1994): 122–34; Calvin Trillin, 'Anne of Red Hair: What Do the Japanese see in *Anne of Green Gables*?' *New Yorker*, 5 August 1996: 56–61.

5 Other items included the last RCMP Northern Dog Team Patrol (silver dollar priced at $17.95 or $24.50, depending upon the case), the National War Memorial (proof loonie priced at $16.95), and the Home Front during the Second World War ($100 gold coin priced at $249.95).

6 See Carole Gerson, 'Canadian Women Writers and American Markets, 1880–1940,' *Context North America: Canadian/U.S. Literary Relations*, ed. Camille La Bossière (Ottawa: U of Ottawa P, 1994) 106–18.

7 Through the 1930s to the 1960s, serious writers such as Morley Callaghan and Hugh MacLennan constantly wrestled with the problem of Canada's viability as an internationally recognizable setting for fiction. Because it sought an American readership, Sinclair Ross's classic novel of Depression life on the prairies, *As For Me and My House* (1941), contains nothing to identify the setting as Canadian.

8 Personal communication from Mary Rubio, Montgomery's current biographer, 13 September 1995. In 1986 the National Archives of Canada acquired eight contracts between Montgomery and L.C. Page as well as a 1919 memorandum concerning their lawsuit (MG 30 D 342). All that survives of McClelland & Stewart's dealings with Montgomery are several pages of notes at McMaster University, taken by George Parker from records that were subsequently destroyed.

9 There is very little information available about Page, other than the entry by Margaret Becket and Theodora Mills in volume 49 of the *Dictionary of Literary Biography*. I would like to thank Sid Huttner at the University of Tulsa for his assistance with references to Page. Montgomery's published journals refer many times to Page's gambling and philandering (e.g., *Journals* 2.117, 226).

10 L.C. Page & Company to Miss L.M. Montgomery, 8 April 1907. This is the only letter from Page in the Montgomery papers at the University of Guelph.

11 Another of his projects that involved Canadian authors was his 'Little Cousin' series of school texts that included contributions by Jane Roberts MacDonald (*Our Little Canadian Cousin 1. The Maritime Provinces*, 1904), Mary Solace Saxe (*Our Little Quebec Cousin*, 1919), and Emily Murphy (*Our Little Canadian Cousin of the Great Northwest*, 1923).

12 Montgomery wanted the second book to be *The Later Adventures of Anne*, not *Anne of Avonlea* (*Green Gables Letters* 85) and disliked the title *Anne of the Island* (*Journals* 2.163). The titles of *Kilmeny of the Orchard* (*Journals* 2.362) and *Chronicles of Avonlea* were also Page's creation, the latter, in Montgomery's view, a 'somewhat delusive title' (*Journals* 2.94). *Further Chronicles of Avonlea* (1920), the unauthorized collection issued by Page, was presented as an Anne book (*Journals* 2.376). The maturity of the red-headed young woman appearing as the cover portrait on all the Anne books predicts the direction of the series.

13 The independent books are *Kilmeny of the Orchard*, *The Blue Castle*, *Magic for Marigold*, *A Tangled Web*, and *Jane of Lantern Hill*. However, it should also be noted that none of her other sequences trailed on as did the Anne books. Rather, she limited them to pairs (*The Story Girl* and *The Golden Road*; *Pat of Silver Bush* and *Mistress Pat*), and then a trilogy (*Emily of New Moon*, *Emily Climbs*, *Emily's Quest*).

14 George Parker's notes on Montgomery's files with McClelland & Stewart, McMaster University, quotation from letter of 29 April 1916.

15 See Laurel Boone, ed., *The Collected Letters of Charles G.D. Roberts* (Fredericton, NB: Goose Lane, 1989) 287, 380, 450, 589, 600, 606; Muriel Miller, *Bliss Carman: Quest & Revolt* (St John's: Jesperson, 1985) 206, 254; Arthur Stringer to John Garvin, 1 December [no year], Queen's University Archives, Lorne Pierce Collection, A.ARCH 2001b B032 F007 I13. Arthur Stringer's correspondence with literary agent Paul Reynolds refers to yet another dispute with Page, eliciting from Reynolds the comment that Page 'is a smart, shrewd fellow but he will bear watching': Reynolds to Arthur Stringer, 30 March 1905, Paul R. Reynolds papers, Box 166, Butler Library, Columbia University. Thanks to Clarence Karr, Malaspina University College, for the Stringer references.
16 That is, according to Andrew Leggatt's analysis earlier in this volume.
17 See Gillian Thomas, 'The Decline of Anne: Matron vs. Child'; Mary Rubio, 'Subverting the Trite, L.M. Montgomery's Room of Her Own,' *Canadian Children's Literature* 65 (1992): 6–39; Jennie Rubio, '"Strewn with Dead Bodies": Women and Gossip in *Anne of Ingleside*,' *Harvesting Thistles: The Textual Garden of L.M. Montgomery*, ed. Mary Rubio (Guelph, ON: Canadian Children's Press, 1994) 167–77.
18 See Alan R. Young, 'L.M. Montgomery's *Rilla of Ingleside* (1920): Romance and the Experience of War,' *Myth and Milieu: Atlantic Literature and Culture, 1918–39*, ed. Gwendolyn Davies (Fredericton: Acadiensis, 1993) 95–122.
19 Journals of L.M. Montgomery, 9 March 1935, XZ5 MS A001, vol. 9, L.M. Montgomery Collection, University of Guelph Library.
20 Journals of L.M. Montgomery, 9 November 1935.
21 Journals of L.M. Montgomery, 12 September 1938.

Works Cited

Becket, Margaret, and Theodora Mills, 'L.C. Page and Company.' *Dictionary of Literary Biography*. Vol. 49 (1986). 349–51.

Berton, Pierre. *Hollywood's Canada: The Americanization of Our National Image*. Toronto: McClelland & Stewart, 1975.

Castle, Terry. *Masquerade and Civilization: The Carnivalesque in Eighteenth-Century Culture and Fiction*. Stanford: Stanford UP, 1986.

Duncan, Sara Jeannette. 'American Influence on Canadian Thought.' *The Week* 7 July 1887: 518.

Feltes, Norman. *Literary Capital and the Late Victorian Novel*. Madison: U of Wisconsin P, 1993.

– *Modes of Production of Victorian Fiction*. Chicago: U of Chicago P, 1986.

Kensinger, Faye. *Children of the Series and How They Grew*. Bowling Green, OH: Bowling Green State U Popular Press, 1987.

Montgomery, L.M. *The Green Gables Letters*. Ed. Wilfrid Eggleston. Toronto: Ryerson, 1960.

– *The Selected Journals of L.M. Montgomery. Volume 1 (1889–1910); Volume 2 (1910–1921); Volume 3 (1921–1929)*. Ed. Mary Rubio and Elizabeth Waterston. Toronto: Oxford UP, 1985, 1987, 1992.

– Unpublished journals, 1929–42. L.M. Montgomery papers, University of Guelph Archives.

Mott, Frank. *Golden Multitudes*. New York: Bowker, 1947.

Reimer, Mavis. *Such a Simple Little Tale: Critical Responses to L.M. Montgomery's Anne of Green Gables*. Metuchen, NJ, and London: Children's Literature Association and Scarecrow Press, 1992.

Ross, Catherine Sheldrake. 'Readers Reading L.M. Montgomery.' *Harvesting Thistles: The Textual Garden of L.M. Montgomery*. Ed. Mary Rubio. Guelph, ON: Canadian Children's Press 1994. 23–35.

Rubio, Mary. 'The Architect of Adolescence.' Reimer 65–82.

Rubio, Mary, and Waterston, Elizabeth. *Writing a Life: L.M. Montgomery*. Toronto: ECW Press, 1995.

Thomas, Gillian. 'The Decline of Anne: Matron vs. Child.' Reimer 23–8.

Donald Barthelme and the Postmodern Sequel

MICHAEL ZEITLIN

The Idea of the Postmodern Sequel

As both material object and analytical concept, 'the sequel' invokes the image of a two-part narrative structure governed by conventional rules and expectations. Where there is a sequel there is a before and an after, an original story and its extension, a part one neatly if not always symmetrically divided from a part two. As one takes up the sequel, gathering up familiar causes and characters in order to unite them with their promised ends, one experiences narrative as nostalgic even as it anticipates its own inevitable progress towards a conclusion. Arriving at the sequel's last sentence, one generally looks back upon a single, self-sufficient fictional world, the borders between two discrete though contiguous books having been virtually dissolved. To be sure, the essays in this volume show that the structure involving a primary text and its sequel is anything but 'simple'; indeed, it can be remarkably complex and unstable at times. And yet, in the final analysis, the logic of the relations between 'part one' and 'part two' is generally visible enough to be mapped with reasonable confidence.

In what follows I want to inquire into the possible value for literary analysis of the idea of the *postmodern* sequel, in which one might expect to encounter a subversion or complication of the narrative structure outlined above. There is perhaps no better place to look for a palpably postmodern sequel than among the unruly narrative fictions of Donald Barthelme (1931–1988), in which narrative codes and readerly expectations are routinely flouted.[1] Accordingly, I will explore the value of reading Barthelme's most important work, *The Dead Father*, as the refractive postmodern sequel of some of the foundational narratives of Freudian psychoanalysis, as published in such texts as *Totem and Taboo* (1912–13) and *The Interpretation of Dreams* (1900).

First, however, it will be necessary to clear some theoretical space for the idea of the postmodern sequel, by which I do not mean what might equally be designated by the term – namely, those books which are labelled, published, and read *as sequels* within our postmodern culture. Such books are primarily residual cultural productions insofar as they repeat, with little essential variation or revision, the narrative conventions of a traditional aesthetic.[2] Instead I wish to move beyond strict generic definitions in the direction of a more broadly conceived intertextuality. A postmodern sequel, in this sense, would be any narrative which extends, revises, or redoubles the already-written, doing so, however, as much to complicate and undermine as to reaffirm and reify the principles of narrative continuity, causality, and tradition. Postmodern sequels tend less to follow, serve, and continue than to select, incorporate, and transform their precursor texts, subjecting them in the process to more or less radical programs of fragmentation, distortion, and rearrangement.

In this sense, the intertextual version of the postmodern sequel also contains a strong residual element insofar as it self-consciously recalls, in order to resist or extend, a genealogy of paradigm shifts traceable to a series of modernist repercussions: 'Freud and Einstein and two world wars and the Russian and sexual revolutions and automobiles and airplanes and telephones and radios and movies and urbanization, and now nuclear weaponry and television and microchip technology and the new feminism and the rest, and except as readers there's no going back to Tolstoy and Dickens.'[3] John Barth's inventory of nineteenth-century formal and ideological values which were subverted or exploded by modernism includes 'linearity, rationality, consciousness, cause and effect, naive illusionism, transparent language, innocent anecdote, and middle-class moral conventions.'[4] Modernism's rejection of those things as 'obsolete notions, or metaphors for obsolete notions'[5] entailed its experimental exploration of the 'contraries of those things': 'Disjunction, simultaneity, irrationalism, anti-illusionism, self-reflexiveness, medium-as-message, political olympianism, and a moral pluralism approaching moral entropy ...'[6] For Jean-François Lyotard, 'modernity, in whatever age it appears, cannot exist without a shattering of belief and without discovery of the "lack of reality" of reality, together with the invention of other realities.'[7] In the modernist attempt to invent more 'real' realities, the very idea of orderly sequence – of beginnings, middles, and ends – could not be expected to survive untransformed.

Nor, accordingly, could the idea of the literary sequel: seen through a (post)modern sensibility, the original or source text – held to constitute the basis of its sequel – readily reveals itself as nothing but the sequel of another prior text, which is itself the shadow or echo of ones prior still. Within this bottomless hierarchy of texts (eventually to be reimagined as an intertextual hyperspace, borderless, sourceless, and unmappable),[8] it is often impossible to tell which end is up: a text conventionally defined as a 'sequel' can work a transformative effect upon its precursor, which thereby becomes derivative, secondary, subsequent. As T.S. Eliot observed in a famous essay, 'what happens when a new work of art is created is something that happens simultaneously to all the works of art which preceded it ... [one] will not find it preposterous that the past should be altered by the present as much as the present is directed by the past.'[9] In the psychoanalytic view of temporality, 'consciousness constitutes its own past, constantly subjecting its meaning to revision in conformity with its "project" ... [T]he subject revises past events at a later date and ... it is this revision which invests them with significance ...'[10] This concept of 'deferred action' radically revises any conventional sense of a linear temporality and determinism capable of 'envisaging nothing but the action of the past [i.e., the earlier text] upon the present [i.e., the later or sequel text].'[11] For Harold Bloom, the uncanny effects of temporal circularity and reversibility are to be enjoyed aesthetically: 'In the exquisite squalors of Tennyson's *The Holy Grail*, as Percival rides out on his ruinous quest, we can experience the hallucination of believing that the Laureate is overly influenced by *The Waste Land*, for Eliot too became a master at reversing the *apophrades* [the return of the dead].'[12] By the time we get to Slavoj Žižek, hallucination yields to deadpan empirical demonstration: '*Richard II* proves beyond any doubt that Shakespeare had read Lacan ...'[13]

Especially vulnerable to (post)modern modes of destabilization and reinvention, then, are the 'already-given' orders of history, chronology, and causality, the apparently commonsensical and natural relation of past to present, primary to secondary, before to after. At the same time, any transgression against the stability of such relations remains remarkably 'dependent on the[ir] persistence ... as a figure depends upon the ground against which it defines itself.'[14] Upon these terms, the reader begins, inevitably, by acknowledging the historical fact of a text's having been written and published earlier or later than another in order to set up an initial pairing of texts, one as the primary text, the other as the sequel. In the imaginative flux of reading, or criticism, or fantasy, however, that fact and that positionality can very easily lose their once privileged status. The text we place (or which finds itself) in the antecedent position inevitably becomes the 'primary' text simply because the 'secondary' text, by definition, may be read as, in some sense, its reflection, repetition, or extension. Seen in this way, the primary/sequel structure is one to be manipulated and shuffled by a reader for whom the question of the relation between the primary and the secondary reduces itself to the mobility of shifting perspectives or the unruly operations of imaginary response.[15]

If readers can manipulate texts, shuffle their positions, forget or confuse chronological and narrative orders, then writing itself, as embodied in published texts and as inseparable from the idea of the author, resists such anti-chronological and distorting effects insofar as it asserts a metaphorical shape, a narrative purpose, and a generic structure, all of which imply the historicity and historical 'positionality' of writing. In one important sense, texts and authors locate themselves with respect to the history of narrative as much as they are located by critics in narratives of literary history. Texts and authors can be seen as adopting (voluntarily or involuntarily) certain affective attitudes towards the past, announcing their affiliations, selecting their burdens of narrative memory. The postmodern text may be linked to earlier texts by complex patterns of influence and emulation, borrowing and 'theft,' imitation and resistance, rereading and rewriting, and sometimes playful and sometimes polemical forms of 'dialogue ... parody ... contestation.'[16]

All of these possible stances, as well as others as yet uncatalogued, may be placed under the sign of 'belatedness,' a term commonly used to denote the predominating affective condition of the postmodern artist. For the early Roland Barthes, the postmodern writer proceeds from a more or less unhappy awareness (one which defines narrative's own unfolding condition) that 'writing still remains full of the recollection of previous usage.'[17] Writing, in this sense, is always a 'compromise between freedom and remembrance' (*Writing Degree Zero* 17), enmeshed as it is in a 'network of set forms [which] hem in more and more the pristine freshness of discourse' (78). The scene of writing is never played out on a blank page but on the palimpsest of the already-written, whether the 'whole previous geology of the novel' (85) or the History of Literature itself: 'History puts in [the writer's] hands a decorative and compromising instrument, a writing inherited from a previous and different History, for which he is not responsible and yet which is the only one he can use. Thus is born a tragic element in writing, since the conscious writer must henceforth fight against ancestral and all-powerful signs which, from the depths of a past foreign to him, impose Literature on him like some ritual, not like a reconciliation' (86).

Along similar lines, for Lyotard, postmodern artists 'must question the rules of the art of painting or of narrative as they have learned and received them from their predecessors. Soon those rules must appear to them as a means to deceive, to seduce, and to reassure, which makes it impossible for them to be "true."'[18] In an effort to be modern, original, new, and 'true,' postmodern art must also proceed, paradoxically, in a polemical (that is to say, a retrospective) direction:

What, then, is the postmodern? What place does it or does it not occupy in the vertiginous work of the questions hurled at the rules of image and narration? It is undoubtedly a part of the modern. All that has been received, if only yesterday ... must be suspected. What space does Cézanne challenge? The Impressionists'. What object do Picasso and Braque attack? Cézanne's. What presupposition does Duchamp break with in 1912? That which says one must make a painting, be it cubist ... In an amazing acceleration, the generations precipitate themselves. A work can become modern only if it is first postmodern. Postmodernism thus understood is not modernism at its end but in the nascent state, and this state is constant.[19]

If postmodernism is fated to be poised on the verge of a perpetually nascent modernism, equally it cannot escape an acute self-consciousness of its genealogical indebtedness to an older modernism that refuses to die. For the hyper-aware postmodern artist, then, the history of art is always in some sense primary material; it is 'always already there' as much to 'produce effects as set limits to choice' (*Writing Degree Zero* 2). If choice is to be limited, all the more reason for the postmodern artist to attempt to transform the scene of resentment and constraint into the scene of identification and self-assertion. As Donald Barthelme has put it, '[e]very artist is the product of a (theoretically infinite) number of predecessors; reversing the usual fathering procedure, these are chosen by the artist, consciously or through the texture of the skin.'[20] Or, in other terms, '[a]ny work of art depends upon a complex series of interdependences.'[21] It is the proper task of the literary historian to attempt to analyse and adumbrate such genealogical complexities.

Barthelme's *The Dead Father*

Will I, nill I, the ineffable thing has tied me to him; tows me with a cable I have no knife to cut. Horrible old man! ... Oh! I plainly see my miserable office, – to obey, rebelling; and worse yet, to hate with touch of pity!
Starbuck, in Melville's *Moby-Dick*

Shall we never, never get rid of this Past? ... It lies upon the Present like a giant's

dead body! In fact, the case is just as if a young giant were compelled to waste all his strength in carrying about the corpse of the old giant, his grandfather, who died a long while ago, and only needs to be decently buried.
Holgrave, in Hawthorne's *The House of the Seven Gables*

These many individuals eventually banded themselves together, killed him and cut him in pieces.
Freud, *Group Psychology and the Analysis of the Ego*

... he was conscious that he had a deep vow unredeemed, and that an unburied corpse was calling to him, out of the wilderness.
Hawthorne, 'Roger Malvin's Burial'

Fredric Jameson has observed that postmodern intellectual activity often implies the 'new work ... of rewriting all the familiar things in new terms and thus proposing modifications, new ideal perspectives, a reshuffling of canonical feelings and values.'[22] The fiction of Donald Barthelme is deeply engaged in this new work of revision, recombination, and retranslation of major (and minor) aspects of the Western literary tradition.[23] Throughout this revisionary project, Freudian psychoanalysis – as a mode of thinking, as a system of ideas, as a complex of narratives – is the necessary medium and context for Barthelme's 'deferred action' upon 'the tradition.' In other words, for Barthelme (whom I take to be exemplary and representative in important ways), postmodern must also mean post-Freudian, and from a post-Freudian perspective there can be no such thing as a pre-Freudian text. The narratives of classical psychoanalysis must act as refracting mirrors, breaking up the integrity of the traditional or the received or the mythological narrative in order to expose an 'inmost' configuration or mobilize a latent logic now decipherable in postmodern terms. If psychoanalysis takes the form in Barthelme's text of a kind of oneiric dynamism, it also governs the ways in which primary loads of narrative material – content, plot, dramatic structure, scene, character – are absorbed into the overdetermined text. An approach to Barthelme's fiction through psychoanalysis, then, promises to shed light on the tone, characteristics, and operative principles of what I have been calling the postmodern sequel.

Freud

As both 'an author of texts' and a 'founder of discursivity' – to deploy the suggestive formulations of Michel Foucault in 'What Is an Author?' – Freud can be seen as 'open[ing] the way for a certain number of resemblances and analogies which have their model or principle in [his] work' even as Freud produces 'the possibilities and the rules for the formation of other texts,' establishing 'an endless possibility of discourse.'[24] Unmistakably, it is Freud in both these 'author functions' whose effects warp the surface even as they structure 'the depths' of Barthelme's major work, *The Dead Father*. In this text a band of 'sons' (or what Freud would call 'a tumultuous mob of brothers')[25] are dragging the Dead Father, who is attached to a cable, across a barren, elemental, and always patently textual landscape. In a manner that we have come to associate with the dynamic operations and fragmentary texture of the Freudian dreamwork, however, the achievement of linear progress is radically disrupted by sudden leaps, bizarre juxtapositions, unintelligible conversations, metafictional antics, typographical pranks. The Barthelme text is analogous, in this sense, to that 'censored political newspaper' that Freud referred to in the *Introductory Lectures* in order to illustrate the fragmentary texture of the dream. With its 'circumlocutions and obscurities,' blanks, gaps, and distortions – the traces, bearing the mark of the censor, of absent phrases – Barthelme's narrative gives us only a parody of intelligible discourse even as it works aggressively to sabotage any drift towards sustained, everyday coherence.[26] In accordance, moreover, with the ruling dreamwork analogy by which Barthelme's text unfolds, the disruption of surfaces and the subversion of coherence signal the presence of a psychic tangle of forces identifiable in classical psychoanalytic terms: the 'indestructible wish,' the backlash of guilt and repression, the activation of 'condensation and displacement' in order to bring about an 'evasion of the censorship,' the mobilization, in turn, of even more determined forces of 'purposive forgetting,' and so on.[27]

In *The Dead Father*, structured as it is upon an extended oxymoron, the forces of censorship and the purposes of amnesia are inseparably fused with 'the repressed contents of the unconscious' themselves.[28] Yes, the Dead Father is dead, but somehow he has recrossed the threshold:

The living did not feel safe from the attacks of the dead till there was a sheet of water between them. That is why men liked to bury the dead on islands or on the farther side of the rivers ... [T]hey are *afraid* of the presence or of the return of the dead person's ghost; and they perform a great number of ceremonies to keep him at a distance or drive him off. They feel that to utter his name is equivalent to invoking him and will quickly be followed by his presence. (Freud, *Totem* 113, 115; Freud's emphasis)

Despite all the work and all the noise, we have failed, it seems, to keep the Dead Father at a distance, let alone to drive him off for good. And, as Slavoj Žižek reminds us, if the dead keep returning, that is *'because they were not properly buried,* i.e., because something went wrong with their obsequies.'[29] Hence the Dead Father serves as an embarrassing acknowledgment of his own non-disappearance, even as he also serves as something of a suggestion, a recommendation: if we can settle our 'symbolic debt'[30] to the Dead Father, then maybe he will sink into his appropriate place at last. Maybe then (in the words of Faulkner's Addie Bundren) he will be 'ready to stay dead a long time.'[31] The intense wish for the Dead Father to be really and truly dead simply confirms, of course, the impossibility of wish fulfilment in this case: any report of a successful and lasting interment will be premature, exaggerated, nakedly wishful, as poignant as it is parricidal. Barthelme sums up the situation in a neat formulation: 'Dead, but still with us, still with us, but dead.'[32] And: 'We *want* the Dead Father to be dead. We sit with tears in our eyes wanting the Dead Father to be dead ...' (*Dead Father* 5; Barthelme's emphasis).

The fact that the Dead Father is dead, then, does not prevent him from assuming a number of living forms. He is, successively and simultaneously, a simple human being; a granite monument; a gigantic serpent; a strange, majestic, awe-inspiring object; a pathetic, dangerous, infantile, and paralytic old man; a figure who comes apart in pieces; a voice who takes up residence inside one's head. His multiple, repetitive, and protean incarnations postulate one central function which no amount of defensive formal play can negate, disguise, or deconstruct. 'The ontic plane' (the phrase is Lacan's) on which the Dead Father exists is best apprehended by focusing on the narrative's representation of what Freud would call his 'group function': the Dead Father is there to organize, overshadow, and intimidate a surrounding community of souls. He is an obsession, a constant focus of conversation, attention, concern, resentment. Diffusing himself throughout the novel's complex of social relations, presiding over a field of erotic competition, contaminating desire with the remorse evoked by his dying, he is James Frazer's Slain King ('the one who keeps the corn popping from the fine green fields' [*Dead Father* 92]), Jessie Weston's Fisher King, the primal father of Freud's *Totem and Taboo*, or the Name-of-the-Father of Lacanian psychoanalysis – the signifier of the group's strangely amorous relation with an essentially absent yet disturbingly potent figure of proscription and authority. The Dead Father looms large, the fig-urehead of mass culture and individual psychology alike.[33]

In this capacity he is the fit object for an intense ambivalence of feeling, his absurd construction the unmistakable signature of a collective and unconscious animosity:

The Dead Father's head. The main thing is, his eyes are open. Staring up into the sky. The eyes a two-valued blue, the blues of the Gitanes cigarette pack. The head never moves. Decades of staring. The brow is noble, good Christ, what else? Broad and noble. And serene, of course, he's dead, what else if not serene? From the tip of his finely shaped delicately nostriled nose to the ground, fall of five and one half meters, figure obtained by triangulation ... He is not perfect, thank God for that. The full red lips drawn back in a slight rictus, slight but not unpleasant rictus, disclosing a bit of mackerel salad lodged between two of the stained four [teeth]. We think it's mackerel salad. It appears to be mackerel salad. In the sagas, it is mackerel salad.

Dead, but still with us, still with us, but dead. (*Dead Father* 3–4)

In *The Interpretation of Dreams*, Freud tells us that 'the construction of col-lective and composite figures is one of the chief methods by which con-densation operates in dreams,'[34] and clearly, in the passage cited above, one encounters a classical representation of the composite nature of the highly condensed dream image, into whose overdetermined form flow currents of admiration and disrespect, idealization and degradation, love and murderous hostility. Suffused, that is to say, by a tone of derision and ridicule, the '*immoderate, exaggerated* and *monstrous*' (*Dreams* 155; Freud's emphasis) features of the passage lie at the heart of the psychoanalytic notion of 'the absurd,' which in the 'work' of imagination (whether dream or artistic production) signals the presence of a 'particularly embittered and passionate polemic' (*Dreams* 436).[35]

Hence, as Freud dryly puts it (in a Barthelmean moment), in dreams 'we may ... assume that there [are] strong reasons present for the activity of the censorship ... ' (*Dreams* 584):

Nor is it by any means a matter of chance that our first examples of absurdity in dreams related to a dead father. In such cases, the conditions for creating absurd dreams are found together in characteristic fashion. The authority wielded by a father provokes criticism from his children at an early age, and the severity of the demands he makes upon them leads them, for their own relief, to keep their eyes open to any weakness of their father's; but the filial piety called up in our minds by the figure of a father, particularly after his death, tightens the censorship which prohibits any such criticism from being consciously expressed. (*Dreams* 565)

Denied a conscious, let alone physical, outlet, the currents of father-directed hostility must swirl upon themselves in the unconscious, where a self-renewing, 'primordial' scene perpetually acts itself out. We may as well call this scene, according to which Barthelme structures his postmodern text, the speculative founding myth and the archaic master narrative of Freud's theory of culture as presented in *Totem and Taboo*:

One day the brothers who had been driven out came together, killed and devoured their father and so made an end of the patriarchal horde. United, they had the courage to do and succeeded in doing what would have been impossible for them individually. (Some cultural advance, perhaps, command over some new weapon, had given them a sense of superior strength.) Cannibal savages as they were, it goes without saying that they devoured their victim as well as killing him. The violent primal father had doubtless been the feared and envied model of each one of the company of brothers: and in the act of devouring him they accomplished their identification with him, and each one of them acquired a portion of his strength. The totem meal, which is perhaps mankind's earliest festival, would thus be a repetition and a commemoration of this memorable and criminal deed, which was the beginning of so many things – of social organization, of moral restrictions and of religion. (*Totem* 209)

In 'Dostoevsky and Parricide,' Freud draws one continuous line between this primordial scene and the origins of the 'modern' superego, of tyrannous conscience itself: 'For men knew that they had disposed of their father by violence, and in their reaction to that impious deed, they determined to respect his will thenceforward.'[36]

This metatheme of murder and remorse is built into the very fictional vision and structure of *The Dead Father* as the mob of brothers are unable to transcend the sheer repetitive insistence of their guilt, their doubt, their rationalization, their self-deception, their 'inner lack of resolution and craving for authority.'[37] Dragging the corpse, they ask,

... for what purpose? are we right? are we wrong? are we culpable? to what degree? will there be a trial after? official inquiry? court of condemnation? white paper? have you told him? if you have told him what have you told him? how much of the blame if there is blame is ours? ten percent? twenty percent? in excess of that figure? and searching our hearts as we do each morning and evening and also at midday after lunch and after the dishes have been washed, we wonder wither? what for? can the conscience be coggled? *are we doing the right thing?* ... (*Dead Father* 92; Barthelme's emphasis)

Beneath the ironic comedy and self-consciousness of such questions lies a narrative ridiculously tragic, a story which, judging from its repetitive treatment throughout Barthelme's *oeuvre*, no amount of parody can succeed in making light of once and for all.

In Barthelme's assimilation and transfiguration of the text of Freud, then, one encounters what Jameson has called the persistence of 'buried master narratives' in the ironically self-conscious but still dark and troubled discourses of American postmodernism. If Jameson posits 'not the disappearance of the great master-narratives, but their passage underground as it were, their continuing but now *unconscious* effectivity ...,'[38] it is a major part of Barthelme's narrative work to make them conscious again. If, moreover, major fragments of the Freudian Father Narrative come to inhabit a postmodernist discourse characterized by formal self-consciousness, stylistic plurality, and 'epistemological self-mockery,'[39] the effect is to amplify and complicate, not to undermine or negate, the significance of the psychoanalytic 'deep material': a narrative obsession with patriarchal figures and the psychologies (individual and collective) they invariably dominate.

With *The Dead Father*, in sum, Barthelme has written a postmodern sequel to *Totem and Taboo*, a story whose life and whose death – like the Dead Father's, like Freud's, like Barthelme's – continues to unfold.

Notes

1 Donald Barthelme is perhaps best known for the humorous and experimental short stories, spoofs, and sketches which he published in *The New Yorker* magazine beginning in the 1960s. The son of a well known and successful architect of the modernist school, Barthelme grew up in Houston, Texas, and attended the University of Houston, where, from 1956 to 1960, he edited the award-winning journal *Forum*. He then took up a position as director of the Contemporary Art Museum in Houston, leaving after two years for Greenwich Village, New York, where he co-edited the journal *Location* and embarked upon a full-time career as a fiction writer. He published many collections of short stories (for example, *Come Back, Dr. Caligari* [1964]; *Unspeakable Practices, Unnatural Acts* [1968]; *Sixty Stories* [1981]) and, depending on how you categorize them, three or four novels (*Snow White* [1967]; *The Dead Father* [1975]; *Paradise* [1986]; *The King* [1990]). In the 1980s he taught creative writing at the University of Houston. A chain-smoker, he died of cancer in 1988.

2 A prime example of the residual postmodern sequel would be a historical romance like Alexandra Ripley's *Scarlett: The Sequel to Margaret Mitchell's 'Gone With the Wind'* (New York: Warner, 1991).

3 John Barth, 'Literature of Replenishment,' *The Friday Book: Essays and Other Nonfiction* (New York: Putnam's, 1984) 202.

4 Barth, 'Literature of Replenishment' 203.

5 John Barth, 'Literature of Exhaustion,' *The Friday Book* 73.

6 Barth, 'Literature of Replenishment' 203.

7 Jean-François Lyotard, 'Answering the Question: What Is Postmodernism?' trans. Régis Durand. Appendix to *The Postmodern Condition: A Report on Knowledge*, trans. Geoff Bennington and Brian Massumi (Minneapolis: U of Minnesota P, 1984) 77.

8 '[T]his latest mutation in space – postmodern hyperspace – has finally succeeded in transcending the capacities of the individual human body to locate itself, to organize its immediate surroundings perceptually, and cognitively to map its position in a mappable external world ... [i.e.] the great global multinational and decentered communicational network in which we find ourselves caught as individual subjects' (Fredric Jameson, *Postmodernism, or, The Cultural Logic of Late Capitalism* [Durham, NC: Duke UP, 1991] 44). See also Jean Baudrillard, for whom a conjuncture of postmodern technological forces reduces the subject to 'a pure screen, a switching center for all the networks of influence' ('The Ecstasy of Communication,' trans. John Johnston, *The Anti-Aesthetic: Essays on Postmodern Culture*, ed. Hal Foster [Port Townsend, WA: Bay Press, 1983] 133). For a splendid discussion of Barthelme as both a 'late-capitalist subject immersed in a sign-saturated, consumer culture' and a 'dissident postmodernist' seeking 'emancipation from the prevailing (reified) forms of language by fragmenting them into novel configurations' see Paul Maltby, *Dissident Postmodernists: Barthelme, Coover, Pynchon* (Philadelphia: U of Pennsylvania P, 1991).

9 T.S. Eliot, 'Tradition and the Individual Talent,' *Selected Prose of T.S. Eliot*, ed. Frank Kermode (London: Faber, 1975) 38–9.

10 J. Laplanche and J.-B. Pontalis, *The Language of Psycho-Analysis*, trans. Donald Nicholson-Smith (New York: Norton, 1973) 112.

11 Laplanche and Pontalis, *Language of Psycho-Analysis* 112.

12 Harold Bloom, *The Anxiety of Influence: A Theory of Poetry* (New York: Oxford UP, 1973) 142.

13 Slavoj Žižek, *Looking Awry: An Introduction to Jacques Lacan through Popular Culture* (Cambridge, MA: MIT, 1991) 9.

14 Brian McHale, *Constructing Postmodernism* (London and New York: Routledge, 1992) 23–4.

15 A classic example of modernist 'reversible sequels' would be Faulkner's *The Sound and the Fury* (1929) and *Absalom, Absalom!* (1936). In *Absalom, Absalom!* Faulkner resurrects as his principal narrator and 'witness' the character of Quentin Compson, who had died in Cambridge, Massachusetts, on 2 June 1910, in *The Sound and the Fury*. That is, the later text, *Absalom, Absalom!*, elaborates and extends the earlier text, *The Sound and the Fury*, even as it returns us to an earlier narrative time: Faulkner sets *Absalom's* main scene of narration in the fall and winter of 1909 – that is, some months before Quentin will drown himself in the Charles River. Faulkner produces thereby a dynamic, unstable, and uncanny structure of repetition, revision, and intertextual elaboration in which each text is 'always already' the sequel of the other.

In the postmodern scene, typically it is no longer the author or formal complexities but television and the technology of the image which become the characteristic modes of chronological confusion. In the technology of videotape montage, for example, '[p]resent and past images are mixed in no necessary order; fact and fiction are made part of the same "scene," not through a painful psychic process or by means of an extraordinary leap of the imagination, but simply because both are edited and interspersed with a frequency that makes the very idea of chronological order seem like slow motion' (Robert Kiely, *Reverse Tradition: Postmodern Fiction and the Nineteenth-Century Novel* [Cambridge, MA: Harvard UP, 1993] 3).

16 Roland Barthes, 'The Death of the Author,' trans. Richard Howard, *Contemporary Critical Theory*, ed. Dan Latimer (San Diego: Harcourt Brace Jovanovich, 1989) 59.

17 Roland Barthes, *Writing Degree Zero*, trans. Annette Lavers and Colin Smith (New York: Hill & Wang, 1968) 17; cited parenthetically hereafter.

18 Lyotard, 'Answering the Question' 74–5.

19 Lyotard, 'Answering the Question' 79.

20 Donald Barthelme, 'Reifications,' *Elaine Lustig Cohen* (New York: Exit Art, 1985) 5.

21 Donald Barthelme, 'Not-Knowing,' *Voicelust: Eight Contemporary Fiction Writers on Style*, ed. Allen Wier and Don Hendrie, Jr (Lincoln and London: U of Nebraska P, 1985) 45.

22 Jameson, *Postmodernism*, xiv.

23 The tradition that Barthelme rewrites extends from S.J. Perelman and Sabatini to Faulkner, Joyce, Freud, and Kafka; from Dostoevski, Melville, Hawthorne, and Poe to Shakespeare, Sophocles, Greek mythology, the Bible, and so on.

24 Michel Foucault, 'What Is an Author?,' *The Foucault Reader*, ed. Paul Rabinow (New York: Pantheon, 1984) 114.

25 Sigmund Freud, *Totem and Taboo, Standard Edition of the Complete Psychological Works of Sigmund Freud*, 24 vols., ed. and trans. James Strachey (London: The Hogarth Press and the Institute of Psycho-Analysis 1966) 13.204; cited parenthetically hereafter as *Totem*.

26 Writing during the First World War, Freud observed: 'Take up any political newspaper and you will find that here and there the text is absent and in its place nothing except the white paper is to be seen. This, as you know, is the work of the press censorship. In these empty places there was something that displeased the higher censorship authorities and for that reason it was removed – a pity, you feel, since no doubt it was the most interesting thing in the paper – the "best bit"' (Freud, *Introductory Lectures, Standard Edition* 15.139).

27 In a brilliant obituary, Thomas Pynchon describes Barthelme's unique gift for emulating oneiric processes, especially their genius at 'evading the censorship': 'Barthelme ... happens to be one of a handful of American authors, there to make the rest of us look bad, who know instinctively how to stash the merchandise, bamboozle the inspectors, and smuggle their nocturnal contraband right on past the checkpoints of daylight "reality." What he called his "secret vice" of "cutting up and pasting together pictures" bears an analogy, at least, to what is supposed to go on in dreams, where images from the public domain are said likewise to combine in unique, private, with luck spiritually useful, ways. How exactly Barthelme then got this into print, or for that matter pictorial, form, kept the transitions flowing the way he did and so on, is way too mysterious for me, though out of guild solidarity I probably wouldn't share it even if I did know. The effect each time, at any rate, is to put us in the presence of something already eerily familiar ... to *remind* us that we have lived in these visionary cites and haunted forests, that the ancient faces we gaze into are faces we know ... '

(Thomas Pynchon, Introduction, *The Teachings of Don B.: Satires, Parodies, Fables, Illustrated Stories, and Plays of Donald Barthelme*, ed. Kim Herzinger [New York: Turtle Bay, 1992] xvi–xvii; Pynchon's ellipses and emphasis). Of his own art, or art in general, Barthelme himself noted: 'All the magic comes from the unconscious. If there *is* any magic' (Interview, 'The Art of Fiction LXVI,' *Paris Review* 23 [Summer: 1981], 182; Barthelme's emphasis).

28 'In so far as desire is articulated ... through phantasy, phantasy is also the locus of defensive operations ... Such defences are themselves inseparably bound up with the primary function of phantasy, namely the *mise-en-scène* of desire – a *mise-en-scène* in which what is *prohibited (l'interdit)* is always present in the actual formation of the wish' (Laplanche and Pontalis, *Language of Psycho-Analysis* 318).

29 Žižek, *Looking Awry* 23; his emphasis.

30 Žižek, *Looking Awry*, 23.

31 William Faulkner, *As I Lay Dying* (New York: Vintage, 1990) 169.

32 Donald Barthelme, *The Dead Father* (New York: Penguin, 1975), 3; cited parenthetically hereafter as *Dead Father*.

33 Cf. Freud's *Group Psychology and the Analysis of the Ego*: '*a primary group ... is a number of individuals who have put one and the same object in the place of their ego ideal ...*' (*Standard Edition* 18.116; Freud's emphasis). As a result, this object, establishing itself in the place occupied by the individual superego (whose nucleus is the narcissistic ego ideal), comes to dominate the subject. Writing in the aftermath of the First World War and the Russian Revolution, Freud has mass psychologies (national, military, ideological, religious) in mind.

34 Freud, *The Interpretation of Dreams, Standard Edition* 5.400; cited parenthetically hereafter as *Dreams*.

35 'Nonsense, absurdity which appears so often in dreams and has brought them into so much undeserved contempt, never arises by chance through the ideational elements being jumbled together, but can always be shown to have been admitted by the dream-work intentionally and to be designed to represent embittered criticism and contemptuous contradiction in the dream-thoughts. Thus the absurdity in the content of the dream takes the place of the judgement "this is a piece of nonsense" in the dream-thoughts' (Freud, *Jokes and Their Relation to the Unconscious, Standard Edition* 8.175).

36 Freud, 'Dostoevski and Parricide,' *Standard Edition* 21.225.

37 Freud, 'The Future Prospects of Psycho-Analytic Therapy,' *Standard Edition* 11.146.

38 Jameson, Foreword, Jean-François Lyotard, *The Postmodern Condition* vii–xxi

39 Barth, 'Literature of Replenishment' 199.

'After the Fact': Marx, the Sequel, Postmodernism, and John Barth's *LETTERS*

THOMAS CARMICHAEL

The [postmodern] artist and writer, then, are working without rules in order to formulate the rules of what *will have been done*. Hence the fact that work and text have the characters of an *event*; hence also, they always come too late for their author, or, what amounts to the same thing, their being put into work, their realization (*mise en oeuvre*) always begins too soon. *Post modern* would have to be understood according to the paradox of the future (*post*) anterior (*modo*).
Jean-François Lyotard, 'Answer to the Question, What Is the Postmodern?' 1982; trans. 1983

If (as Marx says in his essay *The 18th Brumaire*) tragic history repeats itself as farce, what does farce do for an encore?
John Barth, *LETTERS*, 1979

As Fredric Jameson has so accurately observed, 'neither space nor time is "natural" in the sense in which it might be metaphysically presupposed ...: both are the consequence and projected afterimages of a certain state or structure of production and appropriation, of the social organization of productivity.'[1] This is equally true of the forms of narrative discourse, which attempt to represent lived experience in contingent and specific historical configurations. Jameson has suggested that the conspiracy narrative is perhaps the exemplary postmodern narrative form in that it permits us to represent something akin to the individual and collective experience of the contemporary 'system of social productivity'; however, one might well argue that the notion of the sequel as a mode of narrative discourse is even more representative of the often contradictory impulses that inhabit and shape our experience of the postmodern condition.[2] Conventionally understood as a text that manages to repeat and somehow to extend the representational field of a prior text, the sequel is a narrative production whose claim to authority ironically rests upon its intertextual traces. Every image and figure in the sequel stands in differential relation to an earlier representation, with which it is affiliated and from which its authority derives, and to the extent that a narrative is recognized or recognizes itself as a sequel, it inevitably also calls attention to the conventions that govern its own narrative logic. In this respect, the sequel occupies a particularly contemporary representational space in which each element operates simultaneously on the narrative and metanarrative levels.

At the same time, in its fundamental nature as a repetition with a difference, the sequel would also appear to be a particularly suitable narrative mode from which to represent an imagined relationship to a contemporary world system characterized by the frenetic proliferation and circulation of images and by a relentless drive towards homogeneity, or what Jean-François Lyotard has so aptly dubbed the 'degree zero of contemporary general culture.'[3] In addition, in the specific context of modern cultural production, the sequel has often been understood as a mode properly belonging to the fields of mass culture, so that popular serial narratives, for example, can be read as representing a powerfully conservative message through their seemingly inexhaustible repetitions of particular values or forms of social organization.[4] Of course, serial narratives are not necessarily sequels in the strict sense, but the link between repetition and various forms of authority that can be most easily traced in the emergence of the modern popular mass narrative is also connected to a larger crisis in representation that arises with cultural modernity, and not simply on the level of industrialized mass culture. Keeping in mind Lyotard's claim that 'postmodernism is not modernism at its end, but in a nascent state, and this state is recurrent,'[5] I want to consider a historical moment in this larger crisis, or at least a reading of that historical moment, as a means of tracing forward the cultural work of an extravagant and acutely self-conscious postmodern narrative sequel – John Barth's 1979 novel, *LETTERS*.

Barth's *LETTERS* is a postmodern epistolary novel, and as its putative author, variously identified as J.B. and John Barth, explains in the text, 'the letters in *LETTERS* are to be from seven correspondents, some recruited from my earlier stories,' each of whom is preoccupied in the projected narrative with, as the 'author' puts it, 'revolutions and recyclings generally.'[6] More explicitly, Barth himself suggests in a 1980 interview with Heide Ziegler that '[m]y characters in the new novel, *LETTERS*, will act out, whether they know it or not, Marx's notion that historical events and personages recur, the first time as tragedy and the second time as farce.'[7] *LETTERS*, as Barth here suggests, is to be read as a self-conscious return to and reconfiguration of his own previous fiction and also of Marx's famous meditations in *The Eighteenth Brumaire of Louis Bonaparte* on the enactments and re-enactments of history and their representation. Marx's *Eighteenth Brumaire*, written in late 1851 and early 1852, provides an account of how the political upheavals of the 1848 revolution in France and their aftermath led to Louis Napoleon's *coup d'état* in early December 1851, or as Marx puts it in the 'Preface' to the second edition of 1869, 'I show how ... the *class struggle* in France created circumstances and conditions which allowed a mediocre and grotesque individual to play the hero's role.'[8] But while it is an account of immediate political events, Marx's *Eighteenth Brumaire* is also an extended meditation on the very crisis in representation that marked the emergence of the culture of modernity.

David Harvey has argued that the continent-wide European economic depression in 1846–7, 'which quickly engulfed the whole of what was then the capitalist world,' and which 'can justly be regarded as the first unambiguous crisis of capitalist overaccumulation,' occasioned a crisis in representation itself that was produced by what he terms 'a radical readjustment in the sense of time and space in economic, political, and cultural life.'[9] For Harvey, what emerged most conspicuously out of this crisis, and from the transformation in the basic categories of experience of which it was emblematic, was cultural modernism: 'Neither literature nor art could avoid the question of internationalism, synchrony, insecure temporality, and the tension within the dominant measure of value between the financial system and its monetary or commodity base.'[10] According to Harvey, modern formalism and the modernist preoccupation with style and various forms of perspectivism arose out of this particular moment of crisis in the economic order, which in itself was symptomatic of a large and growing separation of the logic of capital from Enlightenment rationality and its notions of progressive spatial and temporal organization. To confirm this reading of a mimetic relationship between cultural production and a more generalized logic of production, Harvey points to Roland Barthes' famous assertion that 'around 1850, classical writing therefore disintegrated, and the whole of literature, from Flaubert to the present day, became the problematics of language.'[11] As Harvey and Barthes both insist, the problematics of language are part of a larger crisis in representation that links cultural production to history and to the motives for historical change, and inevitably links the upheavals from which modernism emerged to the later transformations in the productive and social sphere that mark the arrival of a distinctly postmodern culture.

For Marx, the specific political crisis in France at mid-century, which had its material origins in a panic generated by overproduction, is acted out as purely political spectacle through an elaborate network of self-conscious affiliations that serve ultimately to call their own representational authority into question (*Brumaire* 226–7). 'Hegel remarks somewhere,' Marx so famously begins, 'that all the great events and characters of world history occur, so to speak, twice. He forgot to add: the first time as tragedy, the second as farce' (*Brumaire* 146). As Edward Said remarks in his own reflections on *The Eighteenth Brumaire*, repetition is 'Marx's instrument for ensnaring the nephew [Louis Napoleon] in a manufactured world of analyzed reality,' and, in large part, Marx accomplishes this by distinguishing between forms of historical repetition.[12] Human beings make their own history, Marx insists, but always in situations not of their own making, so that 'the tradition of the dead generations weighs like a nightmare on the minds of the living' (*Brumaire* 146). What the past provides is a language of representation that can give provisional structure to the present, which is why, Marx argues, those involved in revolutionary transformations of themselves and their surroundings 'timidly conjure up the spirits of the past to help them; they borrow their names, slogans and costumes so as to stage the new world-historical scene in this venerable disguise and borrowed language' (*Brumaire* 146). Thus, the revolution of 1789 borrowed the language of republican Rome in order both to overthrow feudalism and to create a bourgeois order in France, and it did so in a guise that enabled the creators of that new form of social organization to 'hide from themselves the limited bourgeois content of their struggles and ... maintain their enthusiasm at the high level appropriate to great historical tragedy' (*Brumaire* 148).

But whereas the revolution of 1789 threw off the costumes of republican affiliation once the new social formations had triumphed, the case of Louis Napoleon and the *coup d'état* of 1851, in Marx's reading, is very different. In the mid-century configuration of this 'world-historical necromancy,' the revolution that brought Louis Napoleon to power borrowed the rhetoric and costumes of the earlier revolution that had eventually enthroned his uncle, but only succeeded in parodying the earlier revolution in its form and consequences.[13] This is true, Marx argues, because the grotesque parody of 1851 is produced in the absence of a language adequate to the transformations in the social organization of productivity at the middle of the nineteenth century. For Marx, the French political crisis of 1851 signifies a failure to find a form of representation for the vast transformations of the historical moment, brought about by the shifting of the scene of world-historical events from the bourgeois revolutions of the eighteenth century to the proletarian revolutions of the nineteenth. Henceforward, Marx insists, poetry will be created from the future and not from the past: 'The social revolution of the nineteenth century can only create its poetry from the future, not from the past, ... Earlier revolutions have needed world-historical reminiscences to deaden their awareness of their own content. In order to arrive at its own content the revolution of the nineteenth century must let the dead bury their dead' (*Brumaire* 149).

However accurate or inaccurate we may take this prediction to be with respect to the rhetoric of social revolution in the later nineteenth century, the modern culture that can be traced forward from 1850 would appear to confirm Marx's anticipation in its increasing preoccupation with style, symbolist aesthetics, and psychological projection. If Marx's *Eighteenth Brumaire* is a meditation on repetition as a trope of historical representation and interpretation, then, as Edward Said has observed, Marx's reflections might be said to turn about a central question: 'does repetition enhance or degrade a fact?'[14] Marx's answer to this question is unequivocal: repetition, as *The Eighteenth Brumaire* so convincingly demonstrates, is always a self-conscious struggle for a pure coincidence which is irretrievable, in which filiation is inevitably replaced by affiliation, coincidence by the anguish of belatedness. 'Thereafter,' as Edward Said so aptly puts it, 'the problems multiply,' and what *The Eighteenth Brumaire* would appear to document is how the grotesque repetitions of revolutionary rhetoric in mid-century France betray a deeply felt anxiety about legitimation brought about by ruptures in the very master narratives that had provided a ground of authority.[15] In Marx's reading, the ascendency of Louis Napoleon occurs amid what we might now understand as a triumph of hyperreal images in which the representations of the past are borrowed to disguise the present from itself, so that the representational field of politics is effectively separated from the social organization of productivity. Although the older representational codes remain in place, they persist as disembodied systems of circulation, both symptoms and confirmations of a systematic transformation beyond reproach.

If Marx's text might be said to be eerily 'postmodern' in its preoccupations with parody, signification, and the relation between representation and the fracturing of master narratives that had once sustained and guaranteed the course of world-historical events, then Barth's postmodern sequel, with its allusions to *The Eighteenth Brumaire of Louis Bonaparte*, might well be said to mark a return to Marx, through its representations of repetition, order, and contingency in the field of postmodern history. As 'the Author' in the text explains of his plans for LETTERS, 'Thus I am hazarding, for various reasons, the famous limitations both of the Novel-in-Letters and of the Sequel, most fallible of genres,' in the form of an epistolary novel by seven correspondents, 'one from each of my previous books (or their present-day descendants or counterparts, in the case of the historical or fabulous works), plus one invented specifically for *this* work, plus ... the Author' (LETTERS 431). Prominent among the preoccupations of the letter-writers in their various 'free-standing sequelae' are the events of 1969, the present time of the novel, and also the events of the War of 1812 (LETTERS 431). For example, the letters of one of the correspondents, A.B. Cook VI, are written in order to influence the course of contemporary political events, but they are also much concerned with the experiences of his several ancestors, particularly those of A.B. Cook IV, whose efforts to influence the War of 1812 are detailed in a series of epistles ostensibly under his own hand, letters that his descendant faithfully transcribes and passes on to his son and to the Author. These past events are also replayed elsewhere in the novel in the avant-garde film that is being made about the works of the Author, a project to which each of the novel's seven correspondents has some connection. As the Author himself admits to A.B. Cook VI in his description of the plans for LETTERS, '[w]hile I don't conceive the work in hand to be a historical novel, ... I evidently do have capital-H History on my mind.' That capital-H History often focuses upon the War of 1812, which is structurally and thematically significant in Barth's text because, as the Author explains, that war is often called, at least in LETTERS, the 'Second War of Independence' or, more tellingly, the '2nd Revolution' (LETTERS 431, 48). In Barth's postmodern epistolary novel, the War of 1812 is the sign of history, but, just as in Marx's account of the events of 1851, history in LETTERS is the scene of a crisis in representation that pervades the personal narratives of each of the seven correspondents. And as in Marx's reading at the beginning of the modern period, this crisis in LETTERS is in each case the product of a conflict between the compulsion to repeat and the contingent demands that confront that compulsion, or what amounts to a choice between a symptomatic postmodern attitude that is resigned to a world system and one that, as Lyotard puts it, '[refuses] the consolation of correct forms' in the pursuit of the difficult reawakening of agency in a world whose only measure of truth is performance.[16]

In his 1979 essay 'The Literature of Replenishment,' John Barth returns us to Roland Barthes' assertion that sometime around 1850 'Classical writing' disintegrated into the problematics of language; however, for Barth, the modernist problematics of language is itself inextricably caught up in the relation of modernism to Cold War consensus culture in North America. As Barth remarks in a footnote to a later essay, 'Postmodernism Revisited,' '[a]s for twentieth-century literary Postmodernism, I date it from when many of us stopped worrying about the death of the novel (a Modernist worry) and began worrying about the death of the reader – and of the planet – instead.'[17] Although a seemingly marginal assertion in 'Postmodernism Revisited,' Barth's repudiation of modernist formalism is central to his prescription for postmodernist, post–avant-gardist fiction. Barth's postmodernism begins with the premise that 'art lives in human time and history,' and it urges in the contemporary moment a fiction that would, as he puts it, 'be more democratic in its appeal than such late-modernist marvels (by my definition) as Beckett's *Texts for Nothing* or Nabokov's *Pale Fire*.'[18] Although his prescription for postmodernist fiction retains the formal self-consciousness that Barth so often associates with modernist practices, narrative self-consciousness now serves as a sign of the world's contingency and as a reaction against the constraining formalist imagination of official Cold War culture.[19] In Barth's fiction, narrative self-consciousness signals the fundamental arbitrariness of every motive and category, while the codes of realistic discourse function as the formal correlative of the finality of history and action. Barth's prescription advances a narrative discourse that would refuse totalization in favour of contingency but that would at the same time insist upon the irresistible demands of lived experience upon the subject in history. As Barth has approvingly remarked of Aristotle, '[o]ur experience of this protean reality – of "human life, its happiness and misery," Aristotle says – is the subject of literature; not *ought to be*, but *is*, as shall be shown. It is an experience that significantly includes our experience of language and even, for audiences as well as for artists, our experience of art.'[20]

In *LETTERS*, the experience of language and of the art of narrative is inextricably bound up with the notions of imitation, representation, and the sequel. To understand this connection we should recall that, in his well-known 1967 essay 'The Literature of Exhaustion,' Barth celebrates what he terms 'an imitation of a novel' in contrast to the traditional realistic narrative, or what he calls 'a proper "naive" novel.'[21] While Barth considers the latter form of narrative to rest upon questionable, if not outright discredited, assumptions about language and representation, 'an imitation of a novel' circumvents this obsolescence by foregrounding the conventions that govern their representational practices. Barth then explains: 'In fact such works are not more removed from "life" than

Richardson's or Goethe's epistolary novels are, both imitate "real" documents, and the subject of both ultimately, is life, not the documents.'[22] As 'an old-time epistolary novel' (*LETTERS* vii), *LETTERS*, of course, literally fulfils the nascent postmodern prescription that Barth sets out in 1967; that is, through the device of the letter, the novel succeeds in simultaneously exploiting, foregrounding, and calling into question the codes of realistic representation as the artifices upon which narrative construction depends.[23]

In *LETTERS*, this formal artifice is extravagant. The novel's eighty-eight letters, one for every alphabetical character in the subtitle, are arranged according to an elaborate scheme: the novel's seven correspondents always write in the same order, each on a different day of the week, but the actual letterhead date of any single letter and the number of letters written by any correspondent in a month are determined by superimposing a letter from the novel's title word upon the calendar for one of the seven consecutive months from March to September 1969. This plan is described, discussed, and graphically reproduced in the novel, so that the fundamentally self-referential order that structures the narrative is repeatedly asserted alongside the codes of plausibility that appear to motivate the events described in the letters themselves. At the same time, like the correspondents in much epistolary fiction, Barth's seven 'drolls and dreamers' (*LETTERS* vii) are very much aware of their roles as writers and narrators in their letters, and Barth's 'Author' extends that awareness by insisting upon the fictionality of the entire enterprise. As he remarks in his initial letter to the reader, dated 2 March 1969, 'If "now" were the date above, I should be writing this from Buffalo, New York'; however, as he points out, 'It is *not* March 2, 1969: when I began this letter it was October 30, 1973,' and still later in the letter, 'Now it's not 10/30/73 any longer, either. In the time between my first setting down "March 2, 1969" and now, now has become January 1974' (*LETTERS* 44–5). As the Author remarks, every letter might be said to belong both to the time of its writing and to the time of its reading, but 'to the units of epistolary fictions yet a third time is added: the actual date of composition, which will not likely correspond to the letterhead date, a function more of plot or form than of history' (*LETTERS* 44). The time of epistolary fiction is not history, as the Author insists, but the letter as a device imitates the form of everyday historical documents.

In this respect, epistolary fiction only represents more acutely the double bind that governs all narrative operating under a realistic imperative: that the conventional expectations of the reader will be met and that the artifice of those conventions will be suppressed. In Barth's text, however, the extravagant formal arrangements and the self-reflexive commentaries of the Author and of the other correspondents foreground the finally arbitrary correspondences and arrangements that structure the narrative, and they do so because Barth's text is fundamentally concerned with relations between order, contingency, and lived experience. As one of the correspondents, Lady Amherst, observes in a hopeful moment: 'My whole romantic life, I am trying to persuade myself, has, like the body of this letter, been digression and recapitulation; it is time to rearrive at the present, to move into a future unsullied by the past' (*LETTERS* 224). Like the other correspondents in *LETTERS*, Lady Amherst desires a sequel to her own past; however, as Barth's novel suggests, an unsullied future may be only the idealized projection of an inescapable past, to which the weight of history demands a more negotiated response.

As a sequel to his six previous volumes of fiction, *LETTERS* includes correspondents drawn from or connected to five of Barth's earlier works, and in keeping with the self-conscious narrative program in *LETTERS*, each of these figures is acutely aware of his prior representation. Even more characteristic perhaps, each of these figures also calls into question the authority or accuracy of that earlier representation. Todd Andrews, for example, the protagonist and narrator of Barth's first novel, *The Floating Opera*, claims that he provided the plot of that novel to the Author in a confessional conversation at a New Year's Eve party in 1954. As Andrews remarks, 'About your *Floating Opera* novel, which appeared the following year, I understandably have mixed feelings. On the one hand it was decidedly a partial betrayal on your part of a partial confidence on mine ...' (*LETTERS* 85). But Todd Andrews, together with Ambrose Mensch, is perhaps the most sanguine of the correspondents about his earlier fictional representation. In contrast, Jacob Horner petulantly suggests in a letter to himself that the Author somehow managed to get hold of Horner's lost manuscript entitled *What I Did Until the Doctor Came*, which became the basis for what he calls 'a slight novel called *The End of the Road*, which ten years later inspired a film, same title, as false to the novel as was the novel to your Account and your Account to the actual Horner-Morgan-Morgan triangle as it might have been observed from either other vortex' (*LETTERS* 19).[24] More aggressively, Jerome Bray accuses the Author of having plagiarized *Giles Goat-Boy* from a divinely authored manuscript in Bray's possession, and also of having plagiarized each of his three earlier novels from Bray's own fiction, while A.B. Cook VI suggests that he and the Author collaborated together to produce *The Sot-Weed Factor*, a claim the Author sharply denies (*LETTERS* 27–8, 406,

533). Although each of the seven correspondents in *LETTERS* is the narrator of his or her own present narrative in letters and, in some instances, volunteers these epistles to the Author for inclusion in his *LETTERS* project, their persistent questioning of narrative authenticity and authority, as reflected in their efforts to distance themselves from their earlier fictional representations or to contest the authority of those representations, returns us to the dynamic of narrative repetition and narrative difference that governs the structure of *LETTERS* and the very notion of the sequel.[25]

In this context, the example of Todd Andrews is emblematic of the function of the sequel in *LETTERS*. Todd Andrews is unable to conceive of his present existence except in relation to a representation of his earlier life, and he is incapable of representing his present to himself as other than a form of repetition, however reconfigured or inverted. In large part, Andrews's sense that 'my life has been recycling' also reflects the concern with the continuing crisis in the political and social course of the American republic that resonates throughout the novel (*LETTERS* 256). The present time of the text is 1969, and the counter-cultural disruptions of that year along with the political and social upheavals of the previous year, or what the Author calls in his first letter to the Reader 'the shocks of "1968" and its predecessors,' echo the theme of revolutions in the text, and more particularly the failure of revolutionary representations to imagine actual or impending social, political, or economic transformations (*LETTERS* 42). As Todd Andrews explains to the political activist Drew Mack, 'North Americans neither needed, wanted, nor would permit anything like a real "Second Revolution"; once its principal focus, the Viet Nam War, reached whatever sorry dénouement, the much-touted Counterculture would in a very few years become just another subculture, of which the more the merrier, with perhaps a decade's half-life in the media' (*LETTERS* 720). As Andrews goes on to explain, his scepticism about the revolutionary potential of the counter-culture has nothing to do with an endorsement of the status quo. Rather, it represents a keen awareness of the difficulties of effecting real political change in America, and, just as important in the light of our present consideration of a return to Marx, in Barth's postmodern program it also springs from an equally strong sense that the discourse of a 'Second Revolution' is produced out of an overdetermined and disembodied network of repetitions that collapses together a largely European tradition of revolutionary Marxist politics, a militant Third World rhetoric of armed liberation, and a native American liberal tradition that would endorse radical individual autonomy. Like the parodic 'Second Revolution' of 1812, the counter-cultural revolution of 1969 in *LETTERS* is another instance of 'world-historical necromancy' that resurrects the spectre of revolution in the cultural imaginary merely in order to make, in Marx's phrase, 'its ghost walk about again' (*Brumaire* 149).

In Barth's novel, these failures of the personal and collective imaginary to present anything but a scene of overdetermined repetitions can in part be attributed to the paralysing effect of an inhibitory self-consciousness. This is the dilemma represented in Todd Andrews's fears about his life's recycling, or more numbingly in Jacob Horner's 'anniversary view of history,' his blandly unhistorical practice of writing down lists of historical events that have occurred on a specific day (*LETTERS* 98). In contrast to these unhistorical repetitions of a 'borrowed language,' the narrative self-consciousness of Lady Amherst, the only correspondent not drawn directly or indirectly from Barth's earlier fiction, points to the means by which the metanarrative impulse might be placed in the service of history. As she remarks in a 26 April letter to the Author, 'Thus has chronicling transformed the chronicler, and I see that neither Werner Heisenberg nor your character Jacob Horner went far enough; not only is there no "non-disturbing observation"; there is no non-disturbing historiography. Take warning sir: to put things into words works changes, not only upon the events narrated, but upon their narrator. She who saluted you pages past is not the same who closes now, though the name we share remains ...' (*LETTERS* 80). Unlike the other correspondents in *LETTERS*, who dwell upon repetitions and recyclings, Lady Amherst refuses the consolation of metanarratives; instead, she embraces the assertion of provisional order in the realm of lived experience as the necessary response to a world that, as Fredric Jameson so accurately describes it, would otherwise inspire a craving for conspiracy, for the security however frightful of 'a potentially infinite network, along with a plausible explanation of its invisibility.'[26]

It is no surprise in this context that *LETTERS* concludes with a seemingly obscure reference to the disappearance of a former CIA agent on Chesapeake Bay, a mystery that will in fact become central to Barth's next novel, *Sabbatical*. With respect to sequels and history in *LETTERS*, however, the notion of conspiracy would seem best to apply to the swirling maze of plots and counterplots in which the seven correspondents are embroiled, and which apparently come to no sure resolution, except that as the novel progresses these plots become vertiginous in their self-conscious designs, increasingly self-cancelling, and curiously homogeneous. What they finally appear mimetic of is not a plan of collective or personal action or transformation, but of a purely imagined relation to a world anachronistically conceived. Conspiracy in *LETTERS* is a sign of the inability to accept merely provisional assertions of order; it is a failed strategy to constrain history and contingency through projection, and it is linked with the equally misguided tactics of the contemporary avant-garde. *LETTERS* contains many figures connected with the notion of an avant-garde, from Lady Amherst's lover André Castine, who already on the eve of the Second World War was entirely taken up with '"action historiography" or the *making* of history as if it were an avant-garde species of narrative,' to Reg Prinz the avant-garde film-maker, to Ambrose Mensch, the avant-garde writer, now Prinz's collaborator and adversary, and Lady Amherst's current lover (*LETTERS* 73). But the logic of the contemporary avant-garde as it would appear in both its cultural and its political projects in the novel leads it simply to repeat the imperatives of the past, however ironically reconfigured, in its nostalgic pursuit of the authentic gesture.[27]

Appropriately, it is Ambrose Mensch, Lady Amherst's lover in *LETTERS*, who alone among the several artists in the text finally comes to recognize the limits of his avant-gardism at the scene of history. In a letter of 12 May, Mensch appears to dismiss history as an endless chain of signification and deferral, 'a code which, laboriously and at ruinous cost, deciphers into HISTORY. She is a scattered sibyl whose oak-leaf oracles we toil to recollect, only to spell out something less than nothing: e.g. WHOL TRUTH, or ULTIMATE MEANIN' (*LETTERS* 332). But as his lover, Lady Amherst, reminds him, when Mensch fancifully lists the correspondences between their current situation and the circumstances surrounding Napoleon's banishment to St Helena: 'it was the same Louis Napoleon's grotesque replay of his uncle's career that prompted Marx's essay *On the Eighteenth Brumaire*, etc., in which he made his celebrated, usually misquoted observation of History's farcical recyclings.' As for her lover's elaborate list of correspondences and echoes, she is simply dismissive: 'Pooh, said I, that's a game anyone can play who knows a tad of history: the game of Portentous Coincidences, or Arresting but Meaningless Patterns ... And none of this, in my opinion, meant anything more than that the world is richer in associations than in meanings, and that it is the part of wisdom to distinguish between the two' (*LETTERS* 384–5). Lady Amherst refuses to be seduced by repetition and coincidence; instead, she insists upon the importance of lived experience and its inescapable demands for distinction and action. Mensch himself comes much later to embrace this view, when he writes in a letter of 4 August, 'our concepts, categories, and classifications are ours, not the World's, and are as finally arbitrary as they are provisionally useful' (*LETTERS* 648).

In this context, the assertion of contingency and action in *LETTERS* would appear also to present a critique of the limits and assumptions of the sequel as a mode of narrative representation and narrative understanding. To the extent that the notion of the sequel is caught up in a dynamic of repetition, it espouses a logic, as Barth's novel would appear to suggest, that is inevitably bound by origins and appeals to representational authority. In this respect, the metahistorical content of the sequel might be said to be curiously unhistorical in that the transformations of a prior text or representation would seem to be inevitably involved in a self-enclosed field of identity and repetition. At the same time, if the modes of narrative logic are themselves historical, then the logic of a contemporary or postmodern sequel would seem to demand its own repudiation. While the sequel in its fully elaborated serial forms might be read as a contemporary expression of the frenetic circulation of depthless images, whose repetition however reconfigured always ultimately reveals the self-referential logic of their proliferation, the sequel as a mode of postmodern interrogation that would seek a space for agency in the postmodern liberal state, as in the case of Barth's *LETTERS*, insists upon a very different reading. In Barth's postmodern epistolary novel, the sequel as self-conscious elaboration of a prior representation is uncovered as a projection of an older logic or as a means of resisting history. What the novel endorses, however, largely through the example of Lady Amherst, is the end of metanarratives, the acceptance of provisionality, and a return to history in the form of contingency and action. In Barth's novel, the letter is never a self-identical projection, nor a text in the well-plotted channels of the structure of symbolic circulation, but rather a field of dissemination, without centre or ground, but within which the contingent scene of human action finds its inevitable and irretrievable logic of representation. In this configuration, the contradictions of postmodern narratology find their truest expression: in order to function as a sequel in the condition of postmodernity, John Barth's *LETTERS*, as Marx, foresaw in a very different context, must repudiate the sequel as repetition or as a field of determined transformations, and must instead embrace the sequel as a representation of contingent consecutiveness, of an infinite chain of history and difference.

Notes

1 Fredric Jameson, *Postmodernism or, The Cultural Logic of Late Capitalism* (Durham, NC: Duke UP, 1991) 367.
2 Fredric Jameson, *The Geopolitical Aesthetic: Cinema and Space in the World System* (Bloomington: Indiana UP, 1992) 9.
3 Jean-François Lyotard, 'Answer to the Question, What Is the Postmodern?' *The*

Postmodern Explained: Correspondence, 1982–1985, ed. Julian Pefanis and Morgan Thomas; trans. Don Barry et al. (Minneapolis: U of Minnesota P, 1992) 8.

4 See, for example, Umberto Eco's 'The Myth of Superman,' *The Role of the Reader: Explorations in the Semiotics of Texts* (Bloomington: Indiana UP, 1979) 107–24.

5 Lyotard, 'Answer to the Question' 13.

6 John Barth, *LETTERS* (New York: Putnam's, 1979) 654. Subsequent references to this work are noted parenthetically in the text.

7 Heide Ziegler, 'An Interview with John Barth.' *Granta* 1.2 (1980): 169–70.

8 Karl Marx, *The Eighteenth Brumaire of Louis Bonaparte*, trans. Ben Fowkes, *Surveys from Exile*, vol. 2 of *Political Writings*, ed. David Fernbach (Harmondsworth: Penguin, 1992) 144. Subsequent references to this work are noted parenthetically in the text.

9 David Harvey, *The Condition of Postmodernity* (London: Blackwell, 1989) 260–1.

10 Harvey, *Condition of Postmodernity*, 263.

11 Harvey, *Condition of Postmodernity*, 263. Although presented as a direct quote from Barthes, taken from an English translation published in London in 1967, this is more accurately a paraphrase of Barthes's remark. The phrase 'around 1850,' for example, which appears as the opening of the sentence in Harvey's quotation, does not conform to the French text or to the American translation, which is ostensibly a reprint of the 1967 Jonathan Cape edition.

12 Edward W. Said, *The World, the Text, and the Critic* (Cambridge MA: Harvard UP, 1983) 124.

13 Although he heaps scorn and ridicule upon Louis Napoleon, Marx does not dismiss the actual changes brought about by the events of 1851. In a passage that appears only in the first edition, Marx in fact argues that rather than constituting an aberration, the grotesque ascendency of Louis Napoleon is to be understood as a necessary step on the road towards a European proletarian revolution: 'In despair and disappointment at the Napoleonic restoration, the French peasant will abandon his faith in his smallholding, the entire state edifice erected on the smallholding will fall to the ground, and *the proletarian revolution will obtain the chorus without which its solo will prove a requiem* in all peasant countries': see Ben Fowkes's comments in Marx, *Eighteenth Brumaire* 245, n. 53.

14 Said, *The World* 125.

15 Said, *The World* 125.

16 Lyotard, 'Answer to the Question' 15.

17 Barth, 'Postmodernism Revisited,' *Further Fridays: Essays, Lectures, and Other Nonfiction, 1984–1994* (Boston: Little, Brown, 1995) 123.

18 Barth, 'The Literature of Replenishment,' *The Friday Book: Essays and Other Nonfiction* (New York: Putnam's, 1984) 203.

19 Barth, 'Literature of Replenishment' 202.

20 Barth, 'Very Like an Elephant: *Reality versus Realism,' Further Fridays* 139.

21 Barth, 'The Literature of Exhaustion,' *The Friday Book* 72.

22 Barth, 'Literature of Exhaustion' 72. In terms of the present discussion, it is worth pointing out that Barth defends his enthusiasm for convoluted imitations in this essay by appealing to Marx's formula. As Barth puts it, '"History repeats itself as farce" – meaning, of course, in the form or mode of farce, not that history is farcical' ('Exhaustion' 72).

23 See my discussion of this point in 'John Barth's *Letters*: History, Representation and Postmodernism,' *Mosaic* 21.4 (1988): 65–72.

24 Those who know Barth's early work will recognize that *What I Did Until the Doctor*

Came was the original title of *The End of the Road*, and that there was a 1970 film version of the novel.

25 Amid this disputation about narrative authority and authenticity, we should not overlook the narrative sleight of hand in *LETTERS* that makes this all possible. Although the correspondents take issue with the accuracy of their portraits in Barth's earlier fiction, their present narratives as sequels depend entirely upon the logic of those earlier representations. Todd Andrews remarks, for example, that although the Author 'altered names and doctored facts for literary effect,' *The Floating Opera* left him feeling 'gratified to see the familiar details of my life and place projected as through a camera obscura' (*LETTERS* 85). But in his own discussion of his life since 1937 in *LETTERS*, Todd Andrews nowhere suggests that there is any distance between this supposedly authoritative representation of his life and the Author's fictionalization. He simply treats these 'altered names and doctored facts' as literal truth, and depends upon the truth of that earlier representation to guarantee the veracity of his current account.

26 Jameson, *Geopolitical* 9.

27 As Peter Bürger so persuasively argues in his account of the function of modern avant-gardes, the contemporary period can best be understood as a 'post–avant-garde' phase in cultural history, one that lives in the wake of the historical failure of the avant-garde movements aligned with modernism to explode the institution of art in the name of reintegrating art as a form of social praxis. Although the contemporary 'post–avant-gardist phase' continues to throw up perfected imitations of earlier Dadaist disruptions, these now themselves have become, in both their earlier and their subsequent incarnations, full members of the institution of art. The true contemporary situation, Bürger argues, is much different: 'Through the avant-garde movements, the historical succession of techniques and styles has been transformed into a simultaneity of the radically disparate. The consequence is that no movement in the arts today can legitimately claim to be historically more advanced *as art* than any other ... The time is gone when one could argue against the use of realistic techniques because the historical development had passed beyond them': see Peter Bürger, *Theory of the Avant-Garde*, trans. Michael Shaw, foreword Jochen Shulte-Sasse, *Theory and History of Literature*, vol. 4 (Minneapolis: U of Minnesota P, 1984) 57, 63.

Not surprisingly, the contemporary situation that Bürger outlines is very much the one in which Barth finds himself in 1967, and it is the one to which 'The Literature of Exhaustion' stands as a long-considered response.

Recurrent Monsters: Why Freddy, Michael, and Jason Keep Coming Back

PAUL BUDRA

Horror movies traditionally have simple plot lines: a peaceful society is attacked by some outside threat – usually embodied in a monster – and, after a period of chaos and sacrifice, order is restored. The narrative is comic, its resolution sometimes heightened with the promise of romance between the stalwart hero of the film and the beleaguered *ingénue* he saves. Comedy is reified through formula: the monster is beaten; the overreaching scientist learns his lesson or falls into a vat of bubbling goo; possessed children are exorcized and become valuable future consumers; American know-how triumphs over alien voodoo; God tests us and finds us worthy; love conquers all.[1]

But horror films changed in the late 1960s. They stopped offering closure; they abandoned the comic formula. The threat was not satisfactorily vanquished at the end of the film.[2] Recent horror films have left the audience acutely aware that the threat still exists, will perhaps always exist. And the nature of that threat has changed. Before the 1960s the majority of monsters were aliens, supernatural entities, creations gone awry, or mad scientists. They were *other*.[3] But after the 1960s the most common threat horror movies have offered is the psychotic, that is, the killers who walk among us, human monsters who are somehow a product of our own society, of the nuclear family, often indistinguishable from ourselves.[4] The films suggest that *we* are the problem.

A further, related change has taken place in horror movies: they never end. While some early horror films, such as the Universal Studios' productions *Dracula* (1931) and *Frankenstein* (1931), were sequelized, each film itself offered a full closure. The sequels to those films revived their monsters, often in the most unlikely of ways, only because box-office receipts for the films had been so impressive. And, often as not, the sequels were not true narrative extensions: they were remakes or tangential spin-off narratives. *Dracula's Daughter* (1936) did not bring back Bela Lugosi's Dracula. But contemporary horror films have had consistent, and at times inexplicable, sequel attention. Though financial argument obviously justified the first sequels to *Halloween* (1978), *A Nightmare on Elm Street* (1985), *The Howling* (1989), and even *Friday the 13th* (1980), by the time these films reached their seventh instalments many film-goers were simply baffled at their persistence. And we must remember that only a handful of horror films have ever been big office draws. Those, *The Exorcist* (1973), *The Omen* (1976), *Alien* (1979), have all been sequelized, but the *cognoscenti* of the genre can point to many more obviously marginal films that have also gone into extensive sequelization. Movies such as *Witchboard* (1987), *Witchcraft* (1988), *House* (1986), *Leprechaun* (1993), *Scanners* (1981), *Critters* (1986), *Piranha* (1978), *Ghoulies* (1985), and *The Hidden* (1987) hardly seem to have merited a first production, much less a sequel, and yet they continue to proliferate.

I want to suggest that these new elements in horror films are linked together, that the sequelization of recent horror movies is tied to the loss of closure and the familiarization of threat. Specifically, the sequelization of horror movies is indicative of the emergence of the postmodern horror film, a subgenre that manifests frightening cultural uncertainty through formal innovations, while seducing the viewer through an alignment with the recurring monster.

It would be surprising if there were no such thing as postmodern horror. Traditionally, the collective nightmare that horror films represent has been tied to the phobias at large in the society for which the films have been designed. On the most basic level, this means that, as the darkest concerns of a society have shifted, horror films have reflected those shifts with the introduction of new types of threats. More specifically, every generation has constructed its own collective nightmare around another liminality, on another threshold (Wood 174) – be it generational, sexual, political – and horror movies body forth those liminalities in the threats they depict. To give some very simple examples, in the 1950s, cold war fears of communist infiltration found their image in monster invasion films such as *Them!* (1954), *The Thing* (1951), *The Blob* (1959), *It Conquered the World* (1956), and *Twenty Million Miles to Earth* (1957) (Carrol 208). The 1960s satanic-baby movies – *The Village of the Damned* (1960), *Rosemary's Baby* (1968), and its little-known TV sequel, *Look What Happened to Rosemary's Baby* (1976) – played to audience fears of the emergent youth culture.

Indeed, at least one attempt has already been made to define postmodern horror films: Kim Newman labels any movie that crosses generic borders and incorporates horror elements as postmodern horror (*Nightmare Movies* 211–15). Leaving aside the fact that this would make both *Abbott and Costello Meet Frankenstein* (1948) and *Pulp Fiction* (1994) horror films, this definition does not address the nature of the postmodern unease in recent horror films, identifying a symptom, perhaps, but not its cause. A specifically postmodern unease is generated, not by encroaching threats, but by the perception that the world is increasingly one in which borders have collapsed, in which preconceptions, hierarchies, absolutes, and perhaps reason itself are being abandoned. Postmodern horror movies, then, would be those films that acknowledge the pluralities and uncertainties of the postmodern condition and make those uncertainties themselves the source of monstrosity and fear.

It is the inescapable nature of this uncertainty that makes postmodern horror films different from earlier horror movies. Those earlier films reify the liminalities and phobias of their respective ages in intrusive monsters who could be banished. In postmodern horror films the interplay of meanings that has arisen from the postmodern rejection of certitude is itself presented in the narratives (and I would argue, in popular culture in general) as a collective madness which is implicitly homicidal, monstrous, because it kills established orders and values, slashes moral certainties, and stomps on ontological assumptions. This madness of unmeaning is indigenous and pervasive. The threat in postmodern horror, then, is not the lurker on the threshold, but the very absence of thresholds that the contemporary condition entails. The same nostalgic impulse that inspires retro-culture finds its dark image, the fear of cultural and even ontological negation, in contemporary horror films. So the postmodern horror movie does not celebrate the radical eclecticism of contemporary culture as, for example, do so many glibly surrealistic music videos, but rather represents that eclecticism, together with its underlying relativism and uncertainty, as a *Zeitgeist* fraught with threat for the majority of the intended consumers of popular culture. This threat is manifested in formal aspects of these films, not the least of which is the sequel.

Robin Wood has introduced a useful categorization of horror films that will help us deal with the innovations of postmodern horror. He designates horror movies as either 'ideologically coherent,' that is, focusing on conventional binaries and offering a reassuring conclusion, or 'ideologically incoherent,' offering neither simple appositions nor closure (197). I would argue that, for the most part, the ideologically incoherent movies are acknowledging the uncertainty of postmodern (and hence their proliferation after 1970) and playing with that fear of uncertainty in the audience, while the recently produced ideologically coherent films are playing to nostalgia for modernity in a reassuring, even campy, way.[5]

Let us look at four postmodern horror films in order of increasing incoherence. The first is George A. Romero's *Night of the Living Dead* (1968). In that film the dead come back to life and begin to feed on the living. Unlike the practice in earlier films, however, no clear explanation is given for the plague of cannibalistic zombies, no 'cure' is discovered, no one falls in love. Most shockingly, at the end of the film the sole remaining survivor of the zombie feeding frenzy emerges from the house only to be shot by some rednecks who assume that he, too, is a zombie. The second, and clearly the most influential film, is John Carpenter's *Halloween* (1978). At the end of that film, a psychiatrist named Loomis shoots Michael Meyers, the masked killer who has been stalking the terrified teenager Laurie through the suburban streets of Haddonfield. Michael falls over a second-storey railing and crashes onto the yard below. But when Loomis and Laurie go to look at his body, it is gone. The final shots of the movie are simply of the streets of Haddonfield. The message is clear: Michael is still here; Michael will always be here.

The next two films not only refuse to offer ideological coherence through comic closure, but refuse as well to offer ontological coherence. Dan Coscarelli's *Phantasm* (1979) was one of the first horror films to utterly break the barrier between dream and reality without offering any sort of resolution at the end.[6] This ontological uncertainty is appropriate to its storyline, which involves another dimension. In short, a boy named Michael, tormented by bad dreams after the death of his brother, suspects that his brother's body has been stolen by the undertaker, who becomes known as the 'Tall Man' (played by the wonderfully named Angus Scrimm). Michael investigates by exploring a huge mausoleum at the cemetery, only to be threatened by killer dwarfs in monks' robes and flying silver globes that are armed with vicious flesh-rending blades and drills. Is this a dream? A dimensional distortion? We are never told.

A Nightmare on Elm Street (1985) took the dream/reality breakdown of *Phantasm* and combined it with the stalker narrative of *Halloween* to create a film that was the first self-conscious reworking of postmodern horror's emerging narrative tropes. The film had everything that *Halloween* offered: randy teenagers who die in gruesome manners, a background of nondescript suburban America, and an ingenious killer. From *Phantasm* it took the dream/reality breakdown, now giving it a new twist: the spirit of Freddy Krueger, a child molester burned to death by the irate parents of Elm Street, has come back to haunt the dreams of a new generation of children. If Krueger succeeds in killing you in your dreams, you really die.

These ideologically and ontologically incoherent films all end poised for a sequel. *Night of the Living Dead* presents an unexplained and ultimately inescapable threat: because the living die and turn into the walking dead, the numbers of the zombies keep swelling – the living *cannot* win. It also denies the possibility of escape by presenting an initial society that was neither stable nor, the ending suggests, just. The film has inspired two sequels and a remake. The last shots of *Halloween*, suggestive, terrifying in their banality – it is just a well-kept residential neighbourhood – imply that the threat cannot be eliminated because it is inexplicably part of contemporary North American reality.[7] That film has spawned four sequels. *Phantasm*, leaving the dream/reality conundrum wide open at the end, has spawned two sequels. The last one, *Phantasm: Lord of the Dead* (1994), ends with the Tall Man's admonition 'It's never over.'

But it is *A Nightmare on Elm Street* that is the most self-consciously open-ended and highly sequelized of these films. This self-consciousness is, in fact, the central plot device of the most recent *Nightmare* sequel: *Wes Craven's New Nightmare* (1994). Wes Craven was the director of the original *A Nightmare on Elm Street*. In this pretentiously eponymous film, the breakdown between film and reality and the impossibility of closure make up the entire subject matter. The movie is about Heather Langenkamp, the actress who played Nancy in *Nightmare 1* and *3*. That is, this actress plays herself, as do Robert Englund, the actor who plays Freddy, several other actors from the original film, and Wes Craven and people at New Line Cinema, the company that produces the *Nightmare* films. Langenkamp finds herself the victim of nightmares and threatening phone calls, both of which invoke Freddy Krueger. While this trauma is going on, Langenkamp is being solicited by New Line Cinema to appear in another instalment of the *Nightmare* series based on a script that Craven is currently working on. Craven explains that he is writing the script based on his nightmares. More, he explains that Freddy is now real: 'When the story dies, the evil is set free. Now that the series [of *Nightmare* movies] has ended, the evil's out of the bottle.' Freddy has 'decided to cross over – out of films and into reality.' The only way to contain him is to make another movie, to keep him in film, to keep turning out sequels.

The acknowledgment of postmodern relativism in these films, manifest in ideological and ontological incoherence and the concomitant phenomenon of sequelization, has had an effect on the nature of the monster.

On a very basic level, the post-1960 shift towards psychotics as the monsters of choice, in a world in which any one of us might be such a psychotic, has made the monster pool potentially huge. This possible ubiquity of psychotic killers has made the personality of the individualized human monster less important. Hence, Michael Meyers wears an expressionless mask: he could be anyone. To put it another way, there is only one Godzilla; there are potentially thousands of Norman Bateses. In George Romero's *Living Dead* movies, everyone on the planet is a heartbeat away from becoming a cannibalistic zombie. Simultaneously, the representation, in recent horror films, of a *Zeitgeist* that is itself the source of terrifying uncertainty means the unique monster is not necessarily central to the *frisson* that the films seek to generate. The combination of these facts would seem to argue for a loss of charisma on the monster's part.

In fact, postmodern monsters are at once charismatic 'stars' and faceless automatons of violence representative of cultural unease. This paradox can be explained by the relation of the monster to the world of postmodern confusion in which he moves. The monsters of the early Universal horror movies were threatening because they were chaotic outsiders who challenged a homogeneous stable society. They were, it is true, occasionally tragic in the knowledge of their otherness (think of Karloff as Frankenstein's monster playing with the little girl). Postmodern monsters, on the other hand, inhabit a society that is chaotic. This makes them heroes, in the sense that, while we are confused, denied simple answers and distinctions in a bewildering cultural condition, monsters are not. Monsters have priorities. Monsters are motivated. The principles that govern them are firmer than our own: do not go out in the sunlight; kill anything that giggles. The monster films of the 1980s and 1990s have tended to present vampires, zombies, and aliens as practitioners of alternative, viable, and often highly sympathetic, lifestyles. They are, like Marlowe's Tamburlaine and Shakespeare's Falstaff, exhilarating. But while those Renaissance figures were heroic because, as Alexander Leggatt explains in this volume, they were apparently 'free even from the laws of nature and common sense' (55), the postmodern monster is heroic because he is consistent in an inconsistent world. Robert Cumbow, discussing the films of John Carpenter and Stanley Kubrik's *The Shining* (1980), puts it this way: 'the truly mad do not suffer from a jumbled view of the world around them, but from a tendency to see things all too simply and clearly' (3). That clarity of vision is increasingly something to be envied as a synecdoche for the certainties of modernity which have been lost. And so it is not surprising that contemporary monsters tend to be socially reactionary, preferring to kill the young and sexually promiscuous.

The appealing stability of the monster is worked out formally through the serialization process. The only constant in, say, the *Friday the 13th* films is the psychotic killer. The monster is the norm. It is he, not his victims, to whom the audience finally relates because he will live on into the sequel. The rest of the cast will not last to the closing credits; they have no narrative significance except as victims (Dika 89). Arguably, we want these people to die. The postmodern horror sequel, then, formally reifies the paradoxical stability of the homicidal psychotic and, therefore, helps to make him sympathetic. The two become interdependent: as the sequel stabilizes monstrosity, so the stable monster creates a demand for more sequels.

But not any monster will do. He must have charisma, and for a postmodern monster that means macabre wit, ingenuity of murder technique, and, above all, stamina. If the monster manifests these qualities, he will be allowed increased screen status (and hence charisma) throughout the sequelization process. A good example might be the character of Freddy Krueger from the *Nightmare on Elm Street* series. In the first of these films Krueger says almost nothing. He laughs maniacally and mutters a few threats, but he is a bogeyman: a shape in the dark, never really seen in full light. The actor who plays him, Robert Englund, did not receive first-tier billing in the credits for the film. In the subsequent films, however, the dynamics of serialization made Freddy the centre of attention. He is the only character who is constant in the series. The sequels, then, increase his presence and his consequent charisma. He is shown in full light; we are given his genealogy; we see his inception, and, most important, he begins to talk. The subsequent films in the series all feature Freddy uttering macabre witticisms as he kills people in increasingly clever ways. When he drowns a boy in a waterbed, for example, he says, 'Now that's what I call a wet dream.' And in the sequels, Robert Englund receives top billing.

Another example, one that is even stranger, given the nature of the monster, is Pinhead from the *Hellraiser* films. In the original *Hellraiser* (1987), a sensual adventurer named Frank buys an oriental puzzle box that opens a door to an alternative world populated by demons named 'Cenobites.' The lead Cenobite, played by Doug Bradley, wears a bizarre leather maxi-skirt, is completely bald, and has had the skin of his face marked into squares with incisions; at the corner of each of these squares there is a pin. The image is strikingly original and plays to the current counter-culture vogue for body piercing and bondage clothes, but the character plays a very minor role in the movie, which is mainly concerned with Frank's attempts to return from the dead by feeding on blood from the victims provided for him by his sister-in-law and lover, Julia. Yet Pinhead, as he came to be known, was such a hit that the subsequent films – *Hellbound: Hellraiser II* (1988) and *Hellraiser III: Hell on Earth* (1992) – focused increasingly on him. In *Hellraiser II*, his background is given: he was a First World War army captain named Spenser who, after the war, lost himself in occult speculation. He discovered the puzzle box and, for his pains, was turned into a demon. In *Hellraiser III*, Pinhead has split into his original self, the good Captain Spenser, and his Cenobite alter-ego, Pinhead.

But humour and fashion sense are not essential to monster charisma. All that is ultimately needed is stamina. Witness the case of Jason Voorhees from the *Friday the 13th* films. In the original *Friday the 13th* (1980), seven camp counsellors come together to reopen Camp Crystal Lake, which has been closed for seven years because of a vicious, unsolved murder. Soon the counsellors themselves are being picked off by an unseen killer who, we eventually find out, was the mother of a child who drowned at the lake when he was eleven years old. In the later films (nine in all) the supposedly drowned child, Jason, emerges as the killer. What is interesting about him is that he is not charismatic in any usual way: he is not given to macabre *bons mots* like Freddy, nor does he make a bold counter-culture fashion statement like Pinhead. He never speaks, and beginning in Part III he wears a hockey mask. He is not very interesting in himself; he is simply a hulking anonymous killer who dispatches his victims with a machete or whatever pointed instrument is at hand. This is driven home in the final instalment of the series, *Jason Goes to Hell: The Final Friday* (1993). Here Jason is ambushed near the beginning of the film by an army patrol and blown into bits. His heart, which is twice the size of a normal man's and filled with a black, viscous fluid, takes spiritual possession of the coroner performing the autopsy on Jason's body parts. The coroner becomes Jason, and then goes on to pass Jason's essence to a policeman, and finally to a TV reporter. Jason, then, does not even need a specific body to be a monster-hero. It is the idea of Jason, the idea of the implacable, unrelenting killer, that is appealing.

Our sympathy with the stable, sequel-enduring monster is manipulated into complicity by camera work. Notice the preponderance of monster point-of-view camera work in contemporary horror films.[8] In *Halloween* we see the murder of the sister through the eyes of the child Michael Meyers. Later, when he grows up and embarks on his rampage, we go with him, seeing the mayhem largely through his eyes. We stalk the victims. 'Habitually in fiction film, vision is equated with access to truth: those who can see more know more of the truth' (Ellis 84), and so we, when looking through the eyes of the monster, know the truth, have a certainty that the feckless victims – lost in a culture of uncertainty – do not. Eventually, over the course of sequels, our association with the monster's empowering, malevolent gaze becomes automatic, and we come to see the world through the monster's eyes, even when not engaged by point-of-view photography. For example, we come to see the objects of the suburban household as potential weapons, and we try to second-guess the maniac: will he use the curling iron, the weed-eater, or the can-opener on his victims? Much of the enjoyment of these films comes in guessing correctly: All right! The weed-eater!

No recent horror movie more neatly captures all that I have been discussing than Sam Raimi's *The Evil Dead II: Dead by Dawn* (1987), a sequel to his *The Evil Dead* (1982). The plot is simple: Ash, the survivor of *The Evil Dead*, returns with his lover to the mysterious wilderness cabin of that film. This in itself is unsettling: Part One ended with Ash being attacked by a demon, apparently fatally. How is it that he is still alive? Why did he come back? Is the story being continued or merely repeated? Once at the cabin, Ash accidentally plays a tape made by a university professor reciting from the legendary *Necronomicon* of H.P. Lovecraft lore. The recorded incantation raises demons, and Ash's lover is immediately possessed. The rest of the film has Ash battle the demons both alone and with the help of others who come to the cabin. The plot is insignificant. Characters are not developed; they are not given time to develop. The film is simply a series of confrontations and shocks. No explanation is given for the presence of the demons; they just *are*. They are wholly and inexplicably malevolent, although, for no apparent reason, they possess only some characters at some times. Anyone may become a monster.

This horrific confusion takes place in a world that is itself radically unstable. The cabin is at times a sanctuary, at other times a trap. It is physically inconsistent: the interior of the building seems much too large and complex for its exterior; inanimate objects in the cabin occasionally, for no discernible reason, come to life. The outside world is little better. The demons cannot attack during the day, but daylight seems to last only a few minutes. The sun does not so much set as crash. The physical laws of nature themselves have been suspended. The film, then, for the purpose of scaring its audience, images forth the unsettling implications of Fredric Jameson's speculation that 'neither space nor time is "natural" in the sense in which it might be metaphysically presupposed' (*Postmodernism* 367). Ash must make his way through a world that only has one exact parallel: the world of *The Evil Dead* Part One. In the words of Thomas Carmichael in this volume:

Every image and figure in the sequel stands in differential relation to an earlier representation, with which it is affiliated and from which its authority derives, and to the extent that a narrative is recognized or recognizes itself as a sequel, it inevitably also calls attention to the conventions that govern its own narrative logic. (175)

The Evil Dead II returns us to the narrative logic of *The Evil Dead* Part One, stabilizing, through repetition, a universe of ontological uncertainty.

Audience reaction to this madness is complicated by what I will call the 'point-of-view demon.' Ash is repeatedly terrorized by a monster whom we never see, the same monster who was apparently triumphant at the end of Part One. This creature is, simply, the movie camera crashing through the woods and chasing Ash through the cabin. The camera lens, our point of view, becomes the threat. This makes for the perfect postmodern monster: a monster with no physical presence, but possessed of the charisma that comes with stability through sequelization; a monster with no personality, but who offers the audience total complicity and knowledge through an omniscient and fluidly mobile gaze. The demon empowers the viewer to kill the postmodern confusion epitomized in Ash's situation. And so throughout the film we oscillate between a fear of the incomprehensible and the inconsistent, epitomized for us in the postmodern predicament of Ash, and an all-powerful certainty that comes with the directed malevolence of the point-of-view demon. The postmodern horror movie sequel has taught us to be monsters.

Notes

1 The content and form of traditional horror movies has been tied to both cultural conservatism and, more specifically, its processes of gender construction. See, for example, Clover 15ff.
2 Andrew Tudor's survey of horror films shows that it is not until 1970 that an open ending becomes common; earlier films that did have open endings, such as *The Birds* (1963), met with audience disapproval (18–19). This is not to be confused with the gag ending that became popular in bad horror films of the 1950s. For example, a movie as forgettable as *Attack of the Giant Leeches* (1959) ends when the words 'The End' roll on the screen, but before the audience can start shuffling towards the door, a mocking question mark appears after 'End.' This sort of ending, designed for a cheap laugh, continued at least up to the Michael Jackson video for 'Thriller.'
3 As Vera Dika points out (138), the monsters in earlier horror films came from someplace else (often space), had unearthly abilities, and faced powerful societal opposition. In more recent films, the monsters are indigenous, use primitive forms of violence, and face ineffectual opposition, if any.

4 For a statistical ranking of monsters, see Tudor 20.

5 Many horror films, like so much of popular culture, simply ignore the complexities and implications of the postmodern condition and offer old formulas and reassurances. Compare *Jurassic Park* (1993), a film of 1950s values and narrative structure (greedy entrepreneur learns that there are some things man was not meant to do), with the bleakly postmodern *Carnasor* (1993).

6 One of the first North American horror films, that is. European horror films have a long tradition of ignoring linear narrative; see Tohill and Tombs 5–6.

7 Indeed, no reason is ever given for Michael Meyers's homicidal mania. As a child, he killed his sister. Loomis, who studied the boy as he grew up in an institution, can offer no explanation for his 'pure evil.' In *Halloween 5* (1989), Michael is finally jailed, only to be set free by a mysterious stranger who may be the devil.

8 Dika argues that the 'slasher' film can largely be defined by the use of killer point-of-view shots; see *Games of Terror* 14.

Works Cited

Carroll, Noël. *The Philosophy of Horror*. New York: Routledge, 1990.

Clover, Carol. *Men, Women, and Chainsaws: Gender in the Modern Horror Film*. Princeton, NJ: Princeton UP, 1992.

Cumbow, Robert C. *Order in the Universe: The Films of John Carpenter*. Filmmakers 23. Metchuen, NJ: Scarecrow, 1990.

Dika, Vera. *Games of Terror: Halloween, Friday the 13th, and the Films of the Stalker Cycle*. London and Toronto: Associated UP, 1990.

Ellis, John. *Visible Fictions*. London and New York: Routledge, 1982.

Heba, Gary. 'Everyday Nightmares: The Rhetoric of Social Horror in the *Nightmare on Elm Street* Series.' *Journal of Popular Film & Television* 23.3 (1995): 106–15.

Jameson, Fredric. *Postmodernism or, The Culture of Late Capitalism*. Durham, NC: Duke UP, 1991.

Newman, Kim. *Nightmare Movies: A Critical History of the Horror Movie from 1968*. Rev. ed. London: Bloomsbury, 1988.

Tohill, Cathal, and Pete Tombs. *Immoral Tales: European Sex and Horror Movies 1956–1984*. New York: St Martin's Griffin, 1995.

Tudor, Andrew. *Monsters and Mad Scientists: A Cultural History of the Horror Movie*. Oxford: Blackwell, 1989.

Wood, Robin. 'An Introduction to the American Horror Film.' *Movies and Methods*. Vol. 2. Ed. Bill Nichols. Berkeley: U of California P, 1985. 195–219.

'I'll be back': Hollywood, Sequelization, and History

LIANNE McLARTY

While the Hollywood sequel is not new (Tarzan and the Thin Man came back; so did the creature from the Black Lagoon and the sons of various monsters), it is arguable that during the last two decades the process of sequelization has become common, indeed expected, practice. Such escalation in the production of sequels is evident in the sequel's 'send-up' in popular representations, a cultural move analogous to the parody stage of genre films: one episode of the television show *The Simpsons* imagines a future Springfield in which *Star Trek: So Very Tired* is playing at the local theatre; in a recent episode of *Mad About You*, Bruce Willis plays an actor filming *Die Hard: Die Already*; the title *Naked Gun 33 1/3* (1994) makes absurd the tendency of producers to milk a film for its most minute possibilities of duplication; and, in a moment of cinematic *déjà vu*, the hero of *Die Hard 2* (1990) wonders 'how the same shit can happen to the same guy twice.' That sequels themselves often draw comic attention to their sequential status suggests a certain sequel saturation within popular-film culture.

This self-consciousness is also to be expected from a phenomenon that depends on the existence of a previous text (or texts) for its motivation; repetition is obviously a key feature of the sequel. This is evident in the sequel's equivalent to the advertising jingle, its 'hook': the terminator's 'I'll be back' and the *Die Hard* series's John McClane's 'Yippee kye aye, motherfucker.' In *Die Hard 2*, the similarities to the first film are self-consciously signalled by John: 'Another basement, another elevator'; 'It's okay, I've done this before.' These intertextual references, and the sense they produce of having been there before, rather than distinguishing sequels from other contemporary popular products, suggest they might be understood within the theoretical frameworks provided by postmodernist readings of popular culture. The outcomes of such an analysis might vary according to one's postmodernism. For instance, in Jean Baudrillard's theorizations of contemporary media, the kind of cultural recycling which seems to account for the sequel has contributed to a situation in which images, referring to nothing beyond themselves, not only replace, but 'murder,' 'the real.' If the sequel is understood as a copy, part of a potentially endless cycle of texts referring (presumably *only*) to previous texts, then it is a site of the disappearance of meaning. When media images produce simulations, rather than representations – when it is their 'reference principle' that must be 'doubted' – they no longer make sense of history; they replace it (and sometimes supersede it).

Similarly, for Fredric Jameson, history and meaning are evacuated from postmodern culture because the inability to think historically is a consequence of the 'cultural logic of Late Capitalism.' Signs of the past are cannibalized, their historical context and meaningful depth are erased: pastiche is the 'neutral practice' of mimicry ('Postmodernism' 65). Within and through this culture, a subject is constructed who is unable to 'organize its past and future into coherent experience' (71). That is, the culture and subjects of postmodernity, defined by a sense of a perpetual present, are prevented from recognizing, not only actual histories (our access to events is always mediated) but, importantly, the material relations that help shape them. Within the logic of this postmodernism, the sequel must be theorized as a form of cannibalism, the final signpost pointing the way to cultural exhaustion. It marks the end of originality and results in the triumph of surface over depth, spectacle over meaning and history. Here, too, the sequel is marked by repetition, and driven by the logic of endless reproduction for its own sake.[1]

If, however, one's postmodernism leans in a less pessimistic direction, the implications of repetition and reproduction for their own sakes are not so bleak. The sequel's evident appeal to the pleasures of familiarity and its acknowledgment of previous texts may be located in relation to a general tendency in postmodern culture to signal to an audience the *awareness* that texts beget texts. Here, postmodernism's central stylistic feature is intertextuality, its central function to 'trouble' the illusion of reality produced through means of representation. Some argue that, in engaging with and exploring multiple textualities, postmodern practices make their audiences sensitive to the discursive character of social reality, to the multiple, diverse, and often contradictory ways in which that reality is constructed, and to the role of cultural texts in that construction. Thus, Tony Wilson contends that postmodernism suspends the 'veridical effect, [that is] an apparent looking on at how things are' (392). While modernism constituted a 'detached' 'scrutiny of the means of representation, postmodernism raises the question of the very possibility of representation itself'; 'the postmodern image ... merely displays another' and 'makes no "pretense to showing me, offering me sight of the Real occurring elsewhere"' (396–401).

What distinguishes this postmodernism from that of Baudrillard and Jameson is that it recognizes the 'radical edge' of the questioning of referentiality (Wilson 400). While in Baudrillard's model images replace, and then pretend to *be*, the real, these images avoid any pretence of reference at all. Lawrence Grossberg refers to this troubling of representation as 'pose-modernism': 'the media's performance of particular poses,' which, as such, 'relate problematically to the real' (39). Referring to the multiple billboards which comprise this culture, Grossberg declares that 'it doesn't really matter whether it is another billboard for McDonalds, an anonymous bank, Pepsi or a political organization. It is not a sign to be interpreted, but rather, a piece of the puzzle to be assembled ... any individual billboard is in-different' (32). Ironically, this argument for postmodern culture's problematic relation to 'the real' has led some to the same conclusion as that of Baudrillard and Jameson: defying interpretation, the postmodern is outside of meaning and history. From this perspective, however, the sequel is merely a playful exchange between producers and consumers in which both sides not only know the rules, but know the other knows they know; it is simply an invitation to play with the pieces of culture, to assemble a puzzle which can be reassembled in different ways, indifferently. Ultimately, it is precisely culture's relation to politics and history that is said to be indifferent.

This postmodernism rightly recognizes that the social world is deeply coded by cultural discourses that lead, not to a self-generating monstrous simulacrum, but to a context defined by the simultaneous presence of various and conflicting styles, through and within which multiple and shifting subjectivities are constituted. Contemporary media environments, and their audiences, are neither unitary nor monolithic, but rather heterogeneous and decentred. This observation has led some to conclude that there is an *equivalence* among cultural texts in a 'field of tension which can no longer be grasped in categories such as progress vs. reaction, left vs. right' (Collins, *Uncommon Cultures* 136). All texts are created equal, and understood in relation to themselves and to each other, rather than to the social and historical contexts in which they are produced and consumed. It seems that postmodern cultural practices have troubled themselves out of any meaningful ideological content at all. When culture is a game and politics is play, there is no trouble.

Yet the argument that postmodern culture 'defies interpretation,' and is therefore politically and historically indifferent, *is* troubling. Even as texts question their referential potential, in their troubled relation to the real, they still make sense of the real for their audiences, and not necessarily in equal ways. The existence of multiple identities and contradictory cultural practices does not mean that there is an equality of expression among identities and practices within the social sphere. Indeed, it is precisely the theoretical recognition that popular culture is a site of conflict and contradiction that brings politics into play, by signalling the importance of sorting out the differences among diverse cultural forms in relation to something beyond themselves. If postmodernism acknowledges difference, then the difference between a misogynist representation and a feminist one is more than a simple matter of a different style. It is a matter of the difference between ways of mapping difference. Here Jameson's analogy between representations and maps is useful. Maps neither replace the territory to which they refer nor instruct the traveller to see another map. Maps have to be read in the context of a particular geography; while various routes are possible, they are not unlimited in number or necessarily 'equal.' As maps, representations are not 'indifferent' to social and historical 'geographies.' Rather, in order to make sense, they require a view of themselves which extends beyond their own boundaries.

While I do not want to underestimate the potential of postmodern textual devices to signal the discursive, ideological character of culture and social relations, the degree to which popular culture has appropriated intertextuality and distanciation devices (such as the refusal of narrative closure) may very well defuse its ability to unmask the textual workings of ideology through such means. It may also signal a need to look beyond formal self-consciousness for the political. Indeed, sequels depend on mainstream cinema's incorporation of the 'open text,' the refusal of closure, said to be a feature of the progressive cinema. Yet, when stories are left open-ended – when Freddy does not die, ever – it seems less a matter of leaving contradictions unresolved, than of securing an audience by advertising the next film.[2] In fact, self-reflexive devices can work to reverse the supposed political 'effects' of distanciation. It is arguable, for instance, that *Die Hard*'s (1988) John McClane's assurance in the first sequel that he has 'done this before' functions not so much to dislodge the film from 'the real' (locating it in relation to the work of ideology) as to lodge its character in that reality: John's memory and his personal history provide him with a degree of psychological depth not often granted the stereotypical characters of genre films. Similarly, the over-the-top special – aural, as well as visual – effects in many recent horror, science fiction, and action films, which may work to foreground the spectacle as such, are just as likely to lend them a verisimilitude that would make Andre Bazin drool.

This kind of intertextual referencing and fascination with spectacle can create its own kind of illusion, ironically not only of the real, but, simultaneously, of culture's absolute disengagement from the real, and from the political, historical, and social relations it implies. Yet a culture which is, in Collins's terms, 'uncommon,' and which plays a key and arguably increasing role in constructing the real and in shaping subjects' relationships to it, suggests, not a disengagement of culture from politics and meaning (expressions of privilege and privileged expressions), but, rather, their inextricable link. It is less a matter of culture's separation from politics than of its shifting relationship to it. The evacuation of politics from postmodern textual 'play' (in some postmodern theory and practice) and the widespread appropriation of self-reflexive strategies in popular culture suggest that cultural politics are best located beyond formal play, and in relation to the multiple and shifting histories and identities which are the landscapes that cultures map. As maps, representations work to make such landscapes, and the changes which occur within them, 'intelligible' through the stories they tell. This is not to deny the importance of textual features, or the degree to which the appeal of popular cinema hinges on 'the spectacle.' Indeed, as Yvonne Tasker argues, contemporary action cinema – one of the most sequelized genres – is an 'enactment of spectacle as narrative' (6). Yet the synchronic escalation of better effects is framed within the diachronic development of the story. In fact, sequels imply a kind of linearity which suggests that their narratives, and the characters who inhabit them, are central to their production of meaning, the site of their politics. They indicate a necessity to read against the grain of a fascination with spectacle and formal play, and towards the 'tales' that sequels tell and the sequential adjustments they make to those tales.

The importance of locating those tales in relation to the 'geographies' they map is underscored by the fact that popular culture is not, primarily, characterized by repetition. All popular products – even those which rely heavily on established conventions (genre films), recycled styles (period revival trends such as *film noir* in the 1980s), or previously successful scripts (remakes and sequels) – depend not only on familiarity, but on the appeal and promise of something new. Otherwise, why bother? Indeed, sequels are often promoted as 'new and improved': the video box of *Robocop 3* (1993) promises 'the best Robocop ever!'; the subtitle of *Die Hard 2*, '*Die*

Harder,' suggests the sequel will deliver more than the first, and the third does it with a vengeance. This promise, not only of difference, but of improvement as well, betrays the sequel's tie to the goods of consumer capitalism such as dish soap, breakfast cereal, and automobiles. It signals the desire to promote continued consumption through a kind of cultural planned obsolescence. On the most basic level, sequels make obvious what is true of all popular culture (stylistically postmodern or not): its drive towards differentiation is tied to the marketplace and motivated by the surplus-value demands of capital. In this sense it can be said that the differentiations enacted in the sequel specifically, and in popular culture generally, are (but never 'just') a practical, 'dollars and cents' attempt to expand its audience base.

Product differentiations do not occur in a vacuum, however; they are enacted in history. If commodity culture's indisputable goal is to sell itself to audiences, it must 'make sense' to its audiences *in order* to make 'cents' for its producers; it must respond to changes in the material relations (or 'geographies') of those audiences which result from social and historical pressures. For reasons built into the very logic of commodity exchange, popular culture must continually reinvent itself in relation to 'actual' history, even as it works to invent 'reality.' It is neither standardized nor static, but, rather, multiple and mutable. As Stuart Hall points out, the 'domain of cultural forms and activities' is a 'constantly changing field' (235). Conceptualizing the popular as diverse and in flux does not, however, mean that it is to be 'cozily embraced under the umbrella of a happy liberal pluralism' (Kipnis 35). Rather, the popular is a vehicle that 'antagonistic social forces attempt to appropriate and utilize in opposing ways'; it is a site where social conflicts are played out (29). The sequel's function as commodity culture invites an analogy with the genre film. A cursory glance reveals that the sequel is a phenomenon primarily within popular Hollywood genres such as horror, science fiction, western, war, and action films (although films less easily categorized within a genre – comedies and children's movies – are also widely sequelized). The genre film's interplay of repetition and difference and its evident appeal to audience expectations make it a logical candidate for sequelization. Like genres, sequels access the 'already said,' and their meanings hinge, in part, on the 'generic knowingness' of their audiences (Tasker 7). Nevertheless, both sequels and genres are necessarily dynamic, rewritten in relation to both their viewers and the historical contexts in which they are produced and consumed.

Rather than being indifferent to history, sequels, like genre films (and commodity culture generally), are inscribed and reinscribed with it. The adjustments that sequels make underscore both the mutability of popular forms and the role they play in the hegemonic struggle over meanings. Sequels are a kind of condensed enactment of commodity culture's 'ability to take account of popular aspirations, fears and conflicts, and to address them in ways that assimilate popular values into terms compatible with the hegemonic ideology' (Gitlin 243). The alterations which occur in their narratives and characters can throw into sharp relief the 'resiliency' of popular culture, that is, its ability to defuse challenges to established power by renovating itself.[3]

This essay argues that, in varying ways, and to different degrees, action and science fiction sequels renovate their narratives and characters in ways which either absorb or displace feminist and postcolonial challenges – features of the social and historical context of their production – to sexual and racial oppression. They absorb, or make allowances for, critiques of dominant power by rehabilitating white patriarchy. The white male hero (and sometimes the villain) is, in a sense, domesticated in the interests, not of ideological containment, but of promoting, in different ways and to varying degrees, a kinder, gentler patriarchy (but a patriarchy nonetheless). This 'new' patriarchy depends on 'others,' in that these films deflect criticism by displacing what feminism and postcolonialism identify as oppressive features of dominant power onto those subjected to it. The sequelizations of the films which foreground a female protagonist sometimes work to vilify the woman by displacing onto her those characteristics that were 'monstrous' in the original film. Similarly, challenges to racial oppression are displaced onto images of either a literally monstrous racial 'other' or one who is made to embody the practices of racism. These shifting representations of gender and race indicate that sequels provide an opportunity for updating, that is, for responding to changing social environments by writing in African-American characters and arming women. In doing so, they also suggest that the political in the cultural is located in relation to the writing and rewriting of social identities, and, importantly, the relationships among them.

Boys beyond Reproach

The white male hero of action films is conventionally an outsider, a renegade who is effective because he defies what is usually a corrupt authority and dares to go beyond established procedures. He is a loner, usually without a family, although typically a dead or absent woman precipitates his heroics. Mad Max loses his wife and child by the end of the first film, becoming the Road Warrior. In *Lethal Weapon* (1987), Martin Riggs is a recent widower; in *Lethal Weapon 2* (1989), the woman with whom he begins a romance is murdered; and, in the third film, dead women serve as motivation for Riggs's heroics – it is here that he, and the audience, learn who was responsible for the dead women in the first two films. Although Holly gets to live in the *Die Hard* series, she is contained within a confined space from which she must be rescued (an office tower in the first and, in the second, an airplane which is unable to land). In the third film, she disappears as a physical presence altogether, literally put on hold as John makes several aborted attempts to call her. Like *Die Hard*, *Robocop* (1987) avoids the dead-woman motivation, but it, too, is premised on a hero separated from his family, so that they are as good as dead to him.

Given that these stories take as their starting points a renegade hero and an 'absent' woman, it is interesting that in the sequels many of these heroes, while they may remain outsiders, are coded in relation to traditional signifiers of the domestic for the heterosexual male: women and children. Although John and Holly are estranged in *Die Hard 3* (1995), the film suggests that there will be a reconciliation (significantly, it is motivated by John as he realizes the break-up was his fault – he even promises to reform). *Lethal Weapon 3* (1992) ends with the coupling of Riggs and the promise of a family (they have adopted a dog). In *Mad Max: Beyond Thunderdome* (1985), Max's main heroic act is not only to save a group of children, but to help them get to the 'home' they have constructed in their mythology. As the female voice-over tells us at the end, it is a home that awaits the hero. Underscoring Max's domestication is the fact that he is coupled romantically: the children construct a story about Captain Walker (an identity they base on a photograph of a pilot), attribute this identity to Max, and, in a moment of heterosexual overdetermination, give him a wife based on the image of a stripper.

Like Mad Max, Robocop fights for the home; in *Robocop 3*, his mission is to prevent the eviction of people from their squats. As one character puts it, 'It's the only thing we've got. And if you don't think our home is worth it, then what the hell is?' The recoding of the male hero as guardian of the domestic is also foregrounded in Robocop's relationship with a child (at one point she falls asleep on his protective metallic lap). The end of the film invokes the heterosexual, nuclear family as Robocop, equipped with a jet pack, flies off with the child and the female doctor who has saved his life. *FX 2* (1991) also employs this kind of domestication. Not only has Rollie Tyler fallen in love with a single parent, securing his place in the family, but he has abandoned creating special effects for horror films, his original occupation, for the more benign (simultaneously nurturing and childlike) endeavour of inventing toys. Like Robocop, Tyler is associated with both children and the domestic: he is told he acts like a twelve-year-old, and he fights the villains with a remote-control clown. He also wards them off in a grocery store with exploding bean cans, and employs signifiers of the domestic, such as hotdogs and powdered potatoes, in his heroics. These, significantly, are motivated by a child – Tyler's mission is to get the men who killed his stepson's biological father.[4]

The Fly 2 (1989) not only sequentially rehabilitates the male through domestication, but also works to recuperate the progressive politics of the original (not the case with the previous examples). While Cronenberg's film is arguably a critique of oppressive power relations based on traditional notions of male aggression, the sequel foregrounds the *son* of Brundlefly, transforming a monstrous adult into a child. Martin, the protagonist, suffers from an accelerated growth rate; though he may have the outward appearance of an adult, he is only a child. In *The Fly* (1986), Seth's monstrous transformation is associated with an increase in aggressive (sexual, and thus adult) masculinity which he demonstrates with physical activity. In contrast to his father, Martin is immobilized by his metamorphosis, which the film imagines as a process of cocooning. Not only does this construct Martin as less threatening (unlike Seth, Martin poses a threat only to those who mean him harm) the cocoon, read as womb-like, reminds the viewer that he is merely a child. The ending of this sequel actually visualizes a process of substituting a monstrous patriarchy with one that is, apparently, not one. In order to shed his monstrosity and become human – that is, in order to dissociate himself from systemic patriarchal power – Martin must swap genes with a normal person and Bartock (the scientist who exploits Martin) becomes his gene donor. Cronenberg's monster, constructed in relation to a complex and public network of information and transportation technologies – the 'postmodern scene' – is rewritten in the sequel as a child, innocent of the worldly and its social and political relations.

Terminator 2: Judgement Day (1991) also employs this strategy of rehabilitating the patriarchal in its renovation of the monster from the original film. The new terminator is coded as childlike: he incessantly asks 'Why?' when John (the child he was sent from the future to protect) instructs him not to kill people; and he takes this instruction literally, as a child might, shooting several cops in the knees, but pointing out, 'They'll live.' There is also a way in which the terminator himself is coded as a toy. When John realizes that the terminator is there to follow his orders, he cheers, 'My own terminator,' and gets the terminator to do 'tricks' (unthinkable in the original). This terminator is not only benign but humanized, indeed victimized: he feels pain, by the end of the film understands why people cry, and plays the underdog in relation to the advanced android, the T-1000, whose primary incarnation is as a police officer. Thus the sequel's terminator is another hero who is dissociated from traditional sites of systemic power. Indeed, he is programmed by John, the adult, a future resistance leader, and sent back in time to protect John, the child. This terminator is not only humanized, but radicalized – he works for the opposition, as well as for the children. Susan Jeffords points out that the sequel's terminator is 'a "new" internalized man, who thinks with his heart rather than with his head – or computer chips' (253). Not only does the terminator come back as the benevolent, 'ideal' father, but he is assigned the traditional maternal role as well, enacting, as he does, the self-sacrifice so frequently attributed to mothers in melodramas.

Tania Modleski argues that this emphasis in popular culture on fathering, on men occupying traditional female roles – *Three Men and a Baby* (1987) and *Junior* (1994) – together with the infantilization of masculinity – Pee Wee Herman and Forrest Gump – are not so much critiques of systemic patriarchal power as evidence of it claiming even more territory. It 'constitutes a flagrant encroachment of the (ever multiplying) fathers onto the mother's traditional domain' (*Feminism* 86). This is especially suggestive, given the role women in action films play as absent motivation for the hero, who in turn undergoes increasing domestication. Modleski's aim is not, importantly, to secure the domestic as 'feminine,' or to discourage men from assuming nurturing roles, but to point out the ability of commodity culture to 'deal with the threat of female power by incorporating it' (7). In relocating 'the struggle of feminism against patriarchy to a place entirely *within* patriarchy and within the psyche of the patriarch himself,' these representations constitute an absorption of feminism and, as Modleski argues, the 'disappearance of the feminine' (10).

Girls with Guns

The rehabilitation of traditional masculinity enacted in some contemporary popular culture does not, however, entail the disappearance of women from the stories it tells. In fact, female characters are often present precisely to give 'birth' to the 'new man': they often provide him with a kind of domestication through association. At other times, they themselves are armed. Lately, action and science fiction films, conventionally considered to be 'male' genres, have incorporated women as 'action figures' into their narratives. It is important, however, not to see the insertion of female characters into stereotypical, traditional male roles as progressive. Thelma and Louise may have guns, but it is arguable that the film diminishes the force of patriarchal power by locating it within individual men (husbands and boyfriends) rather than in systems. Girls with guns are not necessarily feminists, especially if their guns are made to represent an abuse of, rather than a challenge to, oppressive power. This is evident in the transformation of *The Terminator*'s (1984) Sarah from a 'hypermother' whose narrative purpose is to procreate – her guns are a defence – to a militaristic survivalist whose goal is to prevent future destruction by destroying first – her guns are 'preventative,' used as an offence. The credit sequence of the sequel constructs her in relation to the maternal (she helplessly watches as children meet a nuclear end in a playground). Yet this sequence (clearly an establishing allusion to the original) turns out to be only a dream; Sarah's mothering is in her imagination. Indeed, her subsequent construction in the film suggests that mothering is a quality she has lost. In contrast to her (biologically essentialist) reproductive and nurturing role in the first film, in the sequel Sarah is almost an 'anti-mother.' She is unable to bond with her son; her response is to chastise him (not unlike a drill sergeant) for rescuing her, rather than greeting him with a 'motherly' (not to mention appreciative) hug, and, like the traditional image of the father, she signifies work and discipline rather than play and love. Conversely, the new and improved terminator (whom Sarah realizes can teach her to be motherly) serves as a more human counterpoint to her hysterical militarism. Although Sarah is clearly justified in her fears about the future, the film suggests that her means of coping are excessive and dangerous. She fires indiscriminately at the home of the man whom she holds responsible for the apocalyptic future the film imagines, and endangers his family in the process. And in shooting him in the back, she evokes the cowardice of the villain more than the bravery of the hero. In her transformation from the original's 'mother of the revolution' into a gun-toting survivalist for whom the end justifies the means, Sarah not only replaces the terminator as the signifier of excessive aggression – his excess is now a matter of play – but, in taking on that role, allows him to mother. She provides him with an alibi against the charges of feminism – *he* no longer has the 'attitude problem.'

This tendency to cast the female action hero as excessively violent is also apparent in *Aliens* (1986). Vasquez, a female marine, is almost exclusively associated with guns, and her guns even seem much larger than everyone else's. Her violent excess is signalled by her desire for the biggest weapon; guns and the use of them are her central concern. She interrupts a briefing about the aliens to declare that she 'doesn't need to know about them,' just where to 'aim her gun'; for Vasquez, fighting aliens is a physical, not a mental, exercise. Later in the film, she is shown in a fetishistic pose, with an enormous gun resting on the full length of her body. This association between Vasquez's body and guns suggests her overidentification with them, an excess which is attributed to her body and, through it, to her race as well – she is Puerto Rican. This excessive identification with firearms poses a threat to the innocent. Significantly, it is Vasquez who disobeys the order to hold her fire, thus endangering the lives of her fellow marines. As one of the men tells her earlier, 'You're just *too* bad.' *Die Hard 3* also exploits this image of the excessively threatening female in the figure of the strong, silent (she literally has no lines) chiselled blonde who attacks one of her opponents with such zeal that even the ruthless bomber has to tell her to stop ('I think he's dead'). This is in sharp contrast to the original, which labours to locate its female characters largely in relation to the domestic, warning of the consequences if they stray from their 'maternal role.'

The *Alien* series expands this female threat into the realm of the literally monstrous, suggesting an increasing conserativism in response to feminism. These films shift, from a corporate and arguably phallic monster in *Alien* (1979), to a feminine, if alien, one in the second, culminating in planting the seed of the alien within Ripley herself, fusing 'the feminine' and the monstrous. The first film locates the source of the threat firmly within corporate capitalism. The 'company,' for whom the crew is expendable, is vilified: it is embodied in both the threatening android, Ash, and in the alien itself. (The company protects it at the expense of the crew.) Although Ripley avoids vilification in *Aliens*, she must battle a monstrous alien mother. But, by *Alien³* (1991), she is visibly constructed as 'other': she is the only woman in an all-male correctional facility. The prisoners of this facility are referred to as 'the indigenous population,' a phrase which not only demarcates Ripley's difference, but assigns her 'foreign,' monstrous status. The use of the term 'indigenous' to describe what Ripley is not connects her with the aliens, which are not indigenous to the planets they invade. Like the aliens, Ripley is a disruptive presence. We are told that she constitutes a 'break' in the 'spiritual unity' of the men; she is a 'disruption of their order.' The threat that Ripley poses is made literal as she is responsible for introducing the alien into the facility (it stowed away on her ship). In the third film, Ripley's very body incubates a queen alien, 'capable of producing thousands more.' Thus a singular, phallic monster has given way to the monstrousness of female fertility. In *Alien³*, it is against this 'monstrous feminine' that the male prisoners (rapists and murderers) are constructed as victims. The film suggests that Ripley's presence could incite the men's criminal, oppressive behaviour; in this way, they play the victim to her monster.

Far from being written out, then, women seem to be rewritten into the role of monster. Indeed, the renovation of the image of patriarchy as nurturing and childlike is arguably more compelling if women are overpresent in the sequels as threats, if their force is portrayed as excessive. If the rehabilitation of traditional 'masculinity' in part depends on the vilification of female characters, then a further whitewashing occurs in relation to the constructions of racial difference.

Dread of Dreads

In *Mad Max: Beyond Thunderdome*, an African-American woman is the economically and socially privileged leader of the brutal, capitalist Bartertown. Not only is her claim to power illegitimate – the only reason she rules is because she was alive after the apocalypse – but she rules in a particularly violent manner. It is highly ironic, and evidence of the ability of commodity culture to accommodate contradiction, that the film displaces anxieties about capitalism onto an African-American woman, a figure doubly marginalized and disenfranchised by that which she is made to signify. *Robocop 3*, on the other hand, is unusual in that an African-American woman leads the resistance of the homeless. However, another threatening 'other' is conveniently constructed in the Japanese characters: a corporate executive who is figured primarily as a video image, and several identical androids (all played by the same actor). Here, the resiliency of popular culture is evident: a veneer of 'progress' glosses the surface of the screen in the rare presence of an African-American female protagonist, but anxieties (in this case about national and economic security) are nevertheless displaced onto representations of a racial 'other.'[5]

A similar strategy is at work in *Predator 2* (1990) as Danny Glover replaces Arnold Schwarzenegger in the lead role. Yet, like that of Ripley in *Aliens* and *Alien³*, the African-American protagonist's heroic status depends on his defeat of an alien predator who is, in some respects, his likeness. In order for Mike to occupy a central place in the narrative and be a hero, he must do battle with a monstrous self. The predator is drawn to jungles, the 'dark continent' in racist ideology, and has dreads (the Jamaican drug dealers also have dreads). Although the predator has high-tech weapons, the association of him with the jungle, as well as his reptilian appearance, lend him an aura of the primitive. In contrast to this, Mike is 'civilized.' His heroic status depends on him annihilating his 'uncivilized,' 'primitive' (African) 'self,' amounting to an assimilation of himself into that which is figured against the 'other': 'civilized,' 'white' society.

The *Lethal Weapon* series also employs this kind of 'self-assimilation.' In each film, Riggs and Murtaugh demonstrate their increasing bond by sharing quips about what a disaster Murtaugh's wife is as a cook. In *Lethal Weapon 2*, Murtaugh wishes that the South Africans had planted the bomb in Trish's stove, rather than behind the toilet (he is seated on it and if he gets up the bomb will detonate). 'Then,' as he says, 'all the suffering would have ended right there.' During the final moments of *Lethal Weapon*, Riggs manages to prove that he is no longer suicidal by admitting that, despite his earlier claims, he does *not* like Trish's cooking. This running joke clearly works to attribute a comically lethal potential to her. But, more important, it is a key way in which the interracial, male bond is demonstrated. In a sense, by enacting the bond between 'black' and 'white' through this shared put-down of the black Trish, the film works to exclude her; assimilation implies exclusion as 'blackness' is made to deny itself. The idealization of the Murtaugh family also works towards assimilation by containing the African-American male within the contours of a non-threatening, aging, and soon-to-retire family man. These films have it both ways: they offer up various racialized identities and at the same time they erase the possibility of difference by assimilating and/or annihilating it.

Die Hard achieves its project of securing the dominant status of the white male by employing African-American characters as narrative functions against which the white hero's heroics can be showcased. For example, it exploits racist stereotypes like the 'buffoon' and the trusty, but less masculine/threatening, sidekick. *Die Hard 3* marks a significant sequential shift in its *acknowledgment* of raced identities. In contrast to *Die Hard*, which depends on racist representations but writes out racism, *Die Hard 3* writes it in (perhaps in response to the increased visibility of questions about 'political correctness' in the media). This thematization of racism is arguably an example of commodity culture's ability to accommodate, and turn on its head, a critique of dominant power. For example, the practice of racism is displaced onto Zeus, John's African-American sidekick: fed up with Zeus's claims that John is a racist, John turns the tables and accuses

Zeus of being one. This depiction of racism as simply reversible dissociates it from systemic relations, making it an individual matter, and denying the fact that its business is conducted from positions of privilege and power.

Not only are the practices of racism displaced onto African Americans, but *Die Hard 3* makes racism seem like Zeus's attitude problem: it is his self-consciousness at being African American that makes him anticipate racial slurs which are never delivered by the white characters and repeatedly complain that he is in danger because of 'some white man's problems.'[6] 'Resistance is futile' since racism as a social practice, *still* practised, is ostensibly erased in *Die Hard 3*: John declares, in all sincerity: 'I didn't oppress your people.' While this statement acknowledges oppression, it relegates it to the past, exonerating contemporary society of its practices and the privileges it bestows. Indeed, the film confirms John's 'innocence' by suggesting that he is a victim of false accusations. In order to avert the bombing of a building, he is forced by the bomber to stand in an African-American neighbourhood wearing a sandwich-board with a racist slogan. He has been made to *play* the racist (significantly by a German). But it is a role for which he is ill suited; that racism does not motivate John's actions is demonstrated when he risks his life to save a group of African-American schoolchildren.

This rehabilitated white male hero, domesticated and egalitarian, is contructed against 'other' identities. The ways in which 'others' are used by white patriarchy to renegotiate its position of privilege by seeming to erase privileged expressions suggest that the political processes of popular culture are enacted around social identities such as gender and race. That the rehabilitation of the hero hinges, in part, on the construction of threatening 'others' indicates that culture is not indifferent to difference, but, rather, obsessed with it. Having concentrated on some shifts within sequels, I am left wondering, 'What has changed?'

Conclusion: Did He Ever Leave?

When Arnold Schwarzenegger said, 'I'll be back,' in *The Terminator*, who would have thought that the reincarnated version would be such a lovable guy? The 1990s hero is 'a self-effacing man, one who now, instead of learning to fight, learns to love' (Jeffords 245). Jeffords's description of the construction of masculinity in her analysis of *Terminator 2* applies more generally to action and science fiction sequels. She argues that the new hero represents a shift from an 'externalized' to an 'internalized' masculinity; the new masculinity 'reproduces' itself through 'inversion rather than duplication' (248). The new hero offers 'male viewers an alternative realm to that of the declining workplace': the family (258). The ways in which the white male hero of action and science fiction sequels is domesticated bear this out. However, the role of this 'new' hero seems less inverted (or introverted) than doubled. His occupation of the domestic does not imply his evacuation from the public, or from the social action a public position implies. He is *both* father and fighter; the home is merely his 'hideout,' an alibi.

The main currency of action and science fiction sequels is still the exploitation and validation of white male musculature, and the strength and activity it suggests, while African Americans are usually the first to die in these films, often passively serving, like some female characters, as motivating absences for the action. Tasker argues that action films make a spectacle of the male body, serving it up for the gaze, equating it with women's bodies in objectification. However, action and physical power are not divorced from this body; these men are not passive, or seen as excessive. It is their very ability to control the situation eventually through wits and strength (superhuman strength at that – the villain body count is often very high) that defines them as heroic. What is particularly interesting about action and science fiction sequels is that they graft the 'new man' onto this image of masculinity as power and control, recycling the 'old man,' and disguising the oppressive features of patriarchy and white supremacy as not only benevolent, but misunderstood. In 'rewriting' the action hero in relation to the domestic, these films offer, not so much a new man, as the same old patriarch with a few new parts (the new terminator may have human flesh but he is still a machine). Rather than invert, they recondition. They overhaul a 1980s masculinity by hauling out an even older one; it is a 'father knows best' who depends for his validation on the simultaneous construction of racial and/or sexual 'others' onto whom images of aggression and/or oppression can be displaced.

Notes

1 Thomas Carmichael's essay in this collection presents John Barth's LETTERS as a critique of contemporary culture somewhat in these terms. However, Carmichael sees Barth's attack as one on an essentially modernist formalism related to Cold War consensus culture in North America (179–80); against this dominant culture, Barth delineates a prescriptive postmodern aesthetic of contingency and lived experience as the basis of representation.

2 See Paul Budra's essay in this volume for a discussion of the open-ended postmodern horror film.
3 In dealing here with the complicit potential of sequelization, I certainly do not mean to suggest that this is somehow built-in, an inevitable consequence of the process. It is arguable that George Romero's 'Dead' trilogy becomes more progressive in its expansion of the critique from the individual (the family) to the social (the military). For example, Barry Grant argues that the female characters progress from being disempowered to empowered. It is, however, important to point out that Romero's films are produced independently of Hollywood.
4 In replacing the original biological father, a police officer who represents established institutions, with a toy-maker father, the film offers a fun hero, who is also, importantly, not part of the system.
5 This is particularly striking, given the first film's location of the threat within the parameters of white, corporate America.
6 In a parallel strategy, when racism is addressed as a systemic (social) practice in *Lethal Weapon 2*, it is displaced onto another country, South Africa.

Works Cited

Baudrillard, Jean. *The Ecstasy of Communication. The Anti-Aesthetic: Essays on Postmodern Culture*. Port Townsend, WA: Bay, 1983. 126–34.
– *The Evil Demon of Images*. Annandale, Australia: Power Institute, 1987.
Collins, Jim. 'Postmodernism and Cultural Practice: Redefining the Parameters.' *Screen* 28.2 (1987): 11–26.
– *Uncommon Cultures: Popular Culture and Postmodernism*. New York and London: Routledge, 1989.
Creed, Barbara. 'From Here to Modernity: Feminism and Postmodernism.' *Screen* 28.2 (1987): 47–67.
– 'Horror and the Monstrous-Feminine: An Imaginary Abjection.' *Screen* 27.1 (1986): 44–70.
Gitlin, Todd. 'Television Screens: Hegemony in Transition.' *American Mass Media and Mass Culture: Left Perspectives*. Ed. Donald Lazere. Berkeley: U of California P, 1987. 240–65.
Grant, Barry K. 'Taking Back the Night of the Living Dead: George Romero, Feminist of Horror.' *Wide Angle* 1.1 (1992): 64–76.
Grossberg, Lawrence. 'The In-difference of Television.' *Screen* 28.2 (1987): 28–45.
Hall, Stuart. 'Notes on Deconstructing the "Popular."' *People's History and Socialist Theory*. Ed. Raphael Samuel. London: Routledge, 1981. 227–40.
Hutcheon, Linda. 'Beginning to Theorize Postmodernism.' *Textual Practice* 1.1 (Spring 1987): 10–31.
Jameson, Fredric. 'Postmodernism, or The Cultural Logic of Late Capitalism.' *New Left Review* 146 (1984): 53–92.
Jeffords, Susan. 'Can Masculinity Be Terminated?' *Screening the Male*. Eds. S. Cohen and I.R. Hark. London: Routledge, 1993. 245–62.
Kipnis, Laura. '"Refunctioning" Reconsidered: Towards a Left Popular Culture.' *High Theory/Low Culture: Analyzing Popular Television and Film*. Ed. Colin MacCabe. New York: St Martin's, 1986. 11–36.

Mercer, Colin. 'That's Entertainment: The Resilience of Popular Forms.' *Popular Culture and Social Relations*. Ed. Tony Bennett et al. Milton Keynes and Philadelphia: Open UP, 1986. 177–95.

Modleski, Tania. *Feminism Without Women: Culture and Criticism in a 'Postfeminist' Age*. New York and London: Routledge, 1991.

– 'The Terror of Pleasure: The Contemporary Horror Film and Postmodern Theory.' *Studies in Entertainment: Critical Approaches to Mass Culture*. Ed. Tania Modleski. Bloomington and Indianapolis: Indiana UP, 1986. 155–66.

Polan, Dana. 'Brief Encounters: Mass Culture and the Evacuation of Sense.' *Studies in Entertainment: Critical Approaches Mass Culture*. Ed. Tania Modleski. Bloomington and Indianapolis: Indiana UP, 1986. 167–87.

Tasker, Yvonne. *Spectacular Bodies: Gender, Genre and the Action Cinema*. London and New York: Routledge, 1993.

Wilson, Tony. 'Reading the Postmodern Image: A Cognitive Mapping.' *Screen* 31.4 (1990): 390–407.

Yacowar, Maurice. 'The White Man's Mythic Invincibility: DIE HARD.' *Jump Cut* 34 (1989): 2–4.

Zavarzadeh, Mas'ud. *Seeing Films Politically*. Albany: State U of New York P, 1991.

Contributors

Paul Budra is an assistant professor in the Department of English at Simon Fraser University. He has published on Renaissance drama, Elizabethan historiography, and twentieth-century popular culture.

Thomas Carmichael is an associate professor in the Department of English, University of Western Ontario. He is co-editor of *Constructive Criticism: The Human Sciences in the Age of Theory* (1995) and the author of several articles on contemporary American fiction and postmodern culture.

Lynette Felber teaches Victorian and modern British literature at Indiana University–Purdue University in Fort Wayne. The author of *Gender and Genre in Novels Without End: The British Roman-Fleuve* (1995), she is also editor in chief of *Clio: A Journal of Literature, History, and the Philosophy of History*.

Carole Gerson is a professor in the Department of English at Simon Fraser University. Her publications include *A Purer Taste: The Writing and Reading of Fiction in English in Nineteenth-Century Canada* (1989), *Canada's Early Women Writers: Texts in English to 1859* (1994), and a new edition of Agnes Maule Machar's *Roland Graeme: Knight: A Novel of our Time* (1892; rpt. 1996).

Mary Ann Gillies teaches in the Department of English at Simon Fraser University. She recently published *Henri Bergson and British Modernism* (1996) and is completing a book on the literary agent.

Ingrid E. Holmberg is an assistant professor in the Department of Greek and Roman Studies at the University of Victoria. Her interests in Greek poetry include the epic and gender issues. She has published on gender in the *Odyssey* and Euripides' *Helen*; she is currently working on a book about the interrelationships of gender and cunning in early Greek epic poetry.

Alexander Leggatt is a professor of English at University College, University of Toronto. His publications include *Shakespeare's Political Drama* and *Jacobean Public Theatre*.

Lianne McLarty is an associate professor in the Department of Art in History at the University of Victoria. She has published on popular film and horror movies.

Betty A. Schellenberg teaches in the Department of English at Simon Fraser University. She has published *The Conversational Circle: Re-reading the English Novel, 1740–1775* (1996) and is currently working on studies of the early English print sequel and the professionalization of the mid-eighteenth-century woman writer.

June Sturrock, a professor in Simon Fraser University's Department of English, published *'Heaven and Home': Charlotte Yonge's Domestic Fiction and the Victorian Debate over Women* in 1995. Her work in progress includes an edition of *Mansfield Park* in the Broadview Text series.

Andrew Taylor is an assistant professor at the University of Saskatchewan. He has published on minstrel performance and medieval reading practice and is a co-editor of *The Idea of Vernacular*.

Samuel Glen Wong, formerly of the Department of English at Simon Fraser University, is now a Visiting Scholar at the University of Victoria.

Michael Zeitlin is an associate professor in the Department of English at the University of British Columbia. His published work has appeared in such journals as *American Imago, Contemporary Literature, Mississippi Quarterly, Mosaic*, and *College Literature*, and in the essay volumes *Faulkner and Psychology* and *Faulkner and the Artist*.